The First Book of

Microsoft® Works for the PC

D1245636

SAMS

A Division of Prentice Hall Computer Publishing
11711 North College, Carmel, Indiana 46032 USA

The First Book of

Microsoft® Works for the PC

Debbie Walkowski

FIRST EDITION
THIRD PRINTING—1992

International Standard Book Number: 0-672-27360-8
Library of Congress Catalog Card Number: 91-60703

Publisher: *Richard K. Swadley*
Publishing Manager: *Marie Butler-Knight*
Managing Editor: *Marjorie Hopper*
Manuscript Editor: *Katherine Huggler*
Technical Editor: *David Knispel*
Cover Design: *Held and Diedrich Design*
Production Assistance: *Claudia Bell, Sandy Grieshop, Bob LaRoche,
Kimberly Leslie, Howard Peirce, Tad Ringo, Bruce Steed, Suzanne
Tully, Lisa Wilson*
Indexer: *Jill D. Bomaster*

Printed in the United States of America

Contents

vii

ix

X

Introduction

In just under a decade, Microsoft Corporation has taken the world by storm with its variety of innovative and high quality software products. It's no surprise that Microsoft Works lives up to the reputation of its creators. Works is one of the best *integrated* packages available on the market, combining into one package four of the most useful software tools:

► a Word Processor tool for typing text documents
► a Spreadsheet tool for performing numeric calculations
► a Database tool for managing lists of related information
► a Communications tool for communicating with the *outside world*

The fact that the tools are integrated means that they are all designed to work together. And one of the biggest advantages of Works over other integrated packages is its *window* system, which allows you to use more than one tool at a time and exchange information between tools with ease. You may find that Works meets the majority of your software needs, whether you use it at home, at school, or in the office.

You don't have to be a computer expert to use Works. Works is easy to learn and easy to use; it was designed for people who need to be productive quickly. If you've never used Works before, this book is for you.

In this *First Book of Microsoft Works*, you'll get an overview of the entire program; learn the fundamentals of each of the four tools; then discover how you can begin using the tools together to achieve your greatest productivity.

How To Use This Book

The chapters in *The First Book of Microsoft Works for the PC* are organized so that you can learn everything you need to know about each tool separately, then learn how to put the tools together.

Chapter 1, Introducing Works, provides an overview of the four Works tools: Word Processor, Spreadsheet and charting, Database and reports, and Communications.

Chapter 2, Getting Started with Works, shows you how to start the program and introduces you to the screen, menus, keyboard, mouse, and help system. It also provides helpful background information about files and directories.

Chapter 3, Using the Word Processor, takes you through a sample business document, explaining how to create, edit, print, and save a document.

xii

Chapter 4, Expanding Your Word Processor Skills, builds on the information in Chapter 3, showing how to format a document, create footnotes, headers and footers, and use the Search and Replace, Spelling Checker, and Thesaurus features.

Chapter 5, Introducing the Spreadsheet, teaches you how to create, print, and save a simple spreadsheet.

Chapter 6, More about Spreadsheets, takes you further into the subject, with valuable tips on editing, using formulas, formatting, and sorting spreadsheet information.

Chapter 7, Charting Your Spreadsheet, shows you how to display your spreadsheet information in graphical chart form, and how to print and save your charts.

Chapter 8, Introducing the Database, takes you through the process of planning, creating, formatting, organizing, sorting, printing, and saving a database, with useful business examples illustrating each process.

Chapter 9, Creating Database Reports, explains how to create useful reports from the information in your database.

Chapter 10, Using Communications, shows how to set up, initiate, and receive communications and files via modem, if one is installed in your computer.

Chapter 11, Making the Works Tools Work for You, takes the examples from previous chapters and shows how you can combine spreadsheet information and charts in a document, and how to create a form letter and merge it with information from your database for mass mailings.

Appendix A, Installation and Startup Instructions, shows you how to install and start Microsoft Works on both hard disk and floppy disk systems.

Appendix B, Common Works Functions, lists 22 of the most commonly used functions for spreadsheet applications.

Conventions Used in This Book

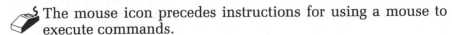

The First Book of Microsoft Works for the PC contains several special features designed to help you learn Works quickly. Watch for the following icons, boxed messages and typeface changes throughout the book.

xiii

Q Quick Steps

1. Look for the Quick Steps icon for lists of step-by-step instructions about frequently used procedures. The left column in color type tells you something to do.	The second column in black type tells you the results of your action.

The mouse icon precedes instructions for using a mouse to execute commands.

The key icon denotes information on keyboard shortcuts to help you perform functions more efficiently.

Boxed tips and notes offer clues about the inner operations of Works. Boxed cautions describe actions that may affect a document or permanently erase data. All of these visual aids are helpful as quick references when you return to this book in the future.

> **Tip:** Helpful tips and notes are included in bordered boxes throughout this book.

> ⊘ **Caution:** Boxed warnings remind you to proceed carefully.

Typeface Conventions

In this book, new terms appear in italic when first introduced. Italic is also used for emphasis or differentiation of terms when needed. Screen messages appear as `computer typeface`. Data that you type in appears as `color computer typeface`. Also, when certain operations require pressing more than one key at a time, this action is expressed with a + symbol, such as Shift+F1 or Ctrl+Shift+F8.

xiv

Acknowledgments

Writing a book is never a solitary effort; no author can do it alone. My sincere appreciation and thanks to Marie Butler-Knight, who provided continuous support, advice, and professionalism; to Kathy Huggler for her excellent editing; and my thanks and gratitude to Amy Perry, who gave me the opportunity to realize my goal.

A special thanks to Frank for his constant encouragement and unfailing support, and to Smokey, who was always a bright spot during those lonely, late nights at the keyboard.

Trademarks

All terms mentioned in this book that are known to be trademarks or service marks are listed below. In addition, terms suspected of being trademarks or service marks have been appropriately capitalized. SAMS cannot attest to the accuracy of this information. Use of a term in this book should not be regarded as affecting the validity of any trademark or service mark.

CompuServe Incorporated is a registered trademark of H&R Block, Inc.

Microsoft Works is a registered trademark of Microsoft Corporation.

Prodigy is a registered trademark of Prodigy Systems.

XV

Introducing Works

In This Chapter

▶ *A Word Processor tool to create text documents*
▶ *A Spreadsheet and Charting tool to do numeric calculations and display numbers graphically*
▶ *A Database tool to manage large volumes of data*
▶ *A Communications tool that lets your PC communicate with the 'outside world'*
▶ *Using all the tools together*

Works Overview

Works contains four of the most popular types of software: word processing, spreadsheet, database, and communications. These four types of software were not chosen by accident; they were chosen because they handle the majority of most users' needs—at home, in the office, or at school. Works refers to the four pieces as *tools*, and you can think of them exactly that way.

Works is referred to as *integrated* software because all four software tools are contained in one package and are designed to work together. There are at least three advantages to using integrated software. The first is that the methods for doing common tasks, like printing, are similar, so you don't have to learn new procedures for each tool. The second is that you can include files from one tool in files from another tool. For example, you can include a chart in a Word Processor document. And third, the built-in window feature in Works allows you to display and work on files in more than one tool at a time. When compared to other stand-alone software packages, these are tremendous advantages.

You could buy four similar software tools separately and try to get them to work together, but they would not be integrated. You wouldn't be able to use two or more tools at the same time without additional software, and you probably couldn't exchange information between them easily. The behind-the-scenes aspects of computer software can be complex, and often you are just not able to use different software programs together with any degree of success. Works is designed for users who want basic functionality from reliable tools that can be used together quickly and easily.

2

Word Processing

A *word processor* is a tool that lets you type all kinds of documents such as letters, memos, reports, notes, contracts, legal documents, papers, articles, resumes, and proposals. Word processors are used for creating almost any kind of a document that contain primarily text.

Word processors have virtually replaced typewriters in the business world. One reason for this is that you can make corrections easily and rearrange text without retyping it. Because you compose the text on a screen and print it later, you can make as many changes as you like before you print the document. You can make characters bold or italic, change the size of characters, change the margins and alignment of paragraphs, rearrange paragraphs, and so on. In addition, the word processor can also do many things for you automatically, such as adding page numbers or other repetitive text at the top or bottom of each page in a document. A sample Works Word Processor document is shown in Figure 1.1.

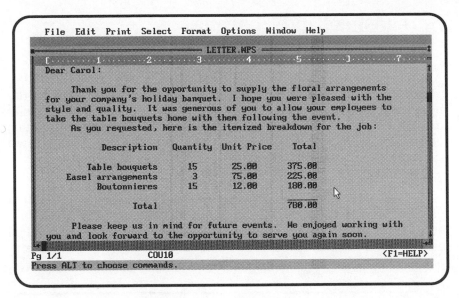

Figure 1.1   A sample Word Processor document.

3

The Word Processor tool in Works has many extra features that make the job of composing text quicker and easier. For example, if you've used a word or phrase frequently in a document and decide you want to change it, you can use the *Replace* feature to replace that word or phrase automatically in the entire document. The *Search* feature alone can save you the time of rereading every paragraph in a document to find the word or phrase you need to revise.

Works also has a built-in *Spelling Checker* and *Thesaurus*. If you have trouble with spelling, the Spelling Checker can locate words that are spelled incorrectly and it can replace the incorrect spelling automatically with the correct one. If you're looking for just the right word or you think you've used a word too many times in a document, the Thesaurus can help you find similar words to use to eliminate repetitiveness.

If you've never used a word processor before, you'll be surprised to learn how versatile it is, and how quickly and easily you'll be creating professional looking documents.

Spreadsheet and Charting

A *spreadsheet* is like an electronic version of a paper worksheet that performs numeric calculations automatically. You can use the Spreadsheet tool in Works to plan your home budget, track financial information for your business, keep track of your records, balance your checkbook, or run financial business models. Without a spreadsheet, you would have to do these tasks on paper with the help of calculator.

The spreadsheet is made up of *rows* and *columns*, just like a paper worksheet. You fill in the column and row headings, then enter numbers into the columns and rows (see Figure 1.2). Once you've entered the numbers, you can enter a variety of formulas to perform calculations on the numbers.

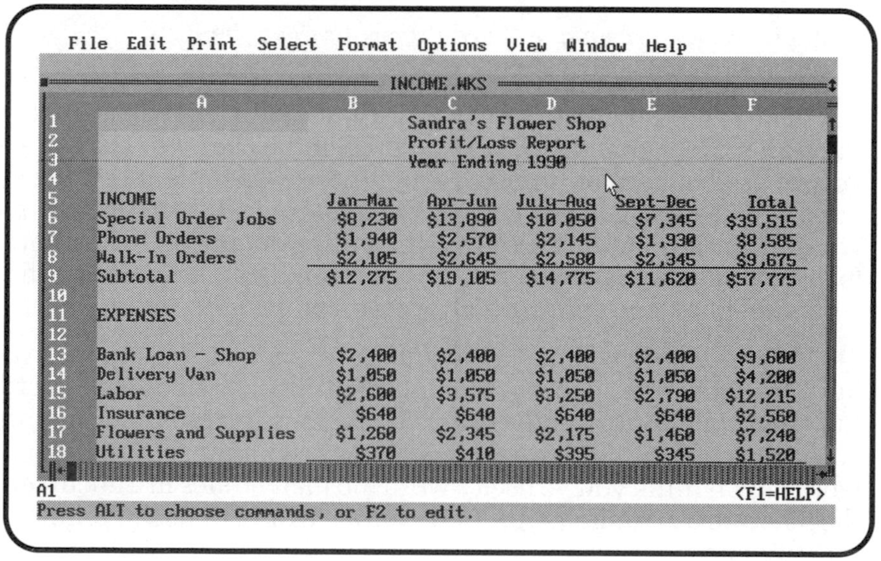

4

Figure 1.2   A sample spreadsheet created with Works.

The biggest advantage to using the Works spreadsheet over a paper worksheet is that the spreadsheet recalculates instantly when formulas are entered or numbers are changed. On a paper worksheet, it can take hours to make changes or move columns and rows of figures; then you still have to recalculate.

Once you've created a spreadsheet, the Charting tool in Works allows you to present your data in a graphical form. Often numeric information is easier to read and understand when presented as a *chart* or *graph*. With Works you can present spreadsheet information in as many as eight different chart styles including bar, line, and pie. Figure 1.3 shows an example of a pie chart generated from Works spreadsheet data.

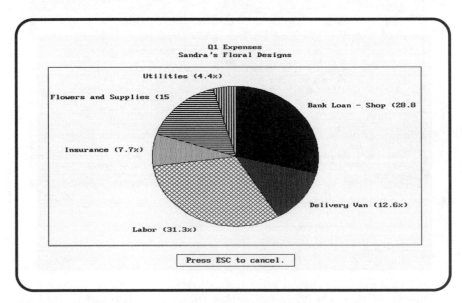

Figure 1.3   A sample pie chart generated from Works spreadsheet data.

5

Database and Reports

Whether you use Works at home or in the office, you probably have a lot of information to record. At the office you might keep lists of customers, suppliers, parts, or prices. At home, you might have a holiday card mailing list, favorite recipes, or a household inventory. These kinds of lists can be very difficult to create and maintain on paper, especially when you want to rearrange the items in a particular order. On your PC, you would store this information in a *database*.

A database is a collection of related information organized in a list-type format. Using the Database tool in Works, you can create and update lists quickly and easily. You can organize, sort, and select certain items on a list, or search for specific items. A sample Database file is shown in Figure 1.4.

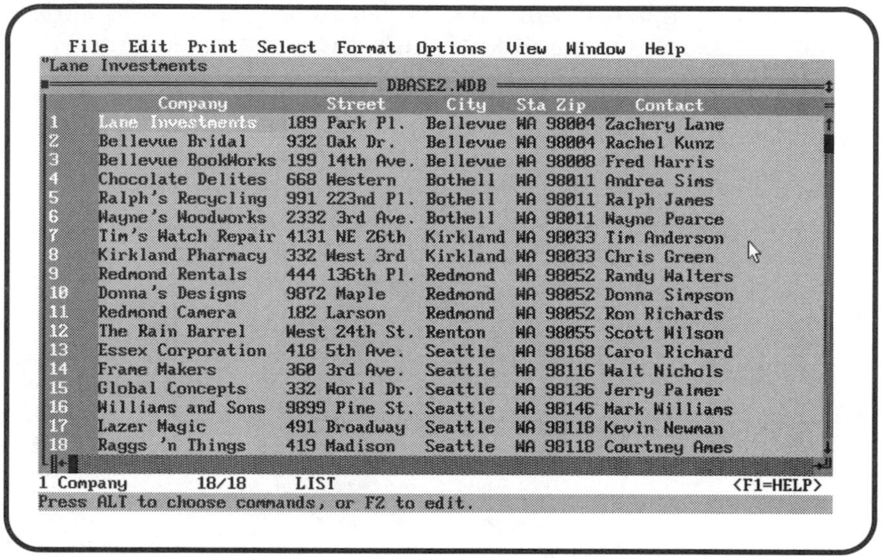

Figure 1.4   A sample Database file created with Works.

Once you've created your lists, Works lets you print *reports* in a variety of formats. You can select the data you want to include, summarize columns of figures, and neaten up the report by adding a title, blank lines for spacing, and special formatting.

Communications

There was a time when a personal computer stood alone; you could use your computer to do your own work, but you had no way of connecting to other computers. If a friend who lives across the country wanted to borrow a file of yours, you had to send a diskette through the mail. If you created a spreadsheet on your PC at home and wanted to use it at work on a mini or mainframe computer, you had to retype it because there was no way to transfer it.

Well, times have changed. Because computers can now be connected, either directly or over telephone lines, you have access to a whole new world of computers and information. Using the Communications tool in Works, you can now send that file from your PC to your friend's PC over the telephone lines, and you can transfer that spreadsheet you created at home to your computer at work.

You can connect to public computer services to do your shopping, or to get information from electronic bulletin boards. There are even national and worldwide mail networks that you can use to send messages back and forth to friends and colleagues. Many people take advantage of this communication capability to develop contacts and establish friendships across the country.

Putting It All Together

7

For most of your everyday tasks, you use the four Works tools separately, but the real power comes when you use the tools together. The following are some examples:

Database + Spreadsheet   Suppose you have a database that includes sales figures for customers. You decide you need to do some calculations on the figures, so you bring the information you need from the database to a Spreadsheet file, then enter the formulas for the calculations.

Word Processor + Spreadsheet + Chart   Suppose you are creating an annual report and need to include financial figures for the year. You can incorporate the Spreadsheet file that contains the figures into your Word Processor file. What if you want to include a chart to show how yearly expenses were broken out? You can create the chart in the spreadsheet and include it in your annual report, too.

Database + Word Processor   You want to send a letter to your customers announcing your latest product. You can use the database that stores your customers' names and addresses together with the Word Processor tool to create form letters and mailing labels.

Database + Spreadsheet + Word Processor +Communications   Suppose you keep track of your monthly sales figures in a database. You can bring the figures into a Spreadsheet file, then include the figures in your sales report in the Word Processor file. Once the report is complete, you can send the file to your boss via telephone lines by using the Communications tool.

What You've Learned

The four tools in Works were carefully chosen to provide you with the most basic software needs at the office, at home, or in school.

8

▶ The Word Processor tool is used for creating documents that contain primarily text.

▶ The Spreadsheet tool is used for performing numeric calculations and includes a Charting tool for presenting figures in a graphical form.

▶ The Database tool helps you manage large amounts of data such as inventory, prices, customer lists, and so on. You can generate a variety of reports from data in the database.

▶ The Communications tool gives you access to other computers. You can use it to send and receive files, and to get information from other computer systems and services.

▶ The four tools in Works are *integrated*, meaning they are designed to work together. You can combine information from one tool, such as the Spreadsheet, with information in another tool, such as the Word Processor.

Chapter 2

Getting Started with Works

In This Chapter

▶ *Using the keyboard and the mouse*
▶ *Using Works screens, menus, and commands*
▶ *Working with files and directories*
▶ *Working with Works windows*
▶ *Getting help*

Setting Up Works

Now you get to actually use Microsoft Works. After you have installed the program (see Appendix A), start it according to the directions for your type of system. For example, if Works is installed on drive C on your hard disk in a directory named WORKS (the default installation directory), follow these steps:

1. Type C: and press Enter to change to drive C.
2. Type cd/ works and press Enter to change to the directory containing Microsoft Works.
3. Type works and press Enter.

You should see the screen shown in Figure 2.1.

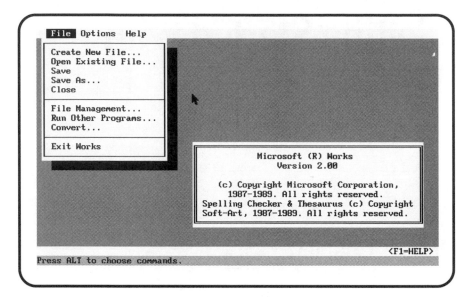

Figure 2.1   The opening Microsoft Works screen.

The Works Screen

Whether you're using the Word Processor, Spreadsheet, Database, or Communications tool, you enter information in a window on the screen. The window is the feature in Works that allows you to view and work on more than one file at a time. (You'll learn more about using multiple windows later in this chapter.)

The screen windows for the four Works tools have several features in common. These are shown in Figure 2.2.

The *menu bar* displays the names of the *menus* available in the Works tool you are using. For example, the menu names on the menu bar in the Word Processor tool are File, Edit, Print, Select, Format, Options, Window, and Help. You'll learn more about menus later in this chapter.

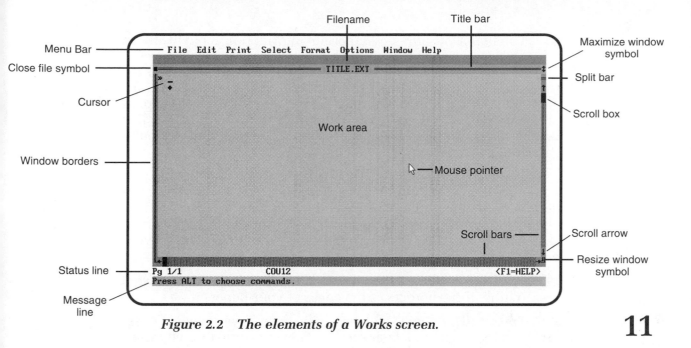

Figure 2.2   The elements of a Works screen.

The *work area* is where you enter information, whether it is text in a word processing document or numbers in a spreadsheet. The appearance of the work area varies depending on the Works tool you are using. For example, in the Word Processor tool, the work area is blank, just like a blank sheet of paper. In the Spreadsheet tool, the work area is divided into rows and columns.

Inside of the work area, the blinking character that looks like an underline is called the *cursor*. The cursor marks the location in the document where text is inserted when you begin typing. You can move the cursor to whatever location you choose. Later on in this chapter you will learn how.

If you have a mouse, you can also see the *mouse pointer* inside the work area. You can move the mouse pointer to any location in the work area and click to position your cursor at that location. You can also move the mouse pointer to any of the menus and click to select menu commands. You'll learn more about selecting commands later in this chapter.

The *title bar* always displays the title, or *filename*, of the file in which you are working. If you have a mouse, you can use the square symbol, or *close file symbol*, at the left end of the title bar to close a file quickly. You can use the double-arrow symbol, or *maximize window symbol*, at the right end of the title bar to expand a window to its full size when you have more than one window open at once.

The *status line* provides important information about the file in which you're working. For instance, it displays what page you are on and the total number of pages in your document. When you press the Caps Lock or Num Lock key, an indicator appears on the status line. The status line reminds you that you can press F1 to get Help. as you'll learn later in this chapter. Other indicators on the status line depend on the Works tool you are using. Later chapters will point these out to you.

The *message line* is usually blank unless Works needs to give you instructions or information. For instance, when you select certain commands, the message line gives you brief instructions about how to use those commands. Or, if you make an incorrect selection, Works displays a message telling you how to correct your error.

The *borders* of your window mark the boundaries of your work area. Think of the borders as the edges of your paper.

12

The *scroll bars* are useful primarily if you have a mouse. These are explained fully in a later section. However, whether you use a mouse or the keyboard, the square symbol on each scroll bar, the *scroll box*, tells you approximately where you are in a document. For example, if the cursor is one-third of the way through a file, the scroll box on the vertical scroll bar is one-third of the way down. This feature can be very helpful, especially for long documents. At each end of the scroll bars are *scroll arrows*, used for moving forward or backward, or right or left. You'll learn more about how to move through a file using the mouse later.

The *split bars* on each scroll bar let you separate the window into horizontal or vertical panes, depending on which Works tool you are using. The *resize window* symbol lets you resize the window to the dimensions you choose, as you will see later in this book.

Using the Keyboard

Before using Works, you should familiarize yourself with your keyboard. Look at Figure 2.3 and find the keyboard that looks most like yours.

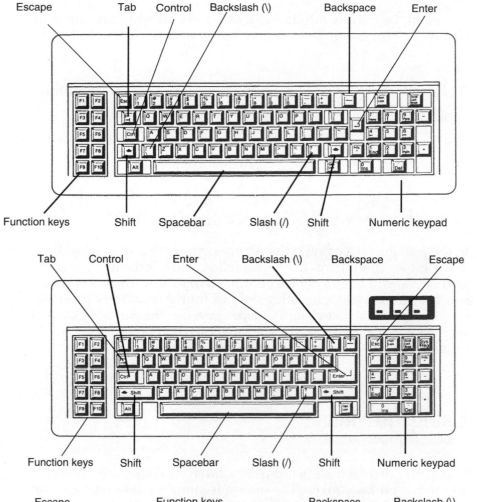

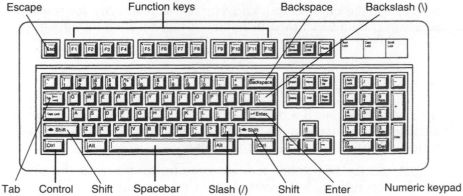

Figure 2.3   Three different types of keyboards.

Next, take a few minutes to locate the following keys on your keyboard. You use these keys frequently in Works.

Enter	Esc	Alt
Backspace	Shift	Ctrl (Control)
Page Up (PgUp)	Page Down (PgDn)	Home
End	Right Arrow	Left Arrow
Down Arrow	Up Arrow	

Using the Keyboard to Move Around in Works

In the previous list of keys, the Arrow keys are the *directional keys*. They move the cursor in the direction they indicate. On some keyboards, you have a choice between two sets of Arrow keys. You can use the keypad consisting only of four Arrow keys (near the bottom right of the keyboard), or you can use the numeric keypad with Num Lock (Number Lock) turned off. (Just press Num Lock to *toggle*, or switch, between On and Off.)

Using the Mouse

You don't need a mouse to use Works, but if you have one it can save you time and keystrokes. The mouse is simply a convenience that lets you make choices quickly. You use it primarily for selecting, whether it be a word in your document, or an item on a menu.

Mouse Buttons and Operation

If you have not used a mouse, practice rolling it around on a hard surface or a mouse pad. As you move the mouse, the mouse pointer follows your movements on the screen.

A mouse has either two or three buttons across the top. In Works you use the left mouse button most often. Throughout this book when an instruction says *click*, press the left mouse button once and release it, unless the directions say otherwise. For some

14

tasks, directions tell you to click the mouse button twice quickly, then release. This is called *double-clicking*. Occasionally you *click and drag* the mouse. To click and drag, press the mouse button and continue holding it down while you drag the mouse to the proper location, then release.

> ▶ **Tip:** If your space is limited and you find that you can't reach every area of the screen when you move the mouse, lift the mouse to reposition it. The mouse pointer stays on the screen right where you left it. Practice pointing to different areas on the screen.

Using the Mouse to Move Around in Works

If you have a mouse, you can use the scroll bars to move the cursor in the document. Click on the arrow at each end of the scroll bars to move forward or backward one line at a time, or one character to the right or left.

15

If you want to move more quickly through a document, click on a scroll box and drag it to the location you want. Your cursor moves to the location you choose. For instance, to move to a point halfway through your document, move the scroll box to the middle of the scroll bar.

Commands and Menus

When you need to tell Works what to do, you use a *command*. To make commands easier for you to find, Works groups related commands together under menus. Menu names are displayed in the menu bar near the top of the window (see Figure 2.4).

To select a menu name with the **keyboard**, press Alt, then type the letter that is highlighted in the menu name. (On your screen the letter is underlined as well as highlighted.)

To select a menu name with the **mouse**, click once on the menu name. When you select a menu name, a *pull-down* menu opens to display the commands on the menu. Figure 2.4 shows the commands on the Options menu after it is opened. If you're using the keyboard to select a command, type the highlighted letter in that command. If you have a mouse, click on the command.

Menu bar

Pull-down menu

Grayed-out command

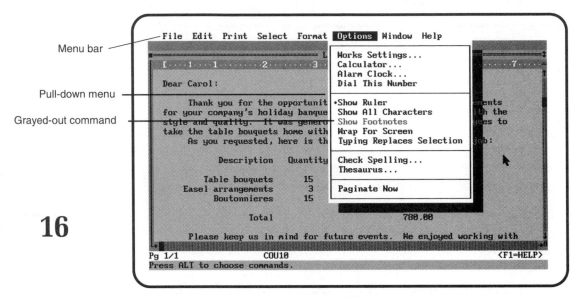

16

Figure 2.4   Pull-down menu listing command names.

When a command does not apply to what you're working on at the time, it is not available to you. These commands appear in gray text and are referred to as *grayed out*. For example, in Figure 2.4 the Show Footnotes command is grayed out because there are no footnotes in the document shown on the screen.

Dialog Boxes

Sometimes Works needs additional information from you to carry out the command you select. In these cases, three dots (...) follow the command name on the menu. When you select one of these items, Works displays a dialog box. In it you can either make choices or give Works instructions (see Figure 2.5).

For instance, when you select the Tab command from the Format menu, the dialog box asks you for more specific information about the tab you want to set, such as its position and alignment. The space in a dialog box where you fill in or change information is called a *field*. Dialog boxes contain one or more of the items listed after Figure 2.5.

List box

Check box

Option box

Command
button

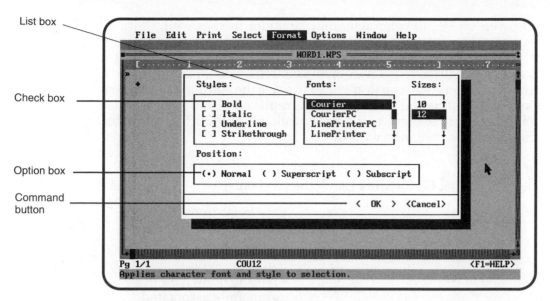

Figure 2.5   A dialog box and its elements.

17

Option box   You can select only one of the items marked by parentheses. The options toggle on and off each time you select them.

Check box   In a check box, you can select one or more of the items marked with square brackets. These options toggle on and off as well.

List box   You can select only one item in a list box.

Text box   When you see text, numbers, or dots between square brackets, the box is a text box. If the box contains text or numbers already, Works has made a suggestion for you. Either confirm the suggested entry or, if necessary, change it. When there are dots, you need to supply information yourself. (Not shown in Figure 2.5.)

Command buttons   At the bottom of each dialog box are two buttons, OK and Cancel. When you choose OK (or press Enter), you confirm all of the current settings in the dialog box. When you choose Cancel (or press Escape), Works takes no action, the dialog box disappears, and you are returned to the pull-down menu.

One character is highlighted in each choice in every dialog box. (This highlight is not visible in the illustrative figures in this book.)

On your screen, the character may be underlined as well. Press the Alt key, then enter the highlighted character to move your cursor to the location you choose in the dialog box. If you prefer, use the Tab key to move in succession from one field to the next. Using either of these two methods, you don't need to erase the setting that's shown; just begin typing and the old setting is replaced. If you have a mouse, click on a field to move to it. Use the following Quick Steps to select menus and commands with the keyboard.

 Choosing Commands Using the Keyboard

1. Press the Alt key.

One letter in each menu name is highlighted on the menu bar.

2. Type the highlighted letter for the menu you want to select.

The menu you selected opens to show you the commands associated with that menu. One letter in each of the commands is highlighted.

3. Type the highlighted letter for the command you want to select.

If the command does not have an associated dialog box, Works carries out the command you request. When the command displays a dialog box, go on to step 4.

4. Supply information or select options in the dialog box that you want to change. Then press Enter.

Works carries out the command you request and returns to your window.   □

If you are using a mouse, you can select menus and commands as described in the following Quick Steps.

 Choosing Commands Using the Mouse

1. Point to the menu name you want to select and click.

The menu opens to show you the command names.

18

2. Point to the command you want to select and click.

If the command does not have an associated dialog box, Works carries out the command you request. If a dialog box appears, go on to step 3.

3. Supply information or click on any of the options in the dialog box you want to change, then click on OK or Done.

Works carries out the action you request and returns to the window.

☐

When necessary, this book gives separate instructions for the mouse and the keyboard for performing certain operations.

Working with Files and Directories

19

You want to save most of the information you type in Works, so it's important to understand how your computer system stores information.

What Are Files?

Files contain information that you have saved on your computer disk. A file might contain a letter, a spreadsheet showing monthly sales figures or a family budget, or a presentation. You can think of computer files just like you think of paper files; they hold information you want to save. Paper files are usually stored in a file cabinet. On the computer, the disk is your file cabinet (see Figure 2.6).

All Works files have a *filename* and a *file extension*. Works automatically adds a file extension to your filename to identify what type of file it is. A period separates the filename from the file extension. For instance, if you used the Word Processor tool to create a sales report for January, you might call it JANSALES. The complete filename is JANSALES.WPS; JANSALES is the name you give the file, and WPS is the file extension. Filenames can be up to eight characters long; file extensions are always three characters. A list of the four file extensions Works uses is as follows.

Extension	Type of file
WPS	Word Processor
WKS	Spreadsheet
WDB	Database
WCM	Communications

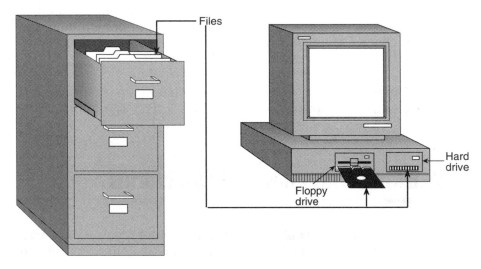

Figure 2.6   Paper and electronic storage of information.

In a color-coded paper filing system, different-colored file folders might represent different categories of files. Think of file extensions as colored file folders; the file extensions indicate different categories of files.

Directories

To help you organize your files, Works creates *directories* for them. Directories on your computer disk are analogous to file drawers in a file cabinet. In a file cabinet, you might reserve one drawer for personnel files and another drawer for customer files, labeling the drawers accordingly. If these drawers existed on your computer, PERSONNEL and CUSTOMERS would be the names of two directories.

Computer directories can be subdivided just as file drawers are. On the computer, these subdivisions are called *subdirectories*. Suppose you divide your customer file drawer into two sections, one for domestic customers and one for international. On your computer, the domestic and international sections are considered subdirectories to the customer directory (see Figure 2.7).

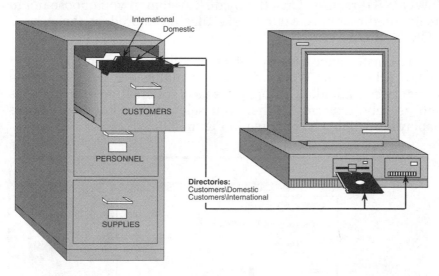

Figure 2.7   *Directories and subdirectories.*

21

If you installed Works on a hard disk, you probably installed it on a section called drive C. The installation procedure created a directory called WORKS. This is the directory where all your Works files are stored. If you wanted to create a subdirectory just for letters, it would be called C:\WORKS\LETTERS. The letter before the colon (:) indicates the disk drive, in this case, drive C. The word LETTERS indicates a subdirectory under the WORKS directory.

The designation C:\WORKS\LETTERS is called a *pathname* because it tells you the path to follow to find your file: start at disk drive C, go to the WORKS directory, then go to the LETTERS subdirectory. If you are running Works on a floppy system, your disk drive is either A or B, so your pathname is either A:\WORKS\LETTERS or B:\WORKS\LETTERS. (You'll learn how to go to a directory in a later section.)

Creating Subdirectories

You don't have to create subdirectories in Works, but if you are going to save a large number of files, creating subdirectories is recommended. If you are using a hard disk system and you choose not to create subdirectories, your Works files are stored in the C:\WORKS directory. On a floppy disk system, if you choose not to create subdirectories, your Works files are stored in the A or B WORKS directory.

To create a subdirectory, select the File Management command on the File menu. Works displays a dialog box with a Create Directory command. (This option is used for creating directories as well as subdirectories.) When you select this command, Works displays the dialog box shown in Figure 2.8.

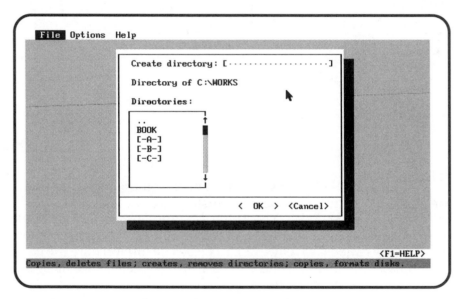

Figure 2.8   Dialog box for creating a directory or subdirectory.

You enter the name for the new subdirectory on the first line in the dialog box. The second line, Directory Of, displays the current drive and directory. In Figure 2.8, the current directory is WORKS on drive C. If you want a directory other than WORKS, you would select one from the Directories box.

Q Creating a Subdirectory

1. Select the File Management command on the File menu.

   Works displays a dialog box with a command for creating a directory.

2. Select the Create Directory command.

   Works displays the dialog box shown in Figure 2.8.

3. Select a directory from the Directory box if the current directory is not the one you want.

4. Type the name of the sub-directory you want to create on the Create Directory line, then select OK.

   Works creates the sub-directory you specify.

   ☐

23

Creating Files

Whenever you want to create a Word Processor, Spreadsheet, Database, or Communications document, you must create a file first. You create each of these types of files using the same command, and Works adds the appropriate file extension.

To create a new file, select the Create New File command on the File menu. Works displays a dialog box with four choices: New Word Processor, New Spreadsheet, New Database, and New Communications. Select the type of file you want to create, then select OK. That's it. Works creates the file and places your cursor in a window for the type of file you select.

Temporary Filenames

Whenever you use any of the Works tools to create a new file, Works assigns a temporary filename and sequence number to your file. For example, each time you enter the Spreadsheet tool, Works assigns the filename SHEET1.WKS. The sequence number keeps track of the number of new files you create while you're using Works. If you create three new files while using the Spreadsheet tool, the second file is named SHEET2.WKS, and the third file SHEET3.WKS.

⊘ **Caution:** Because Works assigns temporary filenames automatically each time you create a file, you must be careful to rename a file when you save it. If you save the file under the temporary filename, SHEET1.WKS, the next time you enter the Spreadsheet tool and create a new file, Works names it SHEET1.WKS, even though the old file named SHEET1.WKS is still in the directory of existing files. If you save the new file under SHEET1.WKS, your original file called SHEET1.WKS is overwritten and lost. To avoid losing your work, it's a good idea to rename every file immediately, even before you enter any information. If you decide you want to change the filename, you can do that later.

Saving Files

You can enter as much information into Works as you like, but unless you save your work, it won't be stored on your computer disk. Everything that you type when you are using Works is held in a temporary storage area in your computer's memory until you save the file. The contents of memory are lost if your power is interrupted or if you turn your computer off, so you must save your files regularly. It's a good idea to get in the habit of saving your work regularly—every few pages.

Works has two commands for saving a file: Save As and Save. Use the Save As command to save a file for the first time when you choose a permanent filename. Use the Save command to save the file in the future. Both the Save As and Save commands use the dialog box shown in Figure 2.9.

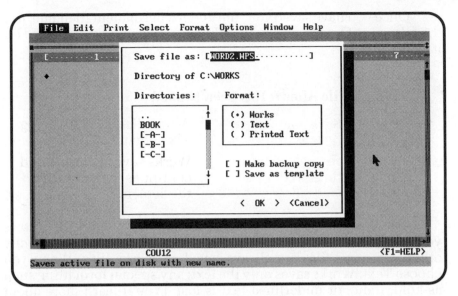

Figure 2.9   Dialog box for saving a file.

25

In the dialog box, the `Directory Of` line tells you which directory is currently chosen. This is where the file will be saved. If you want to save your file under a different directory than the one shown, select a directory from the `Directories` list, then follow the next Quick Steps.

Q Saving a File for the First Time

1. Select the Save As command from the File menu.

   Works displays the dialog box shown in Figure 2.9.

2. Type the new filename in the Save File As field in the dialog box.

   The Save File As field displays the new filename.

3. Make any other changes to the settings in the box and select `OK`.

   Works saves your file under the new name and places your cursor in the new file on your screen.   □

Once you have saved your file under a permanent filename, use the following Quick Steps to save the file when you have worked on it again.

 Saving a File After It Has Been Named

1. Select the Save command from the File menu.

   Works displays the dialog box shown in Figure 2.9.

2. Make any changes to the default settings in the dialog box and select OK.

   Works saves your file and continues to display it on the screen. ☐

The Format box in the dialog box shown in Figure 2.9 allows you to save your file in a number of ways. Unless you specify otherwise, your files are always saved as Works files. When you choose Text, Works saves only the text; any special formatting such as bold, italic, or underlined text is lost. (You'll learn more about when to use the text option in Chapter 10.) When you choose Printed Text, Works saves the file with a carriage return and line feed at the end of each line. Use this option only if you are going to use the file in another word processing program that requires this format.

When you want extra protection for your files, select Make Backup from the Save dialog box. This saves your file along with an identical copy of it. Having a backup means you always have two copies of your file in case something happens to the one you're working on. Backup copies have the same filename, but a different extension.

Extension	Type of file
BPS	Word Processor
BKS	Spreadsheet
BD	Database
BCM	Communications

Recalling A File

Once you have created and saved a file, how do you recall it when you want to work on it again? Instead of using the Create New File command, select the Open Existing File command on the File menu. When you choose this command, Works displays the dialog box shown in Figure 2.10. The options in this box are described next.

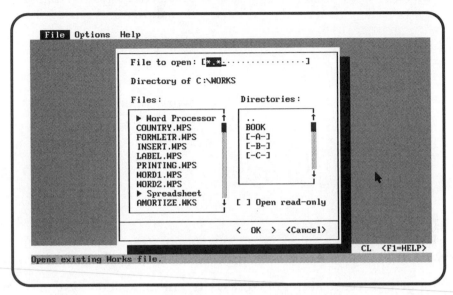

Figure 2.10   The dialog box used for opening an existing file.

File to Open   The name of the file that you want to open is displayed here. You can either type the name, or select a name from the list in the Files box.

Directory Of   This tells you the directory in which you are working. For example, if you see C:\WORKS on this line, you can see all the files in that directory listed in the Files box.

Files   The Files box lists the names of the files in the current directory. Works groups the filenames by file extension. When you select a filename from this box, Works displays its name in the File-to-Open field.

Directories   This box lists the directories that are available for you to choose from. If you want to change directories, select one of the directories in the list. Selecting the .. takes you one level higher in the *directory tree*. For example, if you are still in the C:\WORKS directory, selecting .. takes you back to drive C and shows you all the directories available there.

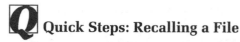

Quick Steps: Recalling a File

1. Select the Open Existing File command on the File menu.

   Works displays the dialog box shown in Figure 2.10.

2. Select the file you want to open from the Files box, then select OK.

   Works opens the file you select.

3. If the file you want isn't listed in the Files box, it must be in a different directory. Select the correct directory, select the file you want; then select OK.

   Works opens the file you select.

□

28

Using Windows in Works

One of the nicest features of Works is its built-in *window* system. The advantage to having a window system is that you can view and work on more than one file at a time. For instance, you can update figures in a spreadsheet in one window and you can type a monthly report that uses those figures in another window. You don't need to close either file to work on the other. Figure 2.11 shows multiple windows on the screen.

Using Multiple Windows

In Works you can have up to eight windows open at once. The windows can contain files from any of the four Works tools. When you have multiple windows open on your screen, Works stacks the windows on top of each other, leaving the title bar of each window visible. The window you are working in is called the *active window*. You can distinguish it from the others in several ways: the cursor blinks in the active window, the work area is a different color, the top border has a double line, and the scroll bars are visible.

To open multiple windows, start by opening one file. It can be an existing file or a new one that you create. Once you have an open file, simply select the File menu and select the Create New File or Open Existing File command. The new window stacks on top of the previous one and becomes the active window.

Title bars of
different windows

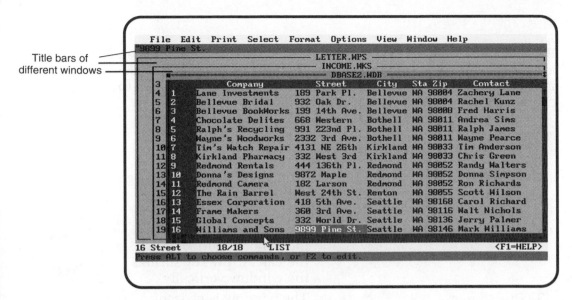

Figure 2.11   Multilple windows open on the screen.

> ▶ **Tip:** Remember to save your work frequently when using
> multiple windows. The Save and Save As commands only
> work with the currently active window.

Moving Your Cursor from One Window to Another

To switch between windows using the keyboard, select the Window
menu, then select the window you want to use from the list in the
menu.

⌨ Ctrl+F6 is a keyboard shortcut for toggling between open
windows. Press Ctrl+F6 to go to the next window. Press
Shift+Ctrl+F6 to go to the previous window.

🖱 With the mouse, you can move your cursor between windows
just by clicking in the window you want to use.

Resizing a Window

Because Works lets you have up to eight windows open on the screen at a time, your screen can become quite crowded. In order to make multiple windows workable on the screen, Works allows you to change window sizes to various dimensions.

Q Resizing a Window Using the Keyboard

1. From the active window, select the Size command from the Window menu.

   The window borders change to black and white.

2. Use the Arrow keys to move the borders of the window where you want them.

   The Up Arrow key shrinks the window horizontally; the Left Arrow key shrinks the window vertically.

3. Press Enter.

   The window is resized to the dimensions you choose. The borders return to normal and the scroll bars are visible again. □

Q Resizing a Window Using the Mouse

1. Click and hold on the resize symbol in the lower right corner of the window border.

   The window borders change to black and white.

2. Drag the mouse until the borders of the window are where you want them, and release the mouse button.

   The window is resized to the dimensions you choose. The borders return to normal and the scroll bars are visible again. □

Moving a Window

When you have multiple windows open on your screen in different sizes, it is often helpful to be able to move them where you want them on the screen. That way you can arrange the screen the way you want it, placing windows side-by-side or one above the other.

Moving a Window Using the Keyboard

1. Select the Move command from the Window menu.

   The borders of the window change to black and white.

2. Use the Arrow keys to move the window where you want it on the screen.

   The window moves to where you direct it.

3. Press Enter.

   The window freezes in the location you choose. The borders return to normal, and the scroll bars are visible again. □

▶ **Tip:** A quick way to move windows on the screen so that they all are visible is to use the Arrange All command on the Window menu. When you select Arrange All, Works chooses the best arrangement to fit all open windows on the screen at once.

31

Moving a Window Using the Mouse

1. Click and hold on the title bar of the window you want to move, and drag the mouse until the window is where you want it.

   The window follows your movements with the mouse around the screen.

2. When the window is where you want it, release the mouse button.

   The window is moved to the location you choose. □

Splitting One Window into Separate Panes

When you are working on a large file, a particularly useful Works feature is the capability to split a window into either two or four panes. Separate panes allow you to view different parts of a document in the same window.

In a Word Processor file you can only split the window horizontally, but in Spreadsheet and Database files, you can split the window either horizontally or vertically. Figure 2.12 illustrates how useful the split window can be in a Spreadsheet file. Notice how the column headings are split horizontally from the body of the spreadsheet, while the row headings are split vertically from the body. This allows you to work on different parts of the spreadsheet in the same window.

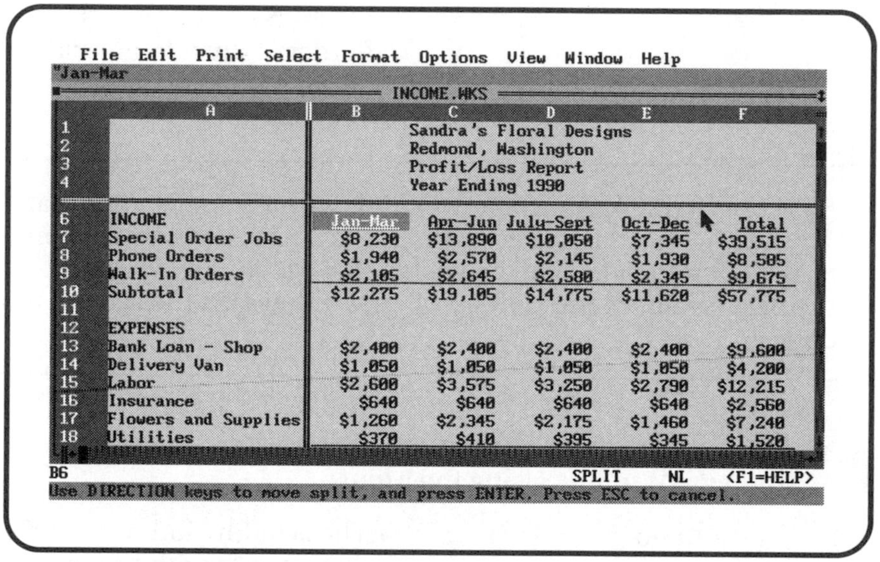

Figure 2.12   Horizontal and vertical split in a spreadsheet.

Splitting a Window into Panes Using the Keyboard

1. Select the Split command on the Window menu.

Overlying the ruler in your window are two horizontal lines that mark the split for the window.

2. Use the Up and Down Arrow keys to set the split lines where you want them in your document.

The lines overlying the ruler move to the location you choose.

3. Press Enter.

The split lines become the border of the new window pane. Your cursor is placed inside the new window pane, where you can then begin editing. □

To move your cursor back and forth from one pane to the other, press F6. The F6 key toggles between window panes.

To close the window pane, select Split from the Window menu and move the split lines back to the top of the window, then press Enter. The window returns to one pane.

Splitting a Window into Panes Using the Mouse

1. With the mouse pointer over the horizontal split bars located in the upper right corner of the window, click and drag the split bars down to the line in your document where you want the window to be split.

The split bars extend horizontally across the window and move vertically through the window as you move the mouse up and down.

33

2. When the split bars are where you want them, release the mouse button.

The split lines become the border of the new window pane. Your cursor is placed inside the new window pane, where you can now begin editing. □

Getting Help

Works is a powerful program with many different functions and commands. It would be almost impossible for you to memorize everything about Works, especially those features that you don't use regularly. To help you remember commands, keystrokes, procedures, and so on, Works provides help on-line.

There are three ways to get help in Works. One way is called *context-sensitive*, because it pertains to the context in which you are currently working. For example, if you select the Footnote command on the Edit menu, then decide you want more information about footnotes before you use the command, just press F1 to get help. Works displays a help screen about using the footnote command.

If you're not sure what topic you want help on, or if you just want to browse through the Help file, select the *Help menu* from the menu bar. From the Help menu, you can select the Help Index, Help on keyboard commands, Help on the active window, and so on.

The third kind of help Works provides is an *on-line tutorial*. The tutorial teaches you various aspects of Works in a lesson format with practice exercises. You may find the tutorial helpful if you are completely unfamiliar with Works. To use the tutorial, select Tutorial from the Help menu, or press Shift+F1 to go directly to a lesson about the task you want to perform.

34

What You've Learned

This chapter introduces you to the things you need to know about Works windows, menus, and commands before you can begin doing productive work.

▶ If you use a mouse, you can point, click, and drag to select commands and text in Works. If you use the keyboard, you usually press Alt to display the highlighted letter for each command.

▶ Among the four Works tools, the windows on the screen have many similarities. The window areas common to each tool are the title bar, menu bar, work area, status line, message line, borders, scroll bars, scroll arrow, and mouse pointer.

▶ Works commands are listed on menus at the top of each window. You open menus to find the commands you want to use. Commands that are followed by three dots (...) have dialog boxes associated with them, in which you either make choices or provide more information about the command you've chosen.

▶ Files contain information that you have saved on your computer disk. Files are categorized within directories and, sometimes, subdirectories.

▶ Select the Create New File command on the File menu to create a new file. Select the Open Existing File to recall a file you want to work on again.

▶ When you are finished working with any of the Works tools, you must save your file under a new filename in order for your work to be saved. The new filename replaces the temporary filename that Works assigns.

▶ Works has a built-in window system that allows you to have up to eight windows open on your screen at a time.

▶ Whenever you need help using Works, select the Help menu or press F1.

35

Using the Word Processor

In This Chapter

- ▶ *About the Word Processor screen*
- ▶ *Creating and editing a document*
- ▶ *Changing the way text and paragraphs look*
- ▶ *Printing and saving your document*

This chapter teaches you how to get started using the Word Processor tool in Works. You'll be guided through the basic steps of creating a simple letter. By the time you finish this chapter you'll have the basic skills to create all kinds of simple word processing documents. Many of the concepts and procedures discussed in this chapter apply to other Works tools, so spend as much time as you need until you feel comfortable with them.

Creating A Document

Before you can use the Word Processor tool to type a new document, you must create a new file. When you start Works, the opening screen displays the File menu, which includes the Create New File option. This screen is shown in Chapter 2, Figure 2.1.

When you select the Create New File option, Works displays the dialog box shown in Figure 3.1.

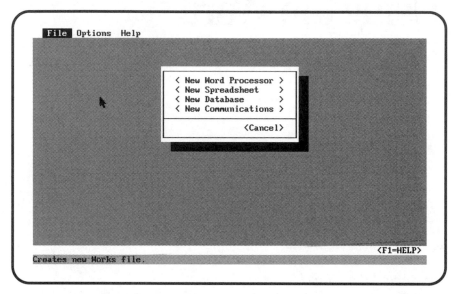

Figure 3.1   The New File dialog box.

From this dialog box, select the New Word Processor option. Works creates a new Word Processor file named WORD1.WPS and places your cursor in the empty window.

 Create a New Word Processor Document

1. Start Works according to the instructions for your screen is displayed type of PC (see Appendix A).	The opening Works on your screen.
2. Select Create New File from the File menu.	The dialog box shown in Figure 3.1 is displayed.
3. Select the New Word Processor option in the dialog box.	Works creates a new Word Processor file named WORD1.WPS and places your cursor in the window. □

About the Word Processor Screen

In Chapter 2 you were introduced to the standard features of the Works screens. Take a minute to review where the menu bar, title bar, status line, and message line are located in Figure 3.2. As you use the Word Processor tool in this chapter, notice the messages that appear on the message line and the indicators that change on the status line. Additional areas on the screen—the *document ruler, new page marker*, and *end-of-file marker*—are described after Figure 3.2. Figure 3.2 shows how the typical Word Processor screen looks before you enter any text.

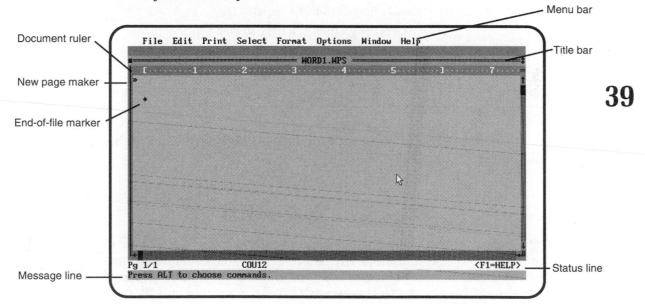

Figure 3.2.   The Works Word Processor screen.

Document Ruler

Across the top of the work area is the document ruler, measured in inches. The ruler measures the size of the document in inches and helps you see where you are relative to the size of the page you will be printing. It contains numbers that mark each inch, a left bracket ([ ) at the far left, and a right bracket ( ]) at the far right. The left and right brackets mark the points at which text will be aligned on the left and right sides. The left marker is set at 0 and the right marker is set at 6. As you type, the text you enter is positioned between the 0 and 6-inch markers.

Other settings that can appear on the ruler are shown in Table 3.1.

Table 3.1   Document ruler symbols and their settings

Symbol	Setting
|	Marks the position of the indent for the first line of a new paragraph
C	Marks the position of a centered tab
R	Marks the position of a right-aligned tab
L	Marks the position of a left-aligned tab
D	Marks the position of a decimal-aligned tab
.,-,_,=	Leading characters to fill the spaces occupied by a tab

You'll learn how to use some of these ruler settings later in this chapter. (See Using Tabs.)

New Page Marker

The beginning of a new page is marked with the >> symbol. As you are typing, Works automatically inserts a page marker at the appropriate place in your document. As you'll learn later, you can move these page breaks or insert new page breaks wherever you like.

End-of-File Marker

The solid diamond-shaped symbol marks the end of the file. If you try to move your cursor past this marker to enter text, the keyboard beeps. Your cursor must be within the document boundaries (that is, between the first line of the document and the end-of-file marker) on an existing line in order to enter text.

40

Using the Document

When you create a new Word Processor file, Works automatically assigns the name WORD1.WPS as a temporary filename until you change it. Now is a good time to use the Save As command to rename your document to the name you want (see Chapter 2). That way you won't lose what you type if you forget to rename the file when you finish working. Rename the sample file you've just created to LETTER.WPS. Remember, you don't have to type the file extension .WPS; Works adds it for you automatically.

Now you can begin typing. The text you type is inserted in the document to the left of the cursor. When you type a short line that doesn't go all the way to the right margin, press Enter to end the line. When you continue typing past the end of the line, as in a paragraph, Works automatically *wraps*, or moves the text down to the beginning of the next line, so that you don't have to press Enter at the end of each line in a paragraph as with a typewriter. When you have finished typing a paragraph, press Enter. This brings the cursor back to the left margin on the next line.

41

Type the text shown in Figure 3.3 to begin creating your letter. Press enter to insert blank lines. For now, ignore any errors that you make as you are typing; you'll learn how to correct them later.

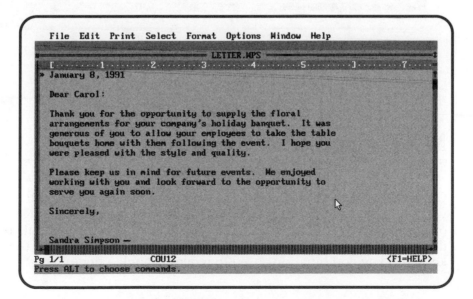

Figure 3.3   A sample letter created using the Word Processor tool.

Works always enters text to the left of the cursor. When you want to add text to a document, move your cursor back to the place where you want to insert text, then begin typing. Works pushes the existing text to the right and inserts the characters you type.

The letter you just typed doesn't include the sender's or receiver's address. Move your cursor to the beginning of the document and type the sender's address as shown in Figure 3.4. Then move your cursor below the date and type the address of the company.

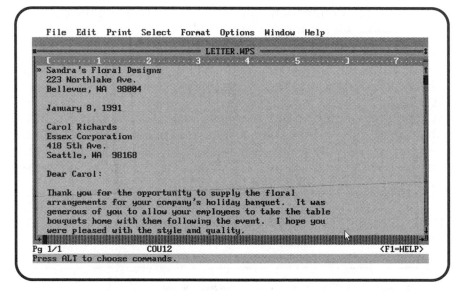

Figure 3.4   Sender's and Receiver's addresses inserted in your letter.

Moving Through the Document

Once you have entered some text in your document, you'll find that you want to move your cursor forward or backward to make changes or enter new text. There are many ways to move throughout a document, some faster than others. Table 3.2 describes some of the keys and key combinations used to move through a document.

Table 3.2 *Moving Through a Document*

Press	To
Right and Left Arrow keys	Move right or left one character at a time
Up and Down Arrow keys	Move up or down one line at a time
PageUp, PageDn	Move forward in the document or backward in the document one window at a time
Home	Move to the beginning of the current line
End	Move to the end of the current line
Ctrl+Home	Move to the top of the document
Ctrl+End	Move to the bottom of the document
Ctrl+PageUp	Move to the first line currently shown in the window
Ctrl+PageDn	Move to the last line currently shown in the window
Ctrl+Right Arrow key	Move forward one word at a time
Ctrl+Left Arrow key	Move backward one word at a time
Ctrl+Up Arrow key	Move backward one paragraph
Ctrl+Down Arrow key	Move forward one paragraph

43

If you want to go to a specific page in a document, select the Go To command on the Select menu. Type the page number in the Go To field of the dialog box and select OK. Your cursor moves to the beginning of the page you select.

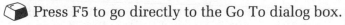 Press F5 to go directly to the Go To dialog box.

With the mouse, you can move the cursor anywhere you like in the document by clicking at the location you choose. You can also scroll forward or backward through the document one line at a time by clicking on the up or down scroll arrows. If you want to scroll continuously, click and hold the mouse button on the scroll arrow.

Selecting Text

In the Word Processor as well as other Works tools, you are selecting text frequently. Selecting text tells Works on which text you want to work. Whenever you want to move, copy, or delete text, change the way the text looks, and so on, you almost always need to select the text first. On your screen, Works highlights your selected text so you can be sure of where you are making changes.

In general, there are four different ways to select text: using the Select menu, using the Shift key, using the F8 key, or using the mouse. The method you choose is entirely up to you. With practice you'll learn which methods work best for the task you want to perform.

Using the Select Menu

44

To select text using the Select menu, start by placing your cursor where you want to begin selecting text, then select the Text command from the Select menu. At this point, there are any number of key combinations you can use to select text. Start by pressing the Right or Left Arrow key repeatedly. This allows you to select text a character at a time. Now try pressing the Up or Down Arrow key. This allows you to select text a line at a time.

You can use any of the keys or key combinations listed in Table 3.2 to select text. Try selecting text using these keys. When all the text you want to select is highlighted, you're ready to choose a command. To cancel any selection, press Esc.

To select the entire file using the Select menu, use the All command rather than the Text command on the Select menu. As soon as you choose All, Works highlights your entire document. Again, to cancel your selection, press Esc.

Using the Shift Key

Using the Shift key to select text is a keyboard shortcut to using the Text command on the Select menu. To select text using the Shift key, place your cursor where you want to begin selecting text. Press and hold the Shift key. At this point, the instructions are the same as for using the Select menu. Start by pressing either the Right or Left Arrow key. The Right and Left Arrow keys allow you to select text a character at a time. Hold down an Arrow key to move quickly. Still holding down the Shift key, now try the Up and Down Arrow keys. This allows you to select text a line at a time.

The Shift key can be used in combination with many other keys to select areas of text. Try selecting text by holding the Shift key in combination with any of the keys listed in Table 3.2. When all the text you want to select is highlighted, release the Shift key. To cancel any selection, press Esc.

Using the F8 Key

Like the Shift key, the F8 key is a keyboard shortcut for using the Text option on the Select menu. Pressing the F8 key signals Works to begin selecting, then allows you to extend your selection of text.

45

Move your cursor to the point where you want to begin selecting text. Press F8. Notice the status line shows EXT, indicating that you can now extend the amount of text selected. Press the Right or Left Arrow key to select text. If you want to select a line at a time, you can use the Up or Down Arrow key after pressing F8.

By pressing F8 repeatedly, you can select text more quickly. You can select a character, a word, a sentence, a paragraph, or the entire file depending on how many times you press F8 (Table 3.3).

Table 3.3   Text selection with the F8 key

Press F8	To
Once	Select character
Twice	Select word
Three times	Select sentence
Four times	Select paragraph
Five times	Select entire file

Try using F8 to select text in the sample letter you typed. If you press F8 too many times, you can press SHIFT+F8 to move your selection backward.

Using the Mouse

The fourth way to select text is to use the mouse. You can select any amount of text by placing the mouse pointer where you want to begin selecting, then click and drag. Release the mouse button when you reach the point where you want to stop selecting text. The text you select is highlighted.

A quicker way to select text using the mouse is to choose one of the methods presented in Table 3.4.

Table 3.4   Text selection with the mouse

To	Click
Select word	The right mouse button anywhere on the word
Select sentence	The right and left mouse buttons simultaneously anywhere in the sentence
Select line	The left mouse button in the left margin (to the left of the first character in the line)
Select paragraph	The right mouse button in the left margin
Select file	The right and left mouse buttons simultaneously in the left margin

To cancel any selection, click anywhere in the window other than the area you've highlighted.

Editing Text

Now that you know how to enter text into a document, what do you do if you decide you want to change it? One of the advantages of using a word processor is that you can change your document whenever you like. You can correct errors, add text, delete text, move text to a new location, copy text, and so on. Any changes you make after you first enter the text is referred to as *editing*.

Correcting Errors

There are several ways to correct errors. The quickest way to correct small errors is to use either Backspace or Delete. Backspace erases the character to the left of the cursor. Delete erases the character at the cursor.

To erase using Backspace, move your cursor to the right of the character you want to erase, press Backspace, then retype the correct character. To erase using Delete, move your cursor to the character you want to erase, press Delete, then retype the correct character. You can press either key repeatedly to erase more than one character. Blank lines that you insert by pressing Enter are read by Works as characters also, so you can delete them just as you delete other characters.

If you made any errors in the letter you just typed, correct them now using the Backspace or Delete keys.

47

Deleting Blocks of Text

The Backspace and Delete keys work fine for small corrections, but often you may want to delete larger blocks of text. For this type of job, it is quicker to select the text first, then delete.

Q **Deleting Text**

1. Move your cursor to the point where you want to begin deleting text.	
2. Using one of the four methods for selecting text, select the text you want to delete.	The text is highlighted.
3. Press Delete.	The text you select is deleted. ☐

If you decide you don't want to delete the text once you've selected it, press ESC. When you begin typing again, the highlight returns to plain text.

Moving Text

Sometimes you need to make major changes to your document, perhaps moving several paragraphs to another place in the document, or reorganizing the document entirely. Without a word processor, you would have to retype the document, but with Works, you can move text wherever you want it. Moving text saves you the time of having to retype.

In order to move text, you must select the text first. Once you select the text, you can decide where you want to move it.

Q Moving Text

1. Select the text you want to move.	The text you select is highlighted.
2. Select the Move command from the Edit menu.	The message line displays the message: `Select new location and press Enter. Press Esc to cancel.`
3. Move your cursor to the point where you want your text to be moved.	
4. Press Enter.	The text you select is moved to the new location. □

 Press F3 to move the selected text.

In the letter you typed, move the sentence in the first paragraph that begins with `It was generous...` to the end of the first paragraph. Select the text using any of the methods you just learned and follow the previous Quick Steps to move the sentence. After moving the paragraph, your letter should look like the one shown in Figure 3.5.

Copying Text

You may want to use some text in more than one location in your document. If so, you can copy the text instead of retyping it. When you copy text, the original text stays in the first location and is copied to the second. The steps for copying text and moving text are similar except that you use the Copy command on the Edit menu.

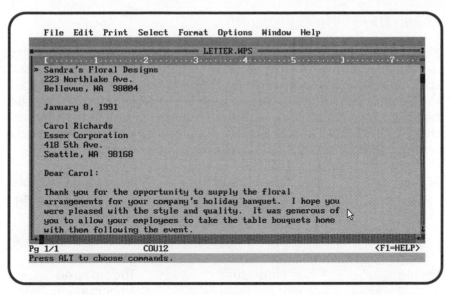

File Edit Print Select Format Options Window Help
```
═══════════════════════ LETTER.WPS ═══════════════════════
[········1·········2·········3·········4·········5·······]·······7·····
» Sandra's Floral Designs
  223 Northlake Ave.
  Bellevue, WA  98004

  January 8, 1991

  Carol Richards
  Essex Corporation
  418 5th Ave.
  Seattle, WA  98168

  Dear Carol:

  Thank you for the opportunity to supply the floral
  arrangements for your company's holiday banquet.  I hope you
  were pleased with the style and quality.  It was generous of
  you to allow your employees to take the table bouquets home
  with them following the event.

Pg 1/1              COU12                          <F1=HELP>
Press ALT to choose commands.
```

Figure 3.5   Your letter after moving a sentence to a new location.

49

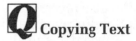 **Copying Text**

1. Select the text you want to copy.

   Works highlights the text you select.

2. Select the Copy command from the Edit menu.

   The message line displays the message: Select new location and press Enter. Press Esc to cancel.

3. Move your cursor to the point where you want the text to be copied.

4. Press Enter.

   The text you select is copied to the new location. □

Press Shift+F3 to copy the selected text. To copy the same selection of text again, press Shift+F7.

Experiment with copying text using the letter you just typed. Try selecting a paragraph and copying it to a new location. When you are finished, delete the paragraph you copied.

Using the Undo Command

Sometimes when you are using the Word Processor tool, you might move a paragraph, delete a word, or change the format of some text, then decide you want to change it back. To change the text back to the way it was originally, you don't have to retype the text, you can use the Undo command on the Edit menu. The Undo command reverses the most recent editing or formatting change you make, which includes all of the following actions or commands:

Move	Insert chart	Normal paragraph
Copy	Footnote	Left, Center, Right, Justified
Copy special	Plain text	Single and Double-space
Delete	Underline	Indents and Spacing
Insert special	Italic	Tabs
Insert field	Font and Style	Borders

50

In addition to all of these, the Undo command also reverses the most recent spelling changes made by the Check Spelling command on the Options menu, as well as any words replaced using the Replace command on the Select menu. (You'll learn about these in Chapter 4.)

> ⊘ **Caution:** Remember that Undo reverses only the most recent action taken. If you delete a paragraph, then decide you want to bring it back, you must use the Undo command immediately. If you make any other changes before you select Undo, Works will undo that change instead of bringing back your paragraph.

Changing The Way Text Looks

One of the things a word processor lets you do that is difficult to do on a typewriter is to change the way text looks. With Works, you can change text to bold or italic, or you can underline it.

Works uses the same keystrokes or procedures for changing the way text looks, whether you want underline, bold, or italic. The basic procedure is outlined in the following Quick Steps.

Q Changing the Way Text Looks

1. Select the text you want to change.

   Works highlights the text you select.

2. Select the Format menu.

   The Format menu opens.

3. Select the feature you want to use to change the text you select (that is, bold, underline, italic, and so on) and press Enter.

   Works changes the text you select to the feature you select.

Press Ctrl+B to make the selected text bold. Press Ctrl+I to make the selected text italic. Press Ctrl+U to underline the selected text.

51

In your sample letter, use the previous Quick Steps to change *Sandra's Floral Designs*, in the sender's address, to bold text.

Changing the Format of Paragraphs

For certain documents or sections of a document, you may want to change the way paragraphs are aligned or spaced. This is referred to as the *paragraph format*. Changing the format of a paragraph adds variety to your document and can help make portions of text stand out. Works gives you many options for changing paragraph format.

Indenting Paragraphs

One of the ways Works allows you to change the format of paragraphs is to use an *indent*. An indent is the distance between the right or left margin and the text in a paragraph. You can indent a paragraph from the right margin, from the left margin, or you can indent just the first line of a paragraph.

To change the margins of a paragraph, you use the Indents and Spacing command on the Format menu. The dialog box for this command is shown in Figure 3.6.

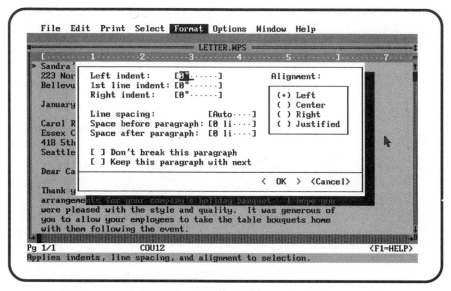

Figure 3.6   The Indents and Spacing dialog box.

Before you indent a paragraph, look for the left and right brackets ([ ]) on the ruler at the top of your document. Earlier in this chapter you learned that these brackets mark the left and right margins of your document. Notice that the left margin is set at 0 and the right margin at 6.

To indent a paragraph, you use the Left Indent, First Line Indent, or the Right Indent fields in the dialog box. Notice that all three are currently set at 0 inches.

The Left Indent marks the point at which Works aligns the text on the left side. (On a typewriter, this is called the left margin.) When you set the Left Indent at 1, Works moves the left bracket on the ruler to 1 and aligns the left edge of the paragraph under that point, leaving a one-inch left margin. The Right Indent works the same way; when you set it at 1, Works moves the right bracket on the ruler to 5 and aligns the right edge of the paragraph under that point, leaving a one-inch right margin.

When you want to indent only the first line of a paragraph, change the First Line Indent setting in the dialog box. Works measures the First Line Indent from the Left Indent rather than from the zero point on the ruler. For example, if the First Line Indent is set at 1 and the Left Indent is set at 0, the first line of your paragraph will be indented one inch; the rest of the paragraph will not be indented at all.

Q Simple Paragraph Indent

1. Select the paragraph you want to indent.	The paragraph you select is highlighted.
2. Select the Indents and Spacing command from the Format menu.	The Indents and Spacing dialog box appears.
3. Change the Left Indent, Right Indent, or First Line Indent to the setting you want.	The settings you choose appear in the dialog box.
4. Select OK.	The paragraph you select is reformatted according to the settings you choose. □

53

In the sample letter you typed, indent the first line of both paragraphs one-half inch. You can change both paragraphs at once if you include both in your selection. Follow the Quick Steps outlined just previously, setting only the First Line Indent at .5. When the paragraphs have been indented, you can delete the blank line between them. Your letter should look like the one shown in Figure 3.7.

Changing Alignment of Paragraphs

Another way you can change the format of a paragraph is to change its *alignment*. Many books use *left-aligned* paragraphs. This means that the characters at the left margin line up vertically while the characters at the right margin are ragged. The paragraph you are reading is an example of a left-aligned paragraph. Works automatically creates left-aligned paragraphs unless you specify otherwise.

In a *right-aligned* paragraph, the characters at the right margin align vertically while the characters at the left margin are jagged. An example is shown next:

Tom's Toys for Tots
1490 Evergreen Drive N.E.
Seattle, WA 98116

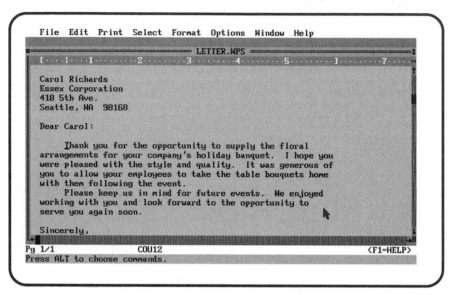

Figure 3.7   Letter with indented paragraphs.

Another option for aligning text in a paragraph is to *justify* it. In a justified paragraph, the characters at the right as well as left margins line up vertically. Works justifies the margins of a paragraph by adding spaces between words where they are needed so that every line measures the same length. The paragraph you are reading is justified.

The other alternative for aligning text is to *center* it. Centered text is often used for titles or for the name and address on a resume. A sample of centered text is shown next.

Resume
Janet M. Michaelson
15439 South Seahurst Drive
Seahurst, WA 98196

Press Ctrl+R to right-align the selected text. Press Ctrl+J to justify selected text. Press Ctrl+C to center selected text. Press Ctrl+X to return selected text to its normal alignment.

The following Quick Steps procedures can be used to format left, center, right, and justified paragraphs.

Q Setting Paragraph Alignment

1. Select the paragraph you want to realign.	Works highlights the text you select.
2. Select the Left, Center, Right, or Justified command from the Format Menu.	The paragraph is immediately realigned to the alignment style you select. □

If you want to change a paragraph back to its normal alignment, select the paragraph, then select the Normal Paragraph command from the Format menu.

In your sample letter, follow the alignment steps listed in the previous Quick Steps to center the name and address for *Sandra's Floral Designs*. Include all three lines in your selection to center all three lines at once. Add three or four blank lines below the address to separate it from the rest of the letter. Your letter should now look like the one shown in Figure 3.8.

55

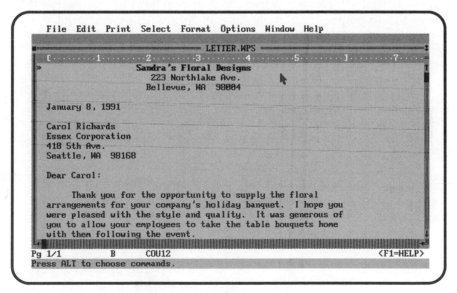

Figure 3.8   The sender's address is now centered.

Changing the Line Spacing of Paragraphs

Works also allows you to vary the *line spacing* of paragraphs. This includes the space between lines, and the number of lines before and after a paragraph. Sometimes you may want to print a draft document double-spaced to make it easier to read and make corrections. To do this, first select the paragraph, then select the Double Space command from the Format menu.

If you want to change the line spacing to something other than single or double-spaced, or you want to add an extra line above or below a paragraph, use the Indents and Spacing dialog box on the Format menu (see Figure 3.6). The Line Spacing, Space Before Paragraph, and Space After Paragraph options in the dialog box are all measured in number of lines.

Works sets the Line Spacing option to *auto* meaning automatic, which is the same thing as single-spaced. The auto setting is the same as a setting of 1, or one line, which is equivalent to $\frac{1}{6}$ inch. You can change the line spacing to fractional numbers, 1.5, 2.25, 1.25, and so on. If you want to add lines before or after a paragraph, change the settings in the Space Before and Space After Paragraph fields. To reset the line spacing of a paragraph, follow the next Quick Steps.

 Changing Line Spacing of Paragraphs

1. Select the paragraph you want to change.

   The paragraph you select is highlighted.

2. Select the Indents and Spacing command from the Format menu.

   The Indents and Spacing dialog box is displayed.

3. Make whatever changes you choose to the Line Spacing, Space Before Paragraph, or Space After Paragraph fields.

   The settings you choose replace the old settings in the dialog box.

4. Select OK.

   The paragraph you select conforms to the new spacing settings that you choose. □

56

Press Ctrl+1 to change selected text to single-line spacing. Press Ctrl+2 to change selected text to double-line spacing.

If you want to change a paragraph back to its normal line spacing, select the paragraph, then select the Normal Paragraph command from the Format menu.

Using Tabs

A *tab* is a point on the line where your cursor moves when you press the Tab key. Tabs are most often used to indent text or create tables. Using tab stops saves you the time of pressing the spacebar to move your cursor and the trouble of having to line up text manually. You should always use tab stops to create tables since text that appears to be lined up on the screen may not actually be lined up when you print it, especially if it contains different type styles or sizes.

In Works, you can use preset—or default—tab stops, or you can set custom tab stops. The default tabs in Works are set at half-inch intervals but they are not displayed on the Works ruler. When you use tabs in your document, you can display the tabs by selecting the Show All Characters command on the Options menu. Tabs are designated by a small right-arrow symbol.

To set custom or default tab stops, use the Tabs command on the Format menu. When you select this command, Works displays the Tabs dialog box. Select Default at the bottom of the box and the dialog box for tab spacing shown in Figure 3.9 is displayed.

In the Spacing field, change the default tab spacing to whatever interval you want. (You'll learn more about the other options in this dialog box in Chapter 4.)

 Changing Default Tab Stops

1. Select the Tabs command from the Format menu.

   The Tab Position dialog box is displayed.

2. Select Default from the Tabs dialog box.

   The Tab Spacing dialog box is displayed.

57

3. In the Spacing box, change the interval to whatever frequency you want, measured in inches. For instance, if you want preset tabs every 1.5 inches, type 1.5.

The Spacing box displays the interval you type.

4. Select OK.

The dialog box disappears and the default tabs are reset to the interval you choose.

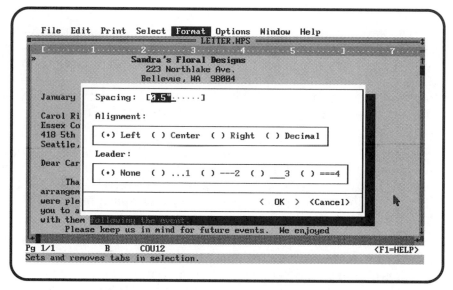

Figure 3.9   The dialog box for tab spacing and alignment.

Printing Your Document

When you're ready to print your document, follow four basic steps:

1. Check your document to see that page breaks fall where you want them. If not, you need to move them using the Insert Page Break command on the Print menu.

2. Use the Print Preview command on the Print menu to see how your document will look when printed according to the current settings. Pay special attention to page layout, page breaks, headers and footers, and so on.
3. If necessary, change any page layout or margin settings using the Page Setup and Margins command on the Print menu.
4. When all settings are correct, print your file using the Print command on the Print menu.

These steps and commands are detailed in the following paragraphs.

Page Breaks

As you type your document, Works automatically determines where page breaks should fall based on the size of paper and margin settings you're using. Works inserts a double-arrow (>>) symbol in the left margin to mark the page break. Works will not leave one line of a paragraph by itself at the top or bottom of a page; it adjusts page breaks to avoid this condition.

Sometimes you may want to force a page break, for instance, when you want a cover page for a document. In these cases, you can insert page breaks yourself using the Insert Page Break command on the Print menu. When you select this command, Works inserts the page break marker in the left margin as well as a dotted line across the window.

There may be times when you want to prevent a particular paragraph from being broken across pages, or you may want to keep two paragraphs together on one page. Use the Indents and Spacing command on the Format menu to set these conditions. Works recognizes these and inserts page breaks accordingly.

Print Preview

The Print Preview feature in Works allows you to see how the printed page will look based on your current print settings. This feature is very helpful for viewing the page layout, page breaks, and so on. Make use of this feature frequently—it can save you a lot of paper. To use Print Preview, select the Preview command on the Print menu. Your window should look like the one shown in Figure 3.10.

59

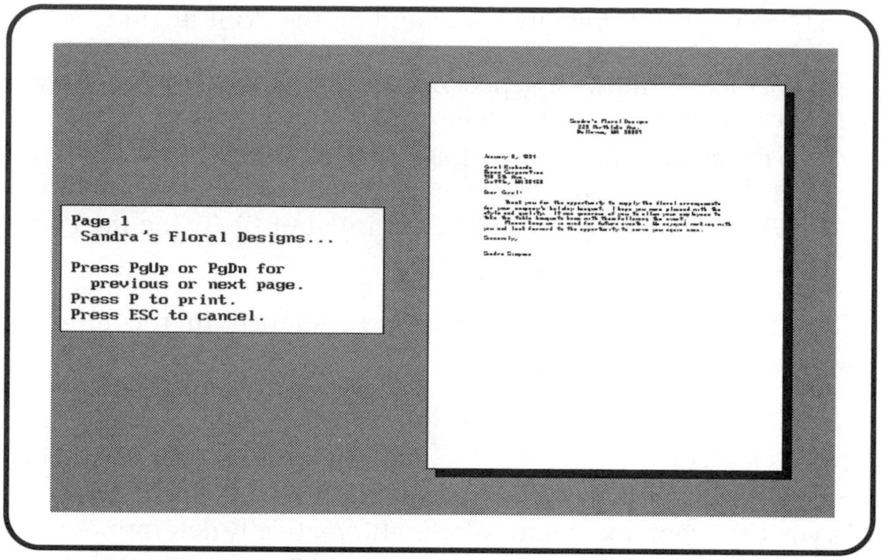

Figure 3.10   Your letter displayed in Print Preview.

Notice that the text is difficult to read because the print is reduced, but you don't need to be able to read the text here, just check the page layout, headers, footers, and page breaks.

Page Setup and Margins

Next, you want to make sure your print margins and paper size are set correctly. If you are using standard 8.5-by-11-inch paper and you are printing from top to bottom, or *portrait* style, chances are you won't need to change any settings. The page setup and margins in Works are preset for this size of paper and print direction. If you want to print on a different size of paper, or if you want to print sideways, or *landscape* style, you need to change some print settings. (Note that not all printers are able to print in landscape mode. If you aren't sure about your printer, check your printer manual.)

When you want to change the margins or the page size of a document use the Page Setup and Margins command on the Print menu. This command deals with the page areas shown in Figure 3.11.

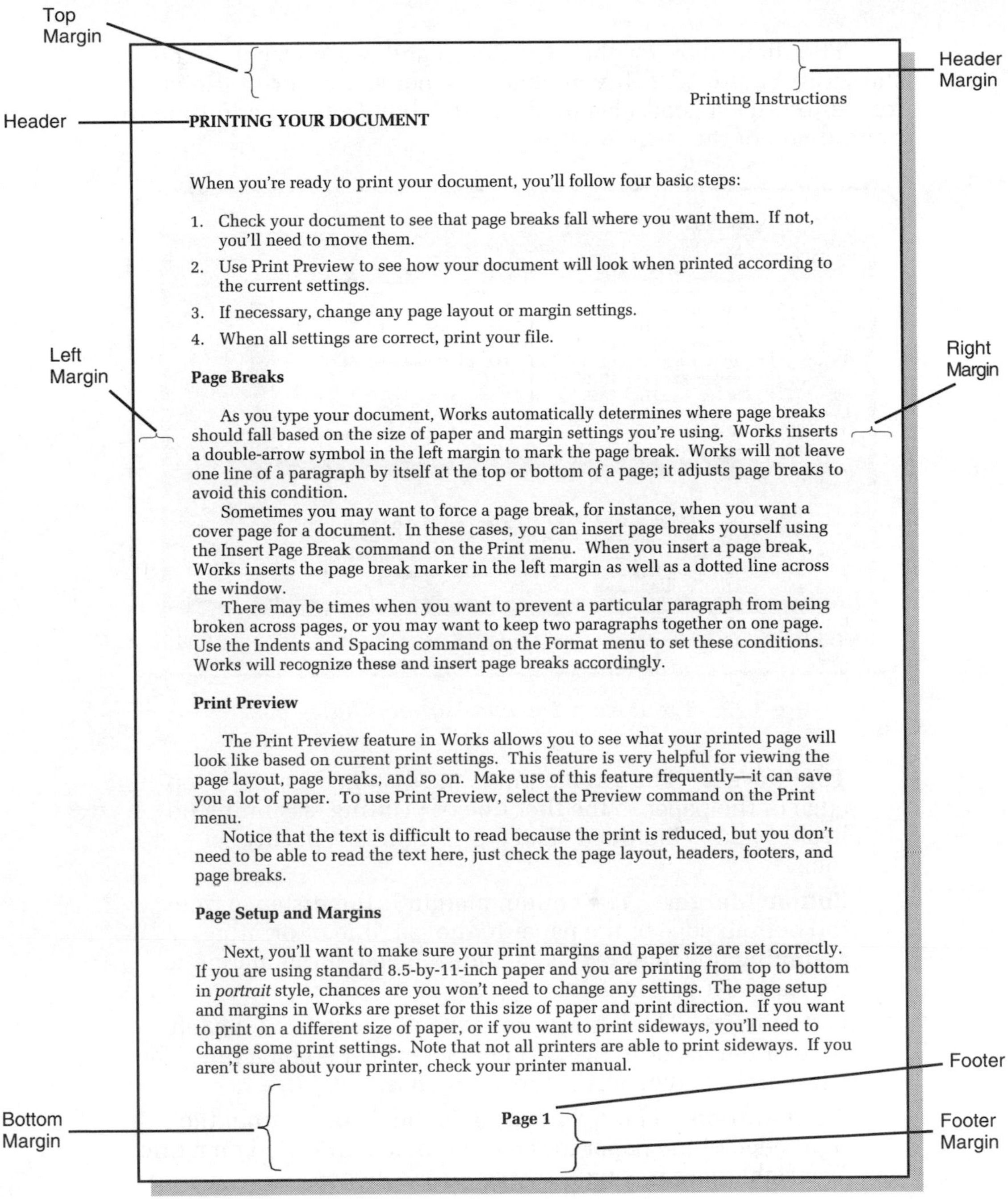

Top
Margin

Header
Margin

Header ——— Printing Instructions

PRINTING YOUR DOCUMENT

When you're ready to print your document, you'll follow four basic steps:

1. Check your document to see that page breaks fall where you want them. If not, you'll need to move them.
2. Use Print Preview to see how your document will look when printed according to the current settings.
3. If necessary, change any page layout or margin settings.
4. When all settings are correct, print your file.

Left
Margin

Right
Margin

Page Breaks

As you type your document, Works automatically determines where page breaks should fall based on the size of paper and margin settings you're using. Works inserts a double-arrow symbol in the left margin to mark the page break. Works will not leave one line of a paragraph by itself at the top or bottom of a page; it adjusts page breaks to avoid this condition.

Sometimes you may want to force a page break, for instance, when you want a cover page for a document. In these cases, you can insert page breaks yourself using the Insert Page Break command on the Print menu. When you insert a page break, Works inserts the page break marker in the left margin as well as a dotted line across the window.

There may be times when you want to prevent a particular paragraph from being broken across pages, or you may want to keep two paragraphs together on one page. Use the Indents and Spacing command on the Format menu to set these conditions. Works will recognize these and insert page breaks accordingly.

61

Print Preview

The Print Preview feature in Works allows you to see what your printed page will look like based on current print settings. This feature is very helpful for viewing the page layout, page breaks, and so on. Make use of this feature frequently—it can save you a lot of paper. To use Print Preview, select the Preview command on the Print menu.

Notice that the text is difficult to read because the print is reduced, but you don't need to be able to read the text here, just check the page layout, headers, footers, and page breaks.

Page Setup and Margins

Next, you'll want to make sure your print margins and paper size are set correctly. If you are using standard 8.5-by-11-inch paper and you are printing from top to bottom in *portrait* style, chances are you won't need to change any settings. The page setup and margins in Works are preset for this size of paper and print direction. If you want to print on a different size of paper, or if you want to print sideways, you'll need to change some print settings. Note that not all printers are able to print sideways. If you aren't sure about your printer, check your printer manual.

Footer

Bottom
Margin

Page 1

Footer
Margin

Figure 3.11 Page layout for a Works document.

The dialog box for the Page Setup and Margins command is shown in Figure 3.12. If you change paper size or print direction frequently, it's a good idea to check this box from time to time to remind you of the current settings.

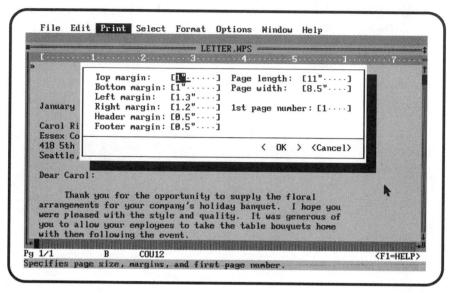

Figure 3.12   The Page Setup and Margins dialog box.

Top Margin   The top margin is the distance from the top edge of the paper to the first line of printing, assuming no header text is included. The top margin is typically set to 1 inch.

Bottom Margin   The bottom margin is the distance from the bottom edge of the paper to the last line of printing, assuming no footer text is included. The bottom margin is typically set to 1 inch.

Left Margin   The left margin is the distance from the left edge of the paper to the first character printed on a line. The left margin is typically set to 1.3 inches.

Right Margin   The right margin is the distance from the right edge of the paper to the last character printed on a line. The right margin is typically set to 1.2 inches.

Header Margin   The header margin is the distance from the top edge of the paper to the first line in the header. Because the header is printed within the top margin, the top margin must always be larger than the header margin. The header margin is typically set to .5 inch.

Footer Margin   The footer margin is the distance from the bottom edge of the paper to the last line in the footer. Because the header is printed within the bottom margin, the bottom margin must always be larger than the footer margin. The footer margin is typically set to .5 inch.

Page Length   The length of the sheet of paper being printed. Typically 11-inch paper is used.

Page Width   The distance from the left edge of the paper to the right edge of the paper, typically 8.5 inches.

First Page Number   This box is used to specify the first number to use to begin page numbering. Typically set to 1, you may want to change it under special circumstances.

Whenever you print on a nonstandard size of paper or in a different print direction, you need to change some of these settings. For example, if you want to print on legal size paper, you need to change the Page Length to 14. If you want to print sideways in landscape mode on 8.5-by-11-inch paper, you need to change the Page Width to 11 and the Page Length to 8.5.

Even when you are using 8.5-by-11-inch paper in portrait style, you still may need to change some settings. For example, if you use a paragraph header or footer in your document, you probably need to change the Header Margin or Footer Margin to a larger setting. If you want the print area on the page to be wider, you need to set the Right Margin and Left Margin to smaller numbers.

63

Q **Changing Word Processor Page Setup and Margins**

1. Choose the Page Setup and Margins command on the Print menu.

   The dialog box shown in Figure 3.12 is displayed.

2. Press the Arrow keys, or Tab to select the setting you want to change.

   Works highlights the selected setting field.

3. Type new settings for any of the options in the dialog box, then select OK.

   Works reformats your document to the settings that you enter.   □

Printing

When you've checked your page breaks and all of the settings discussed previously, you're ready to print your document. Your printer must be turned on and ready to print before you give Works the command to print. Select the Print command on the Print menu. The dialog box shown in Figure 3.13 is displayed.

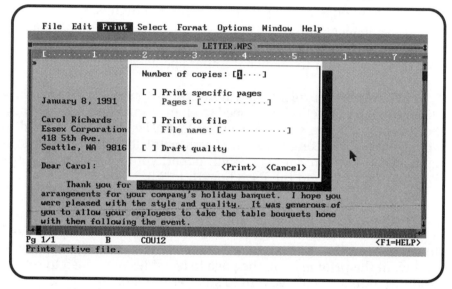

Figure 3.13   The Print dialog box.

Number of Copies   In this field, type the number of copies you want to print.

Print Specific Pages   You don't have to print the entire document each time you print. If you want only one page, type that page number. If you want a range of pages, for example, pages 6 through 9, type 6:9. Or if you want a variety of pages, type 3,5,7,10.

Print to File   When you use this option, Works saves your document with all the special printer instructions it needs to print the file. When you save your file this way, you can print it from DOS without having to start up Works. You can also send the file to another computer where it can be printed without having Works.

Draft Quality   Some printers are able to print in *draft* mode, meaning they print a lower print quality, but at a faster speed. If your printer can print draft quality, use this option when you want faster printing. Note, however, that if you include charts in your document they will not print, and text that you have justified in your document may print normally instead.

When all options are set the way you want them, check to see that your printer is turned on and is ready to print, then select `Print`.

Saving Your Document

It's a good idea to save your document every page or so as you are entering or editing text. This is particularly important in areas that are subject to power fluctuations so that you won't lose any work that you've done.

65

You may recall from Chapter 2 that all Works files are saved in the same way. Chapter 2 includes a discussion of files and directories, temporary filenames, and saving files. Please refer to Chapter 2 for specific instructions for saving your file.

Use the Save or Save As command from the File menu now to save the LETTER.WPS file you created in this chapter. You'll use it again in Chapter 4.

What You've Learned

This chapter introduces you to the most commonly used features of the Word Processor tool. You've learned how to create Word Processor documents and how to make basic changes to them. The main points covered in this chapter are summarized next.

▶ Create a new document using the Create New File command on the File menu.

▶ Select text using the Select menu, the Shift key, the F8 key, and the mouse.

▶ Correct errors and delete blocks of text by selecting the text first, then pressing Delete.

▶ Move and copy selected text using the Move and Copy commands on the Edit menu.

▶ Use the Undo command on the Edit menu to reverse your most recent editing or formatting change.

▶ Use the commands on the Format menu to add bold, underline, or italics to your text.

▶ Use the commands on the Format menu to change the alignment of text from normal to center, right, or justified, or to make your document double-spaced.

▶ Use the Indents and Spacing command on the Format menu to change the line spacing in a paragraph.

▶ Use the Tabs command on the format menu to change the default tab interval from .5 inch.

▶ Use the Print menu to print standard 8.5-by-11-inch documents in portrait style or change page setup and print settings for special printing conditions.

Chapter 4

Expanding Your Word Processor Skills

In This Chapter

67

► *Changing the font and style of text and paragraphs*
► *Finding a word or phrase and replacing it automatically*
► *Adding repetitive text at the top or bottom of each page*
► *Checking your spelling and finding the right words to use*
► *Inserting footnotes and bookmarks*

In Chapter 3 you learned the most basic skills you need to create Works Word Processor documents. In this chapter you'll build on those basic skills by learning some of the professional touches you can add to your documents. You'll be using the document, LETTER.WPS, that you created in Chapter 3. Recall this document now if you want to follow along.

Formatting Features

The term *formatting* refers to text characteristic (bold, centered, left-aligned) as well as paragraph characteristics, (justified alignment, indented, or bordered). In Chapter 3 you learned how to use some

simple text formats such as bold, underline, or italic. You also
learned how to create simple paragraph indents using commands on
the Format menu. In this section you'll learn how to make other
changes to the text and paragraph format including *subscript* and
superscript, hanging indents, custom tabs, and *borders.* You'll also
learn how to change the *font* style and size as well.

Changing the Font and Style of Text

A *font* is a term that is often misunderstood because it is defined in
many different ways and frequently misused. For our purposes, a
font refers to a particular style or design of character that Works
displays on your screen or prints when you print your document.
Each font has a particular shape, weight, and character detail that
makes it unique.

68

When you change the font in Works, you won't see the change
on the screen, only in your printed copy. Works always uses a *screen*
font for its display regardless of the font you choose for your printed
copy. When you select the Font and Style command on the Format
menu, Works displays the Font and Style dialog box shown in Figure
4.1. To enter a special font to appear in your printed copy, select a
font from the font list shown in the dialog box.

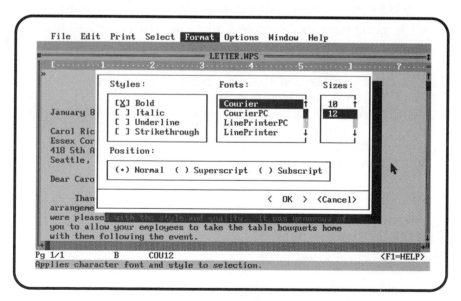

Figure 4.1   The Font and Style dialog box.

The list of available fonts and sizes is entirely dependent upon the type of printer you have. Some printers may offer multiple choices while others may offer just one or two. Check your printer manual to see which fonts and sizes your printer is capable of printing. As you select different fonts from the list displayed in the dialog box, notice that Works also displays the available sizes for each. If you want to change the size as well, select the font first, then the size.

Using the Font and Style command on the Format menu, you can change selected text to *strikethrough*, which is often used in legal documents. When you need to mark a paragraph to be deleted but you still need to be able to read the original text, use the strikethrough option. Strikethrough retains the original text but types a dash or hyphen through the text so that it's still readable.

In your sample letter, select the last sentence in the first paragraph, then select the strikethrough option in the Font and Style dialog box. Figure 4.2 illustrates the strikethrough text in the letter.

69

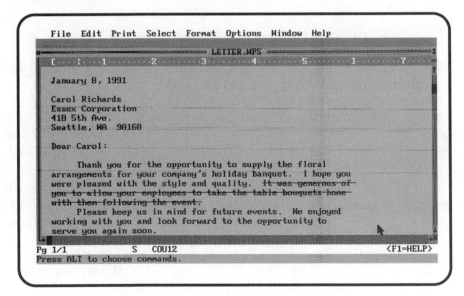

Figure 4.2   A sample of strikethrough text.

⌨ Press Ctrl+S to strike through the selected text.

The dialog box for the Font and Style command also contains options for positioning text: normal, superscript, and subscript. The subscript and superscript options change the horizontal positioning of characters. Superscript raises the selected character slightly above the normal line level while subscript drops the selected character slightly below the normal line level. Superscript is most often used for scientific notation such as 1.835×10^4, or in formulas such as $E=MC^2$. Subscript is most often used for footnotes or mathematical terms such as $\log_a x$.

If after using any of the features in the Font and Style dialog box you decide you want to change the text back again, select the text, then select the Plain Text command from the Format menu. ⌨ Works changes the selected text back to its normal style.

Press Ctrl+Spacebar to change selection back to normal text.

Copying a Paragraph or Character Format

You already know how to copy text from one location to another. Sometimes instead of copying text you may want to copy the *format* of a paragraph or character. For instance, suppose you are typing an article that contains quoted paragraphs. You decide you want the quotations to be indented one-half inch on the right and left. Once you set up that format for the first quotation, you can copy the format to the point where you type the next quotation.

To copy the paragraph format, select the paragraph, then select the Copy Special command on the Edit menu. The status line tells you to select the new location to copy to, then press Enter. When you press Enter, Works displays a dialog box from which you choose to copy either the Paragraph Format or Character Format. Select Paragraph Format, then select OK or press Enter. Works copies the original paragraph format to the paragraph you select.

Using the Character Format option in the same dialog box, you can copy text characteristics such as bold, italics, and underline. You usually copy the character or paragraph format when you are going to enter new text.

Creating a Hanging Indent

In Chapter 3 you learned how to do simple paragraph and first line indents. A variation of the first line indent is the *hanging* indent, which gets its name from the first line of the paragraph that *hangs out* to the left of the following lines. To create a hanging indent, select the paragraph you want to indent, then select the Indents and Spacing command on the Format menu.

The settings for a hanging indent are a little trickier to calculate than a simple first line indent. For example, if you want the first line of your paragraph to hang one inch to the left of the rest of the paragraph, you might guess that the Left Indent would be set at 1 and the First Line Indent set at 0. This seems logical, since the first line will line up under the zero on the ruler and the following lines will line up at the one-inch mark on the ruler. Unfortunately, this is a case where logic doesn't apply.

To create this format, you must set the Left Indent to 1 and the First Line Indent to –1. This is because Works measures the First Line Indent from the Left Indent rather than from the left margin. This can be very confusing at first. It may be helpful for you to think of the Left Indent as the *zero point*, even though it may not be set to zero on the ruler. The hanging indent is always measured to the left of that zero point. It helps to remember that for a hanging indent, the First Line Indent is always set to a negative number.

71

Create a hanging indent for the first paragraph in your sample letter. Begin by selecting the paragraph, then the Indents and Spacing command on the Format menu. Set the Left Indent at 1 and the First Line Indent at –1. Your paragraph should look like the one shown in Figure 4.3. Notice the Left Indent marker on the ruler is now at 1 and the First Line Indent marker is at 0.

Figure 4.4 illustrates an example of a more complex hanging indent. Suppose you want to set up a paragraph that is indented two inches from the left margin and has a one-inch hanging indent. Begin by setting the Left Indent at 2 to align all lines except the first one two inches from the left margin. Then set the First Line Indent at –1.

First
Line
Indent
marker

Left
Indent
marker

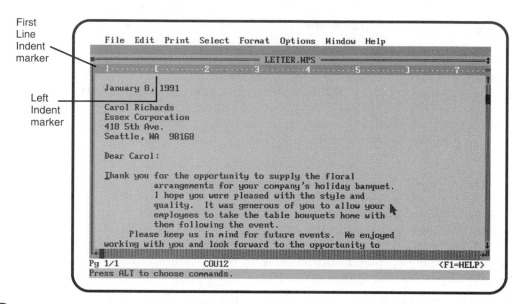

Figure 4.3   A hanging indent created with a Left Indent of 1, a
First Line Indent of –1.

First
Line
Indent
marker

Left
Indent
marker

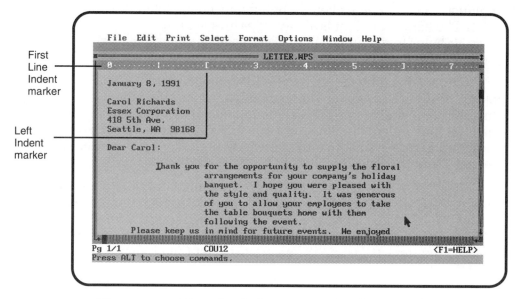

Figure 4.4   A hanging indent created with a Left Indent of 2, a
First Line Indent of –1.

Notice that the ruler settings have changed again. The Left Indent marker is now at 2 and the First Line Indent marker is at –1.

Hanging indents are most often used for numbered lists. Suppose you wanted to create a paragraph with a set of steps like the following list:

1. Loosen lock ring (A) by using a crescent wrench or a hammer and soft punch.
2. Then tighten adjusting cone (C) gently until the top turns freely without play.
3. Tighten adjusting cone (D) onto crank counterclockwise until tight, then turn back $\frac{1}{8}$ inch.

The list just previous uses a hanging indent as well as a tab. Both the Left Indent and Right Indent are set to 1 inch. The hanging indent is created by setting the First Line Indent to –5. Each step number in the paragraph is followed by a period, then a tab. The tab moves the cursor to the one-inch mark, where the left indent is set so the paragraph will wrap at one inch.

73

Setting Custom Tabs

Works sets default tab stops every half-inch, but by using custom tab stops, you have more options for setting up your document. Works lets you set left, right, center, and decimal-aligned tabs.

You can set custom tabs for a selected paragraph or for the entire document. To set tabs for a specific paragraph, you must select the paragraph first. If you want to set tabs for the entire document, set them before you enter any text. If the text is already entered, select the entire document using the Select All command on the Select menu.

When setting custom tabs, you can also designate *leaders*, such as a decimal point. This feature is often used in a table of contents or tables such as price or parts lists. The leader characters fill in the blank spaces between tabs. Works lets you choose between dots, hyphens, underscores, and equal signs.

In our sample letter, shown in Figure 4.5, we entered four columns of data, each using a different type of tab.

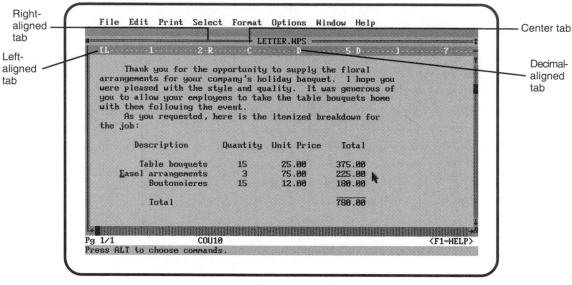

Right-aligned tab

Left-aligned tab

Center tab

Decimal-aligned tab

Figure 4.5 *Left-, right-, center-, and decimal-aligned tabs used in sample letter.*

74

Text entered at a left-aligned tab aligns at the left edge. Text entered at a right-aligned tab aligns at the right edge. Text entered at a center-aligned tab is centered underneath the tab. And text that is entered under a decimal-aligned tab aligns at the decimal point. To set these tabs, select the Tabs command on the Format menu. Try duplicating the tabs and text we added to the sample letter just shown in Figure 4.5.

Q Setting Custom Tabs Using the Keyboard

1. Select the paragraph or paragraphs you want to set custom tabs for.

   The text you select is highlighted.

2. Select the Tabs command from the Format menu.

   The Tabs dialog box is displayed.

3. Type the position where you want the tab to be set.

   The position you select is displayed in the dialog box.

4. Select the alignment and leader, if any, then select `Insert`.

   The tab position you choose is displayed on the ruler. The dialog box remains on the screen so you can set more tabs.

5. Repeat steps 3 and 4 until all tabs are set, then select Done.	The dialog box disappears and all the tabs you set are displayed on the ruler. ☐

If you want to use your mouse to set tabs, the procedure is slightly different.

Q Setting Custom Tabs Using the Mouse

1. Select the paragraph or paragraphs you want to set custom tabs for.	The text you select is highlighted.
2. Select the Tabs command from the Format menu.	The Tabs dialog box is displayed.
3. Point your mouse to the position on the ruler where you want to set the tab, then click.	The position you select is displayed in the dialog box.
4. Select the alignment and leader, if any, then select Insert.	The tab position you choose is displayed on the ruler.
5. Repeat steps 3 and 4 until all tabs are set, then select Done.	The dialog box disappears and all the tabs you set are displayed on the ruler. ☐

75

The steps just outlined for the mouse can also be used to move custom tab stops. When you get to Step 3, instead of pointing to the position where you want a new tab, click and drag an existing tab to the position where you want it to be. There is no need to delete the tab and reset a new one.

In Figure 4.6, the center tab at 3 and the decimal tab at 4 were deleted, then leading characters were added to the final decimal tab at 5.2.

> ▶ **Note:** When you set custom tab stops, Works deletes all default tab stops to the left of the first custom tab you set. Works also deletes all default tabs that are within $^1/_{10}$ inch of any custom tabs.

Indicates leading character added

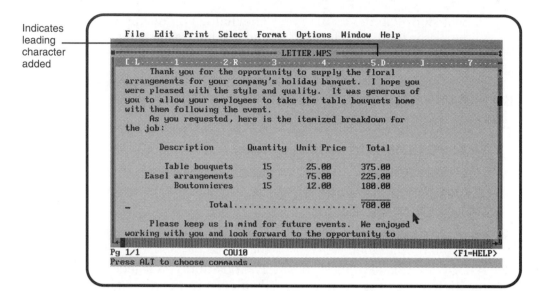

Figure 4.6   Leading characters used with a custom tab.

Bordering Paragraphs

Sometimes you may want to call special attention to part of your document without using bold or italic text. In these cases, a *border* might be most appropriate. Works allows you to add several different types of borders around selected text. You can specify borders on the right and left, top and bottom, or you can specify a complete outline. You also have a choice between normal, bold, or double outline. The dialog box shown in Figure 4.7 lists the three line styles available.

Adding Borders to Text

1. Select the text where you want to add borders.	The text is highlighted.
2. Select the Format menu.	The Format menu opens.
3. Select the Borders command.	The Borders dialog box shown in Figure 4.7 is displayed.

4. Select the border type and border style, then select OK.

Works returns to your document and creates the border type and style you select. □

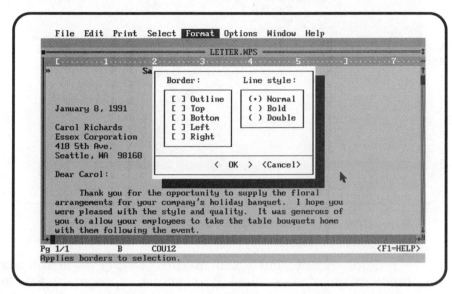

Figure 4.7   The Borders dialog box.

In your sample letter, create a border around the sender's address by selecting all three address lines, then selecting the Borders command on the Format menu. Experiment with the different line styles and types of borders. Figure 4.8 illustrates a double border around the sender's address in our sample letter. Notice that we changed the Left Indent and Right Indent settings to 1.5 to make the border narrower.

Using Search and Replace

Works has two commands that can help you either find text in a document or find text and replace it with something else, called Search and Replace. You use the Search command mostly when you're looking for a specific word or phrase in a document. The Search command can save you the trouble of reading through a document to find just the word you're looking for.

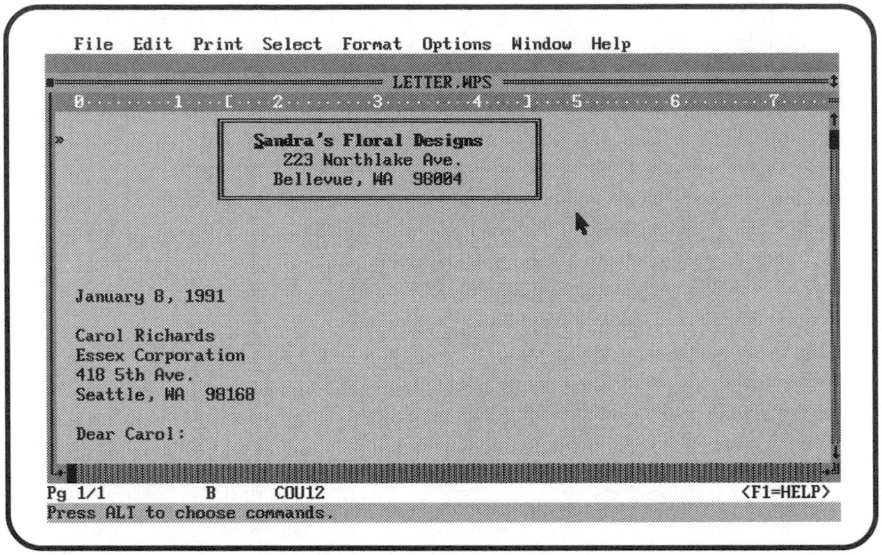

Figure 4.8   A double border around the sender's address.

78

The Replace command is often used to correct errors or to create multiple versions of a document. For example, suppose you want to send the same letter to two different companies but in the letter, the company name is used repeatedly. You could create and save the letter to the first company, then save the file again under the second company's name. Then in the second file you could use the Replace command to change all the occurrences of the first company's name to the second company's name. Now you have two personalized versions of the same letter, and you don't have to retype anything.

Search

Let's begin by explaining how Search works. The Search command gives you the option of matching the entire word or phrase, and matching in upper and lower case. When you select the Search command on the Select menu, the dialog box shown in Figure 4.9 appears.

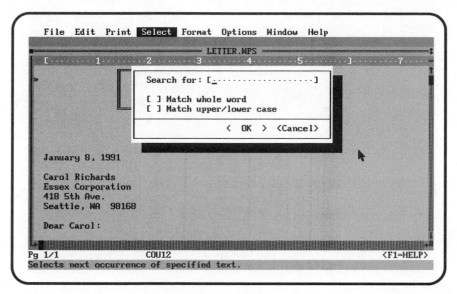

Figure 4.9   The Search dialog box.

In the Search For field, you can type either a word or a phrase. If you're not sure of one of the letters, you can type a question mark. For example, if you are searching for the name Anderson, but can't remember if it is spelled Ander*son* or Ander*sen*, type Anders?n.

If you want Works to search only for whole words, select the Match Whole Word option in the dialog box. Otherwise, if the word you're looking for is contained in another word, Works will find it, too. For instance, the word *explain* contains the word *plain*. If you want to search for the word *plain*, you would want to choose the Match Whole Word option so Works won't find *explain*.

If you want Works to match upper and lower case exactly, select this option in the dialog box. When you select this option and you are searching for the word *The*, Works will not find *the*.

 Searching for a Word or Phrase

1. Place your cursor in the document where you want the search to begin.

   Works searches forward through the document.

2. Select the Search command from the Select menu.

   The dialog box shown in Figure 4.9 is displayed.

3. Type the word or phrase to search for, select the Match Whole Word or Match Upper/Lower Case option, if needed, then select OK.

   Works returns to your document and finds the first occurrence of the word or phrase you specify.

   ☐

 Press F7 to repeat the search.

Replace

Now let's look at how Replace works. As with the Search command, the Replace command can match the whole word or match upper and lower case if you choose. But with Replace, you have an additional choice of replacing only the first occurrence, or all occurrences of the word or phrase. The Replace dialog box is shown in Figure 4.10.

80

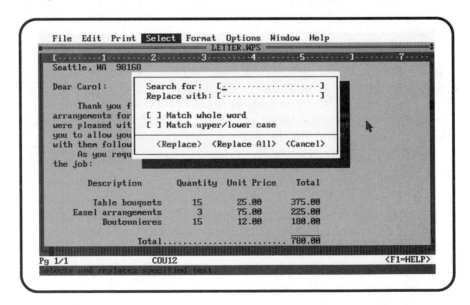

Figure 4.10   The Replace dialog box.

To use the Replace command, use the following Quick Steps.

Q Replacing a Word or Phrase

1. Place your cursor in the document where you want the search and replace to begin.

   Works searches forward through the document.

2. Select the Replace command from the Select menu.

   The dialog box shown in Figure 4.10 is displayed.

3. Type the word or phrase to search for, then type the replacement word or phrase.

   The word or phrase to search for and the replacement word or phrase are displayed in the dialog box.

4. Select the Match Whole Word or Match Upper/ Lower Case option, if needed, then select `Replace`, or `Replace All`.

   Works returns to your document and replaces either the first occurrence or all occurrences, depending on what you specify. □

81

Adding Headers and Footers to Your Document

Works lets you print text such as page numbers or a document title at the top or bottom of every page. When the text appears at the top of the page, it is called a *header*. When it appears at the bottom, it is called a *footer*. You may use one or the other, or both in a document. Headers and footers print in the top and bottom margins of your document. In Works, there are two types of headers and footers, one-line (standard) headers and footers, and paragraph headers and footers.

One-Line Headers and Footers

One-line, or standard, headers and footers are quick and easy to create. Use them when you know your header or footer will not be longer than one line. The words *Company Confidential* centered at the bottom of each page in a document is an example of a simple one-line footer.

Q Creating One-Line Headers and Footers

1. Select the Headers and Footers command from the Print menu.

   The Headers and Footers dialog box appears.

2. Turn off the Use Header and Footer Paragraphs option if it is on.

3. Type the text for the header or footer in the appropriate field of the dialog box.

   The text you type is displayed in the dialog box.

4. Select the No Header on First Page or No Footer on First Page option if appropriate, then select OK.

   The dialog box disappears, saving the header or footer that you type in until you print. □

> ▶ **Note:** Header and footer text is not displayed on your screen. If you need to view it or change it, select the Headers and Footers command in the Print menu.

Inserting Special Text or Characters

In addition to the text you type, you may want to insert special text or characters such as the date, the filename, or page numbers. Chances are you would not need a footer for your sample letter, but suppose you wanted one that looked like this:

82

In the footer field of the dialog box, you must type special codes to get Works to automatically print the filename, the page number, and the date (see Figure 4.11). Special codes are also added to specify the alignment of each phrase. The filename is aligned at the left, the page number is centered, and the date is aligned at the right.

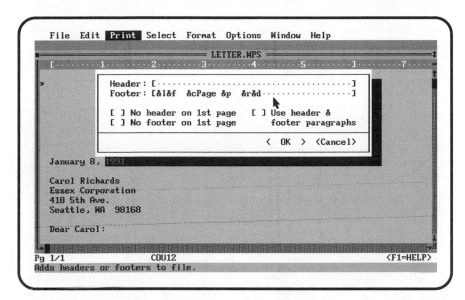

Figure 4.11   The dialog box with settings for a left-aligned name, centered page number, and right-aligned date.

In the example, the spaces in between each phrase are not required; they are inserted only to make the footnote easier for you to read. Notice that to get the word *Page* to print before the page number is inserted, you must type Page followed by a space; Works will not insert it for you. If you want the page number to look like *- 3 -* when it prints, type - &p - . The complete list of codes used for headers and footers is shown in Table 4.1.

Table 4.1   Header and Footer Codes

Press	To
&l or &r	Align text that follows at the left or right margin
&c	Center text that follows
&p	Print page numbers
&f	Print the filename

(continued)

83

Table 4.1   (continued)

Press	To
&d	Print the date at the time of printing
&t	Print the time at the time of printing
&&	Print an ampersand (&)

Paragraph Headers and Footers

Use *paragraph* headers and footers when you know your text is longer than one line. When you create a paragraph header or footer, Works places an H and an F marker at the top of your document on the first and second lines (see Figure 4.12). This is where you will enter the text for the header or footer. Unlike one-line headers and footers, paragraph headers and footers remain displayed on the screen.

84

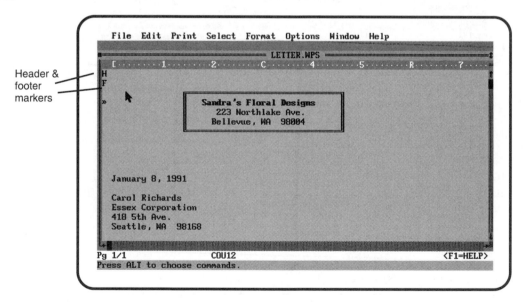

Header & footer markers

Figure 4.12   A document with paragraph header and footer markers.

Since headers and footers print in the top and bottom margins of your document, the margins must be wide enough to hold multi-line headers and footers. If you need to widen your margins, see Printing Your Document in Chapter 3. To create a paragraph header or footer, follow the next Quick Steps.

Q Creating a Paragraph Header or Footer

1. Select the Headers and Footers command from the Print menu.	The Headers and Footers dialog box is displayed.
2. Select the Use Header and Footer Paragraphs option in the dialog box, then select OK.	Two markers are placed at the far left position on the first and second line of your document, H for the header, and F for the footer. The footer contains a placeholder for a page number.
3. Move your cursor to the top of your document and begin entering text for the header next to the H. Then move your cursor next to the F and begin entering text for the footer. You may change the font or add enhancements (bold, italic, underline) to any of the text you type.	The text you type is entered as the header or footer.
4. If you want a multiple-line header or footer, type all the text you want for the first line, then select the Insert Special command from the Edit menu.	The Insert Special dialog box shown in Figure 4.13 appears.
5. Select the End-of-Line Mark option in the dialog box, then select OK.	Works automatically adds another line to your header or footer. □

85

If you only want to use a header, just leave the footer line blank. Or, if you only want a footer in your document, leave the header line blank.

Paragraph headers and footers are treated like any other paragraph in your document: they can be more than one line of text; they can be left-, center-, or right-aligned; they can be formatted; or they can include different fonts and styles such as bold, italic, or underline.

To make your text left-aligned, just start typing next to the H or F marker. To center your text, press the Tab key once. The cursor moves to the center tab and as you type, Works centers the text. To make your text right-aligned, press the Tab again and the cursor moves to the far right margin. Works pushes the characters you type to the left as it right-aligns your text.

Insert Special Text and Characters

86

As with one-line headers and footers, Works also allows you to insert special text and characters into multiple-line paragraph headers and footers. To print page numbers, the date, the time, or the filename in a header or footer, use the Insert Special command on the Edit menu instead of inserting special codes. The Insert Special dialog box is shown in Figure 4.13. The options are defined in the following paragraphs.

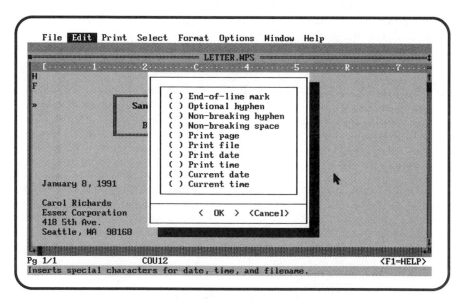

Figure 4.13   The Insert Special dialog box.

End-Of-Line Mark   Use this option when you want to create a multiple-line header or footer. You cannot press Enter at the end of a line when typing a header or footer; you must use this option to insert a new line.

Press Shift+Enter to insert a new line in a header or footer.

Optional Hyphen   If you want to designate how a word should be hyphenated near the end of a line, use this option. You won't see optional hyphens on the screen unless you use the Show All Characters command on the Options menu.

Non-Breaking Hyphen   Use this option if you are typing hyphenated text and don't want it to be broken at the end of a line. Non-breaking hyphens are displayed on the screen.

Non-Breaking Space   This option works much like the non-breaking hyphen, except using a space. If you type two words in your header or footer that you don't want separated at the end of a line, place a non-breaking space between the two words as you type them.

87

Print Page   This option inserts a placeholder, *page*, for a page number. This placeholder is specially coded by Works; don't confuse it with an asterisk followed by *page*, followed by another asterisk. If you try to type in *page* instead of using Insert Special, Works will print the actual characters *-p-a-g-e-* instead of the desired page number.

Print File   If you want the name of your file printed in your header or footer, use this option.

Print Date   If you want the date on the day of printing to print in your header or footer, use this option.

Print Time   If you want the time at the time of printing to print in your header or footer, use this option.

Current Date   When you use this option, the current date is typed into your header or footer. This option differs from the Print Date option in that it inserts the numbers for a specified date into the header or footer. If you use this option today and print the document tomorrow, the printout will still show today's date.

Current Time   When you use this option, the current time is typed into your header or footer. This option differs from the Print Time option in that it inserts a specified time into the header or footer. If you use this option at 9:00 a.m. then print your document at 3:00 p.m., the printout will still show 9:00 a.m.

As you type the text for your header or footer, choose the Insert Special command from the Edit menu to insert any of the characters or text defined just previously. For example, type in a paragraph footer for your sample letter that looks like:

```
Essex Corporation
1/9/91                    LETTER.WPS                    Page 1
```

The first three lines of your document should look like the ones shown in Figure 4.14, including one blank line.

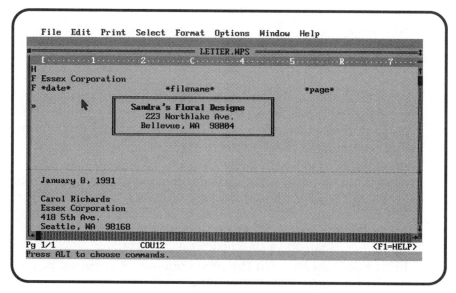

Figure 4.14   A document with a two-line footer.

Creating Footnotes

Footnotes are generally used to provide additional information about a subject in your document or to provide references. When you create a footnote, the footnote mark appears in the text of your document, and the footnote text prints at the end of the document. In Works, you can use either numbers or symbols for footnote marks. If you use numbers, Works automatically numbers them in sequence throughout your document.

When you create a footnote, Works opens a pane at the bottom of your document window where you enter footnote text. Follow the next Quick Steps to create a footnote.

Q Creating Footnotes

1. Move your cursor to the location where you want a footnote mark inserted in your document.

2. Select the Footnote command on the Edit menu.

   A footnote dialog box is displayed.

3. Choose either the Numbered or Character Mark option for the style of footnote mark you want If you choose Character Mark, type the character or characters you want to use. (The character mark can be up to 10 characters.) Select OK.

   The dialog box disappears and Works returns to your document. Works creates a footnote pane at the bottom of your document window and places your cursor in the footnote pane so you can enter text.

4. Enter the footnote text in the footnote pane. When you are finished entering text, press F6.

   Works moves your cursor back to the document pane. You may now continue working on your document. □

89

> ▶ **Note:** If you want to hide the footnote pane, select the Show Footnotes command on the Options menu and the footnote pane disappears. The Show Footnotes command works like a toggle switch to turn the footnote pane on and off.

Once you have entered your footnote, you many want to edit it later. To edit the footnote, start by redisplaying the footnote pane using the Show Footnotes command on the Options menu. When the footnote pane is displayed, your cursor will be located inside the footnote pane where you can edit the footnote text. The F6 key moves your cursor back and forth between the document pane and the footnote pane. When you finish editing, you can either press F6 to move to the document pane or select the Show Footnotes command on the Options menu again to hide the footnote.

Using the Spelling Checker and Thesaurus

Two of the nicest features of the Works Word Processor are the built-in Spelling Checker and Thesaurus. These two tools can save you hours of time spent proofreading for spelling errors and redundancy in your documents.

Correcting Your Spelling

Works has a built-in dictionary that can check your document for incorrectly spelled words, words that are capitalized incorrectly, words that are hyphenated incorrectly, and words that are inadvertently repeated (such as *it it*, *the the*, *is is*, and so on). When a word is spelled incorrectly, you can ask for suggestions and Works will display a list of possible spellings.

When you use a word in a document that isn't in the Works dictionary, Works questions it as a misspelled word. This can happen frequently when you use specialized or technical terms in a document. To prevent Works from questioning these words each time they occur, you can add them to the Works dictionary. When you select the Check Spelling command on the Options menu, the dialog box shown in Figure 4.15 is displayed. Notice that the phrase or word that Works is checking is highlighted in the document window beneath the dialog box. The Check Spelling options are defined next.

Replace With   Use this field to type the corrected word. If you choose a word from the Suggestions list, Works automatically places it in this field.

Suggestions   When you ask Works for a list of suggested words, they are displayed in this box.

Skip Capitalized Words   Check this box if you want the spell checker to ignore acronyms, such as DOS, and other words that consist of all capital letters.

Change All   When you choose this option, Works changes all occurrences of the word in the entire document.

Change   When you choose this option, Works changes only the current (highlighted) occurrence of the word.

Ignore All   When you choose this option, Works leaves all occurrences of the word as they are.

Ignore   Works leaves the current occurrence as is when you choose this option.

Suggest   When you select this option, Works supplies suggested words in the Suggestions box.

Add   If you want to add a word to the Works dictionary, choose this option.

Done   When you are finished using the Spelling Checker, select this option.

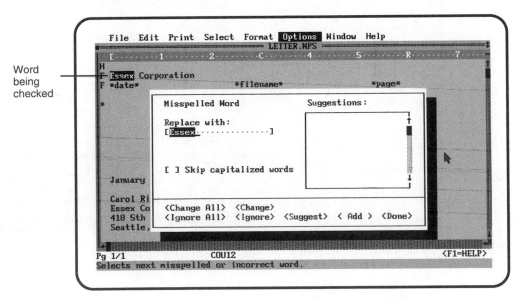

Word being checked

Figure 4.15   ***The dialog box for the spell checker.***

When you choose the Check Spelling command and the dialog box is displayed, Works highlights the first misspelled word in the document window. You can edit the word by typing the correction in the Replace With field or you can ask for suggestions from Works by selecting Suggest. Choose one of the suggested words in the Suggestions box, then select Change. You must select either Change or Change All for the word to be changed in your document.

Q**Using the Spelling Checker**

1. Place your cursor in the document where you want to begin checking the spelling.

2. Choose the Check Spelling command on the Options menu.

   The dialog box shown in Figure 4.13 is displayed and the first misspelled word is highlighted in the document window.

3. If you want to correct the selected word, type the correct spelling in the Replace With field or select Suggest for a list of suggested spellings, then select Change or Change All.

   The spelling of the selected word is corrected in the document.

4. If you don't want to correct the word, select Ignore or Ignore All.

   The selected word is not changed.

5. When you are finished using the Spelling Checker, select Done.

   The dialog box disappears and Works returns you to your corrected document. □

If you don't want to change the word but want to add it to the dictionary, make sure it is spelled correctly, then select Add. The word is added to the dictionary and the Spelling Checker continues to check for other misspelled words in the document.

Finding the Right Word

The term, thesaurus, means a list of synonyms. When you want to find a word that has the same or similar meaning to one you've used, you use the Works Thesaurus. It can help you find just the right word to use as you're typing and help you eliminate repetitiveness in your document. The Thesaurus in Works defines the word you've used as well as suggesting synonyms for it.

When you select the Thesaurus command on the Options menu, Works displays the dialog box shown in Figure 4.16.

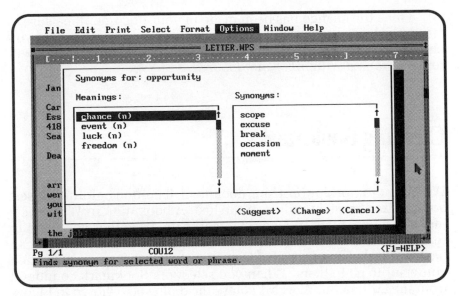

Figure 4.16   The Thesaurus dialog box.

93

To use the Thesaurus, follow the next Quick Steps.

Q Using the Thesaurus

1. Select the word in your document that you want to find a synonym for.

2. Choose the Thesaurus command on the Options menu.

   The dialog box shown in Figure 4.16 is displayed. The word you select is displayed in the Synonym For field. Its meanings are displayed below in the Meanings box and synonyms are displayed in the Synonyms box.

3. Choose one of the meanings in the Meanings box, then select Suggest.

   A list of synonyms for the meaning you choose are listed in the synonym box.

4. If you want to use one of the synonyms in your document, select it from the list, then select Change.

   The word in your document is changed to the word you choose.

   □

Once the change has been made in your document, be sure to check the tense and form of the word. For example, if the word you choose is *worked* and the suggested synonym is *labor*, Works will replace *worked* with *labor*, not *labored*.

Creating Bookmarks

When you're working on a long document, it is often helpful to insert *bookmarks* at certain points in the text. A bookmark in Works acts just like a bookmark in a book; it marks the page that you want to return to. In Works, you name your bookmarks. That way you can have multiple bookmarks, and you can choose them by name when you want to go to them. When you select the Bookmark command from the Edit menu, Works displays the dialog box shown in Figure 4.17. The options are defined next.

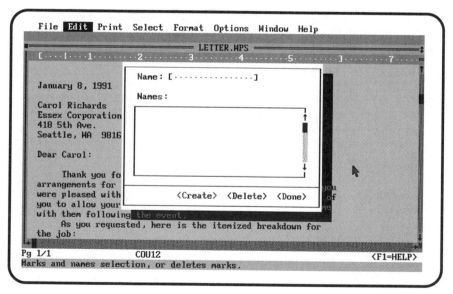

Figure 4.17   The Bookmark dialog box.

Name   Enter the bookmark name in this field.

Names   Once you have created a bookmark, the name is displayed in the Names box.

To create a bookmark, use the next Quick Steps.

Q Creating a Bookmark

1. Place your cursor in the text where you want the bookmark to be inserted.

2. Select the Bookmark Name command on the Edit menu.

   The dialog box shown in Figure 4.17 is displayed.

3. Type the name of the bookmark in the Name field, then select `Create`.

   The dialog box disappears and Works returns to your document.   ☐

Works doesn't display the bookmark on the screen, but you can be sure that it's there by checking the Bookmark dialog box. The names you choose as your bookmarks are listed in the Names box. When you want to delete a bookmark, follow the next Quick Steps.

Q Deleting a Bookmark

1. Select the Bookmark Name command on the Edit menu.

   The dialog box shown in Figure 4.17 is displayed. The list of current bookmarks is displayed in the Names box.

2. Select the bookmark that you want to delete, then select `Delete`.

   The bookmark you select is deleted from the list. The dialog box is still displayed.

3. If you want to delete other bookmarks repeat step 2. When you are finished, select `Done`.

   The dialog box disappears and Works returns to your document.   ☐

95

To move your cursor to a bookmark, you use the Go To command on the Select menu. When you select this command, Works displays the dialog box shown in Figure 4.18.

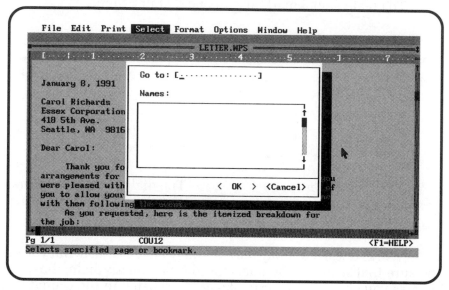

Figure 4.18   The Go To dialog box.

This dialog box is almost identical to the Bookmark dialog box, except for the OK and Cancel options. The bookmarks that exist are displayed in the Names box. Select the one you want to go to, then Select OK. Works moves your cursor to that location.

What You've Learned

This chapter helps you build on your basic Works Word Processor skills by teaching you some of the advanced features. In this chapter you have learned how to add some of the professional touches to documents such as special formatting, headers and footers, footnotes and bookmarks. In addition, you have learned how to use the Search and Replace features of Works, the Spelling Checker, and Thesaurus. The main points covered in this chapter are summarized next.

► Use the Font and Style command on the Format menu to change or add text and paragraph formatting features such as strikethrough, subscript, superscript, and borders around text. Using this command you can also change the style and size of the font in your printed copy.

► Use the Search command on the Select menu to search for a word or phrase in a document and the Replace command to replace the word or phrase with new text.

► Use the Headers and Footers command on the Print menu to create special repetitive information at the top and bottom of your document pages. Headers and Footers can include page numbers, the filename, the date, or any other text that you choose, and you can align the text at the left, center, or right.

► Use the Footnotes command to create footnote references for your document. Works automatically numbers them and prints them at the end of your document.

► Use the Check Spelling and Thesaurus commands on the Options menu to correct spelling errors, add words to the dictionary, and find synonyms for words you select.

► Use the Bookmark command on the Edit menu to create bookmarks, locate them once you have named them, and delete them when you no longer need them.

97

Chapter 5

Introducing the Spreadsheet

In This Chapter

- ▶ *Entering the Spreadsheet tool and creating a new spreadsheet file*
- ▶ *Finding your way around the spreadsheet window*
- ▶ *Selecting cells and cell ranges*
- ▶ *The process of building a spreadsheet*
- ▶ *Printing and saving your spreadsheet*

This chapter teaches you how to get started using the Works Spreadsheet tool by taking you through the steps of creating a simple spreadsheet. First you'll learn about the spreadsheet itself, and how to select cells and move through the window. Then you'll learn about the process for creating, saving, and printing a spreadsheet.

Entering the Spreadsheet Tool

In Chapter 3 you learned that you need to create a new file to type a new Word Processor document. The same is true for spreadsheets, only this time you'll be creating a spreadsheet file. Works will automatically assign the name SHEET1.WKS to the new Spreadsheet file.

Q Create a New Spreadsheet File

1. Select Create New File from the File menu.

   Works displays a dialog box with four choices.

2. Select the New Spreadsheet option in the dialog box.

   Works creates a new Spreadsheet file called SHEET1.WKS and places your cursor in the window for you to begin entering text. ☐

A new Spreadsheet file looks like the one shown in Figure 5.1. It is a good idea to rename the file and save it under its new name as soon you create it. That way you won't lose any of your work if you forget to rename the file when you're finished working.

100

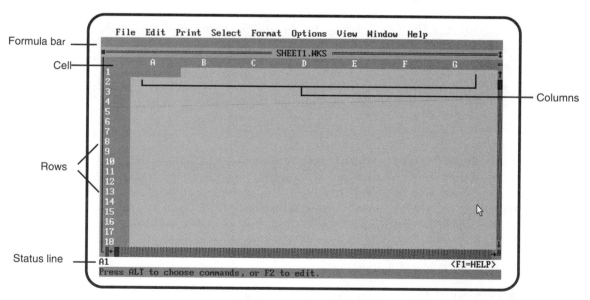

Figure 5.1   The opening screen in the Spreadsheet tool.

The Spreadsheet Window

Certain parts of the Spreadsheet window should look familiar to you from using the Word Processor tool. For instance, the window has a menu bar, title bar, status line, message line, borders, and scroll bars. The spreadsheet also has a work area, but it is a grid made up of rows and columns.

The entire spreadsheet is actually much larger than it appears in the window. The portion of the spreadsheet that you see in the window relative to its actual size is shown in Figure 5.2. You can use as much or as little of the spreadsheet as you need.

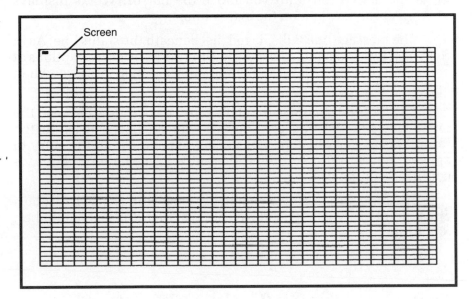

Figure 5.2   *The portion of the spreadsheet that you see on the screen.*

The spreadsheet's rows are numbered down the left side. When you create a new spreadsheet, you can see rows 1 through 18 on the screen, but there are actually 4096 rows in all.

The columns of the spreadsheet are labeled across the top of the window underneath the title bar. The first 26 columns are labeled A, B, C...Z, then AA, AB, AC...AZ, then BA, BB, BC... BZ, and so on. The spreadsheet has 256 columns, so the last column is labeled IV.

The points at which rows and columns intersect are called *cells*. This is where you enter text or numbers into the spreadsheet. Cells are referred to by their location on the spreadsheet, column first, row second. The first cell in the upper left corner is cell A1 because it is located in column A at row 1. The last cell you can see in the window is cell G18 because it is located in column G at row 18.

When you first create a new spreadsheet, cell A1 is highlighted. The highlighted cell is called the active cell. In the spreadsheet, you work with the active cell rather than a cursor.

The status line is located at the bottom of the spreadsheet. The active cell location is always displayed at the far left on the status line. When you create a new Spreadsheet file, the status line displays A1 as the active cell until you move the cursor. Works displays F1=Help at the far right on the status line.

The message line is displayed just beneath the status line. As in the Word Processor tool, the message line offers brief descriptions of commands as well as suggestions and informational messages when appropriate.

102

The *formula bar* is located at the top of the window between the menu bar and the title bar.You type spreadsheet entries in the formula bar after you choose the cell where you want the entry to appear. When you press Enter, the entry from the formula bar is confirmed in the cell.

The term *formula bar* is somewhat misleading since it displays any kind of entry you type into a cell, whether it is text, a number, or a formula.

Getting Around in the Spreadsheet

Before you enter any data, you need to know how to maneuver through the spreadsheet. You can use the keyboard, the mouse, or a combination of the two. Table 5.1 lists keys and key combinations for moving to different parts of the spreadsheet. Practice moving to different locations on the spreadsheet using these keys.

Table 5.1 Keys used to move the cell selector around the spreadsheet

Press	Moves the cursor
Arrow keys	One cell to the right, left, up, or down
Page Down	Down one window
Page Up	Up one window
Ctrl+Page Down	Right one window
Ctrl+Page Up	Left one window
Home	To the current row, column A
Ctrl+Home	To the upper left corner of spreadsheet, cell A1
End	To the last cell containing data in the current row
Ctrl+End	To the last cell in spreadsheet containing data
Ctrl+Arrow keys	By one block of data to the left, up, or down

103

Selecting Cells

When working with spreadsheets, you select cells frequently. Selecting cells in the spreadsheet tells Works which cells you want to calculate, move, copy, delete, and so on. Whenever you want to use a command on a cell or group of cells, you need to select it first.

To select one cell at a time using the keyboard, move your cursor to the cell you want using the Arrow keys. The active cell is the *selected* cell. To select a larger group of cells using the keyboard, use one of the following commands on the Select menu:

Choose the Row command on the Select menu to select an entire row in a spreadsheet.

Choose the Column command on the Select menu to select an entire column in a spreadsheet.

Choose the All command on the Select menu to select the entire spreadsheet.

Press Ctrl+F8 to select an entire row in a spreadsheet. Press Shift+F8 to select an entire column in a spreadsheet. Press Ctrl+Shift+F8 to select the entire spreadsheet.

To cancel any range of cells you have selected, press Esc.

![mouse icon] If you have a mouse, you can use either of the following methods, as well as the keyboard shortcut methods just listed to select cells:

Select an entire row by clicking on the row number.

Select an entire column by clicking on the column letter.

To cancel any selections you've made with the mouse, click on any other cell in the spreadsheet.

Selecting Ranges of Cells

Often you many want to select a range of cells larger than just a row or a column. A range of cells can span multiple columns, multiple rows, or a combination of the two.

Figure 5.3 illustrates several ranges of cells. Ranges are designated using the colon (:) key. For example, A1:C5 includes all cells in columns A through C and rows 1 through 5. Figure 5.3 illustrates the range C2:E7, as noted in the status line.

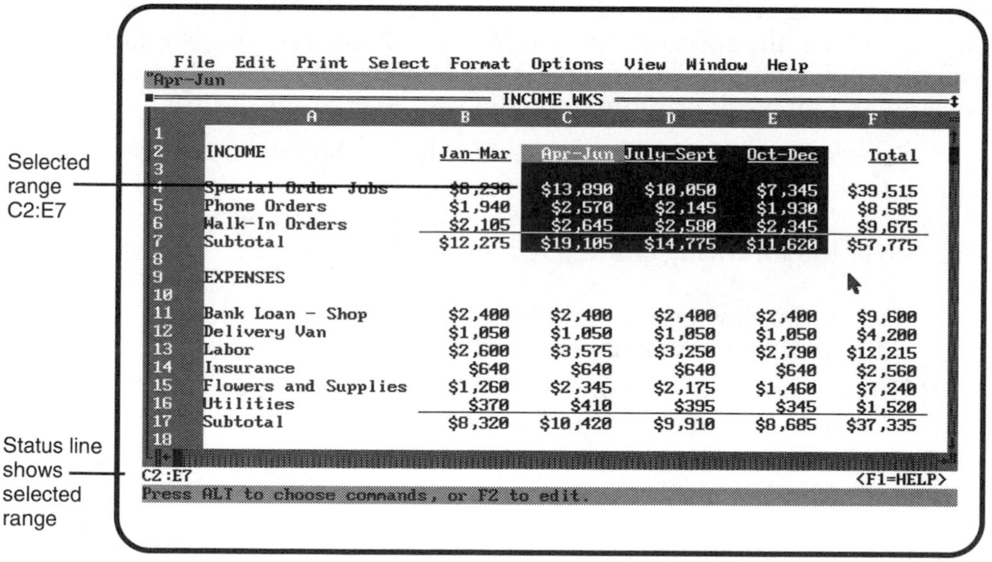

104

Figure 5.3   A spreadsheet showing the range of cells C2:E7.

To select a range of cells using the keyboard, press F8 followed by any of the Arrow keys. If you prefer, you can press and hold the Shift key instead of F8, then press any of the Arrow keys.

Using the mouse, select a range of cells by clicking and dragging from the upper left cell, then releasing the mouse button in the lower right cell, as shown in figure 5.4. Or, you can click on the first cell in the range, press F8, then click on the last cell in the range. Cancel any selection by clicking outside the highlighted area.

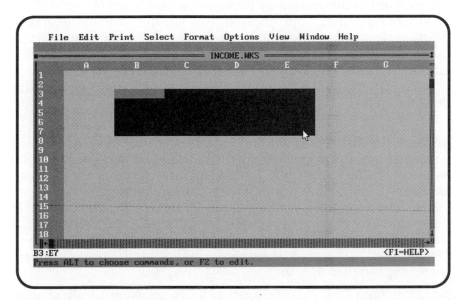

Figure 5.4 Select a range of cells using the mouse by clicking in the upper left and dragging to the lower right.

Building a Spreadsheet

If you've never used a spreadsheet before, your first question after seeing the opening screen might be, *Where do I begin?* Well, you can relax because building a spreadsheet is really quite easy, but it's helpful to follow a logical process. That process begins with planning.

Planning

In any type of project or process, planning is one of the most important steps. The same is true with spreadsheets; planning can save you a lot of time and trouble in the long run. To plan your spreadsheet, begin by asking yourself some questions.

Suppose you want to set up an income statement for your florist business. Income is your first category, so you need to think about all your different sources of income. Do you want to list walk-in business separately from large jobs like weddings? Or do you want to show your income as one lump sum? Next, list expenses. How many expense items do you have? Do you want to categorize them or enter them as one long list? What is the time period you want to specify? Do you want to set up the statement to show twelve months, four quarters, or just year-end numbers?

In this example, you already know the basic structure of an income statement: income and expenses are listed down the left side, and months or the year are displayed across the columns. But when you don't know the basic structure for your spreadsheet, sometimes it's helpful to draw a rough outline of the layout you want to use. For example, if you're creating a sales report, do you want to show months or quarters across the columns, and dollars in the rows, or vice versa? Trying to reverse columns and rows after you've begun creating the spreadsheet can be difficult and time-consuming, so it's best to plan ahead.

You don't necessarily have to have answers to all of your questions before you begin, but it helps to think about them first. Remember, nothing you enter in the spreadsheet is cast in concrete; you can always change your entries later.

The Process

When you've done all your planning and gathered all the information you need, you're ready to create your spreadsheet. The process to follow is outlined next. Read over these steps now and later you'll build your own spreadsheet.

1. Begin by entering column and row headings. Think about how many rows you need for your spreadsheet title and leave those rows blank at the top of the spreadsheet. Then enter your column headings on the next row. Entering column and row headings first gives you an idea of how

large your spreadsheet is going to be, even though you may add rows or columns later.

2. If your row headings are longer than 10 spaces, change the column width now. If the numbers you are going to enter are larger than 10 digits, widen the columns where you'll be entering numbers, too.

3. Enter the spreadsheet title next. Now that you know approximately how wide the spreadsheet is, you can gauge in which column to put your title so that it's centered.

4. Now you're ready to enter numbers into the spreadsheet. You need to have them entered before you can enter the formulas that will perform the calculations.

5. When you have entered the numbers, check to make sure the format is acceptable. If you want numbers displayed as percentages or as currency (that is, with dollar signs), you need to change the format. For now, just change the format for columns or rows; you'll change the format for individual cells later.

6. Once you've entered all the numbers, you're ready to start creating formulas. When you've created the first formula, check to see that the column width is adequate. Cells that contain formula results often need to be widened, especially if the formula is set up to multiply large numbers. If the column is not wide enough, it will display ########.

7. When you have entered all the formulas and all calculations have been made, you'll want to make your spreadsheet easy to read. You may want to add some ruling lines to make certain columns or rows stand out, change some characters to bold or italics, and so on.

107

A Simple Spreadsheet Example

In this section, you'll get the chance to build a simple spreadsheet yourself, following the steps in the process outlined previously. If you'd like to follow along, open up a new Spreadsheet file now and rename it INCOME.WKS. We will build an income statement for a floral shop called *Sandra's Floral Designs*. Assume that all your planning has been done and you've gathered all the information you need to begin.

Step 1: Enter column and row headings.

To enter text in the spreadsheet, move your cursor to the cell where you want the entry to appear, type the text, then press Enter. Watch the formula bar as you type. Even though you have selected a cell, you are actually typing the entry in the formula bar until you press Enter. Pressing Enter confirms your entry and records it in the cell.

When you type a letter on the keyboard, Works recognizes your entry as text rather than a number. Works also recognizes most punctuation marks as text entries. When you press Enter, a quote mark (") is inserted in the formula bar at the beginning of your entry to remind you that you have made a text entry. The quote mark does not appear in the cell entry. If you want to enter a number as text, for instance, a part number such as 13993, type a quote (") at the beginning of the number, otherwise Works reads it as a number on which a calculation can be performed.

108

In our spreadsheet, we want to show quarters on the income statement, so our column headings beginning at cell B5 are Jan-Mar, Apr-Jun, Jul-Sept, and Oct-Dec. We have three sources of income and six types of expenses. (You can only see five types of expenses— the sixth is out of sight on row 19.) These are entered in column A beginning at cell 5. Enter the column headings as well as the income and expense items shown in Figure 5.5.

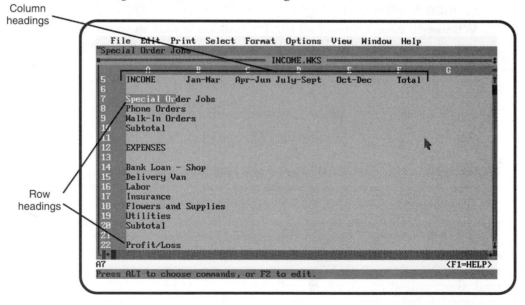

Figure 5.5   The spreadsheet column and row headings.

Step 2: Adjust column widths.

All columns in the spreadsheet are ten spaces wide unless you change their width. Text entries longer than ten spaces fill into the cell to the immediate right if it's empty. If it's not empty, the cell is filled up to the column width, then truncated, or cut off. When numbers or dates exceed the column width, Works fills in ####### in the cell until the column is widened. This is a precaution that Works takes to prevent you from making errors based on incomplete data.

To change the width of column A in our spreadsheet, use the following Quick Steps, entering 25 for the new column width:

Q **Changing Column Width**

1. Select the column you want to widen.	The column is highlighted on the spreadsheet.
2. Select the Column Width command from the Format menu.	The column width dialog box is displayed.
3. Type the width you need, then select OK.	Works returns to your spreadsheet window and changes the column width. □

Step 3: Enter the spreadsheet title.

We want our spreadsheet title to be centered over the columns, so enter the three-line title starting in cell C1. Our title is: *Sandra's Floral Designs, Profit/Loss Report, Year Ending 1990.* The spreadsheet should now look like the one shown in Figure 5.6.

Step 4: Enter numbers into the spreadsheet.

To enter numbers into the spreadsheet, select the cell you want, type the number, then press Enter. You'll be typing the number in the formula bar, just as with text. When you press Enter, the number is recorded in the cell. Type a hyphen (-) preceding any negative numbers. Don't, however, type a hyphen to signify subtraction; we'll create a formula later that subtracts figures in one row from another.

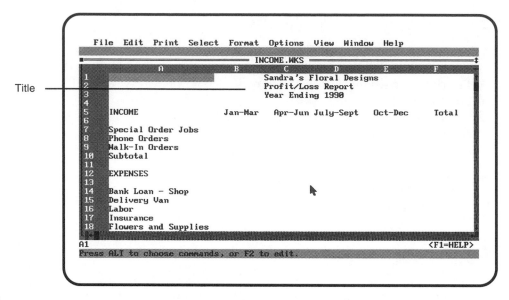

Title

110

Figure 5.6   Column A has been widened and a title has been added.

Begin filling in numbers starting with cell B7 (the numbers are shown in Figure 5.7). Fill in all the income and expense numbers for the year. The spreadsheet should now look like Figure 5.7.

Notice that cells B13 through F13 contain a fixed number of 2400. Since this number is repeated, we can use the Fill Right command on the Edit menu rather than typing an entry in each cell repeatedly. The Fill Right command copies the entry in the active cell to the cell or cells you select immediately to the right. The Fill Down command works exactly the same way, except it fills cells in a downward direction. Use the following Quick Steps to operate the Fill Right or Fill Down command. (The Fill Series command on the Edit menu is detailed in Chapter 6.)

Q Filling Cells

1. Type the entry in the first cell of the series and press Enter.

   Works highlights the cell where you make the entry.

2. Select the current cell and all the cells you want to fill, either to the right or down.

   All the cells in the series are highlighted.

3. Select the Fill Right or Fill Down command on the Edit menu.

The cells you select are filled in with the repeated entry. ☐

When you use a Fill command, the cell's format is copied along with the contents of the cell.

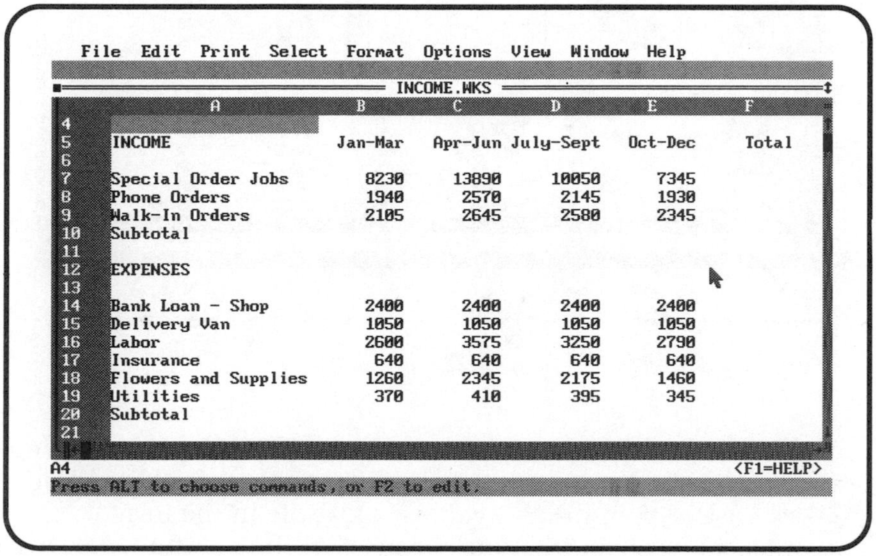

Figure 5.7   ***Figures have now been added to the spreadsheet.***

Step 5: Change the format of the numbers.

Works allows you to display cell entries in a variety of formats. For example, when the numbers in your worksheet represent dollars, you may want to use the Currency format, which displays numbers with dollar signs and commas as well as decimal points if you want them. If some of your entries represent percentages, you can type just the number and Works displays the percent sign for you when you select the Percent format.

Works displays all cell entries in the General format, unless you specify otherwise. When you choose the Format menu, Works displays the commands shown in Figure 5.8.

111

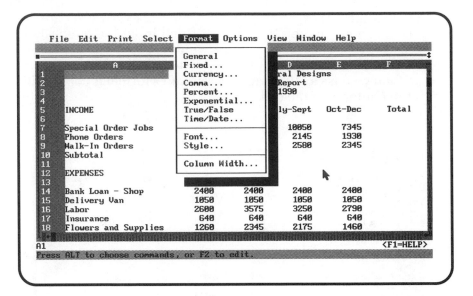

Figure 5.8   The Format menu.

General   Using the General format, Works displays text left-aligned and numbers right-aligned. Numbers are displayed as close to their precise value as possible in the form of integers, decimal fractions, or in scientific notation. Negative numbers are displayed with a minus (–) sign.

Fixed   When you choose Fixed format, you can specify the number of decimal places Works should display. For example, if you specify 0 for the number of decimal places, the number 10992.969 is displayed as 10993. If you specify 2 decimal places, the same number is displayed as 10992.97. Using the Fixed format, Works rounds numbers where appropriate.

Currency   When the numbers in your spreadsheet represent dollars, you can specify the Currency format so that Works displays dollar signs before each number. In Currency format, Works also inserts commas every three places to the left of the decimal point. Works displays the number 8120987 as $8,120,987.00. If you choose to type the $ symbol in the cell, Works recognizes the Currency format and adds commas, but does not add zeros to the right of the decimal point.

Comma   When you choose the Comma format, Works adds commas every three places so that the number 8797245 is displayed as 8,797,245. Using this format, you can also specify the number of decimal places. If you choose two, the number is displayed as 8,797,245.00. When using the Comma format, Works displays negative numbers enclosed in parentheses.

Percent   Numbers are expressed as a percentage when you choose this format. For example, 125 is displayed as 12500.00%, .87 is displayed as 87%. If you choose to type a % symbol following the number you enter, Works recognizes the format and displays the number correctly. Negative numbers are displayed with a minus sign using the Percent format.

Exponential   This format displays numbers in exponential, or scientific, notation. For example, the number 729231 is displayed as 7.29E+05 when you specify two decimal places. When you specify zero decimal places, Works displays the number as 7E+05.

113

True/False   The True/False format in Works displays numbers in terms of logical values. All nonzero numbers are displayed as TRUE; cells containing zero are displayed as FALSE.

Time/Date   If you want to be able to use times or dates in a formula, use this command. For example, if you want your spreadsheet to display weekly dates across ten columns, you can type the date in the first column, then create a formula to add seven days to it and fill the dates in the remaining columns. Refer to the Microsoft Works Reference book for more details.

To change the format of the cells in your worksheet, you need to select the cells first. You can select a cell, a row, a column, or a block of cells. To format cells, follow the next Quick Steps.

Formatting Cells

1. Select the cell or cells you want to change.

   The cells you select are highlighted.

2. Select the Format menu.

   The list of Format commands is displayed on the menu.

3. Select the Format option you want to use.

   The dialog box specific to the option you choose is displayed.

4. Specify whatever changes you want to make in the dialog box, then select OK if necessary.

   Works returns to your Spreadsheet window and reformats the selected cells to the format you choose. □

In our sample worksheet, we want the numbers to be displayed with dollar signs, so we choose the Currency format, specifying zero decimal places. The spreadsheet now should look like the one shown in Figure 5.9.

114

```
   File   Edit   Print   Select   Format   Options   View   Window   Help

=====================================  INCOME.WKS  ==========================
              A              B          C         D         E         F
 1                                Sandra's Floral Designs
 2                                Profit/Loss Report
 3                                Year Ending 1990
 4
 5    INCOME             Jan-Mar   Apr-Jun July-Sept  Oct-Dec    Total
 6
 7    Special Order Jobs   $8,230   $13,890   $10,050    $7,345
 8    Phone Orders         $1,940    $2,570    $2,145    $1,930
 9    Walk-In Orders       $2,105    $2,645    $2,580    $2,345
10    Subtotal
11
12    EXPENSES
13
14    Bank Loan - Shop     $2,400    $2,400    $2,400    $2,400
15    Delivery Van         $1,050    $1,050    $1,050    $1,050
16    Labor                $2,600    $3,575    $3,250    $2,790
17    Insurance              $640      $640      $640      $640
18    Flowers and Supplies $1,260    $2,345    $2,175    $1,460

A1                                                        <F1=HELP>
Press ALT to choose commands, or F2 to edit.
```

Figure 5.9   The spreadsheet figures are displayed with dollar signs.

Step 6: Enter the formulas into the spreadsheet.

A formula is an equation that calculates on one or more values that you specify, and returns a result. In Works you can use formulas to do basic arithmetic calculations such as addition, subtraction, multiplication, and division. Works also has built-in functions for a variety of calculations such as square root (SQRT), average (AVG), and addition (SUM). Formulas and functions are discussed in more detail in Chapter 6. For this spreadsheet example, we'll be using just two types of simple formulas.

When you enter formulas in Works you must type an equal symbol (=) at the beginning of the formula so that Works knows to treat your entry as a formula instead of numbers or text. When you enter a formula for the active cell, the formula is displayed in the formula bar. When you press Enter, the results are calculated immediately and placed into the active cell. If you ever forget what formula you used to calculate the results in a cell, select that cell to display the formula in the formula bar.

115

Figure 5.10 shows the cells in our sample spreadsheet where we will enter formulas. Since formulas can be copied to other cells, we only need to enter four basic formulas in this spreadsheet.

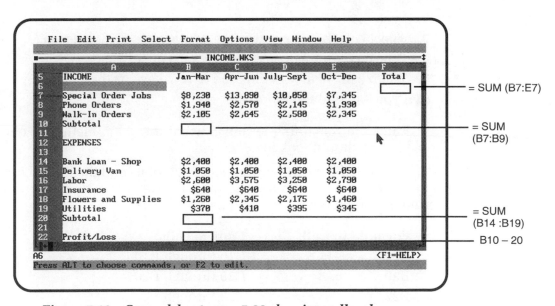

Figure 5.10   Spreadsheet rows 5-22 showing cells where formulas will be entered.

Formula =SUM(B7:B9)   The first formula we enter in Cell B10 calculates the subtotal of the income figures in column B. The formula says to calculate the sum of the figures in cells B7 through B9. The colon (:) means *through* and is used to specify a range of cells.

Formula =SUM(B14:B19)   In cell B20, we enter a similar formula to subtotal the expense figures. This formula figures the sum of expense numbers in cells B14 through B19 and records the result in cell B20.

Formula =B10–B20   To calculate the profit/loss figure, we enter a formula in cell B22 that subtracts the expense subtotal from the income subtotal.

Formula =SUM(B7:E7)   We enter the last formula in cell F7 to sum the figures across row 7 and place the result in column F.

To enter formulas into your spreadsheet, you need to type certain parts (such as the = and the function name, operators, and parentheses), then you can use either the keyboard or mouse method to enter the cell references. Enter the first formula in Cell B10.

1. Select B10.
2. Type =SUM(
3. Select cell B7 using either the Arrow keys or the mouse.
4. Type a colon (:) to designate a range of cells.
5. Select cell B9 using either the Arrow keys or the mouse.
6. Type) to end the formula.

Enter the remaining formulas using the same method. Your spreadsheet should look like Figure 5.11.

To fill in the income and expense subtotals and the Profit/Loss figures across all columns, use the Fill Right command for the formulas shown next:

Formula in Cell:	Copy to cells:
B10	C10 through E10
B20	C20 through E20
B22	C22 through F22

File Edit Print Select Format Options View Window Help

```
========================= INCOME.WKS =========================
         A                B           C         D         E         F
5   INCOME          Jan-Mar      Apr-Jun  July-Sept Oct-Dec   Total
6
7   Special Order Jobs 8230       13890    10050     7345      =SUM(B7:E7)
8   Phone Orders    1940         2570     2145      1930
9   Walk-In Orders  2105         2645     2580      2345
10  Subtotal        =SUM(B7:B9)
11
12  EXPENSES                                                    ▶
13
14  Bank Loan - Shop 2400        2400     2400      2400
15  Delivery Van    1050         1050     1050      1050
16  Labor           2600         3575     3250      2790
17  Insurance       640          640      640       640
18  Flowers and Supplies1260     2345     2175      1460
19  Utilities       370          410      395       345
20  Subtotal        =SUM(B14:B19)
21
22  Profit/Loss     =B10-B20
```
A6   <F1=HELP>
Press ALT to choose commands, or F2 to edit.

Figure 5.11   Formulas entered into spreadsheet.

117

▶ **Tip:** When you use the Fill Right command, remember to
select the initial cell as well as all the cells you want to fill.

For the last formula in F7, we use the Copy command first, then
the Fill Down command. The Copy command is similar to the Fill
command except that it is used when you want to copy to non-
adjacent cells. We want to use the formula in cell F7 in cells F8 and
F9 as well as cells F14 through F19. Since F14 through F19 are non-
adjacent cells, we start by copying F7 to F14. Follow the Quick Steps
outlined next.

Q Copying Cells

1. Select the cell whose contents you want to copy.	The cell is highlighted.
2. Select the Copy command on the Edit menu.	Notice the message line says to select the new location, then press Enter.
3. Select the cell you want to copy to, then press Enter.	The contents of the original cell are copied to the new location. ☐

Press Shift+F3 to copy instead of selecting the Copy command from the Edit menu.

When you use the Copy command, Works copies the cell contents as well as the cell format. The format of the original cell is copied to and remains with the new cell.

In this case, we copied the contents of only one cell to another cell. In Chapter 6 you'll learn how to copy blocks of cells. Now use the Fill Down command to copy F7 to F8 and F9. Then use the Fill Down command again to copy F7 to F14 through F19. Your spreadsheet should look like the one in Figure 5.12.

118

```
 File  Edit  Print  Select  Format  Options  View  Window  Help
"INCOME
============================ INCOME.WKS ============================
         A            B         C          D         E         F
5   INCOME          Jan-Mar   Apr-Jun  July-Sept  Oct-Dec    Total
6
7   Special Order Jobs  $8,230  $13,890  $10,050   $7,345   $39,515
8   Phone Orders     $1,940    $2,570   $2,145    $1,930    $8,585
9   Walk-In Orders   $2,105    $2,645   $2,580    $2,345    $9,675
10  Subtotal        $12,275   $19,105  $14,775   $11,620   $57,775
11
12  EXPENSES
13
14  Bank Loan - Shop  $2,400   $2,400   $2,400    $2,400    $9,600
15  Delivery Van     $1,050    $1,050   $1,050    $1,050    $4,200
16  Labor            $2,600    $3,575   $3,250    $2,790   $12,215
17  Insurance         $640      $640     $640      $640     $2,560
18  Flowers and Supplies $1,260 $2,345   $2,175    $1,460    $7,240
19  Utilities         $370      $410     $395      $345     $1,520
20  Subtotal         $8,320   $10,420   $9,910    $8,685   $37,335
21
22  Profit/Loss      $3,955    $8,685   $4,865    $2,935   $20,440

A5                                                  NL     <F1=HELP>
Press ALT to choose commands, or F2 to edit.
```

Figure 5.12   The spreadsheet now contains all figures and formula values, rows 1-18 shown.

You may be wondering how we can copy formulas from one cell to another and still get accurate results. After all, if a formula adds numbers in column B and we copy it to column C, won't the total reflect the figures in column B? The answer is no, and the reason has to do with using *relative* versus *absolute* cell references in the formula. Relative and absolute cell references are discussed in detail in Chapter 6. For now, just trust that it's all right to copy the formulas and that they will calculate the results correctly.

Step 7: Add final touches to make your spreadsheet easy to read.

To make the title stand out, we want to set the title of the spreadsheet in bold type. Use the Style command on the Format menu to do this. The Style command is also used to change text to italic or underline.

To set the Spreadsheet title in bold, begin by selecting cells C1 through C3, then follow the next Quick Steps.

Q Changing the Way Text Looks in Spreadsheets

1. Select the cells you want to change.	The cells are highlighted on the spreadsheet.
2. Select the Style command on the Format menu.	The Alignment and Style dialog box is displayed.
3. On the left side of the dialog box, select Bold, Italic, or Underline. You may choose more than one option, then select OK.	Works returns to your spreadsheet and changes the cells to the option you choose. □

119

Notice also that this dialog box can be used to change the alignment of text in cells. This is discussed further in Chapter 6.

We want to underline the last row in the income list and in the expense list since subtotals appear directly beneath them. Again, we use the Style command on the Format menu to do this. Select cells B9 through F9, select the Style command on the Format menu, select Underline in the dialog box, then select OK. When Works returns to your spreadsheet, the figures in these cells are underlined. Use the same procedure to underline the last expense figure in each column (cells B18 through F18). If you like, you can also use the same procedure to underline the column headings.

Congratulations! You have just created your first spreadsheet and it should look like the one shown in Figure 5.13. Scroll down to see rows 19-22.

In Chapter 6, you'll learn how to edit the spreadsheet, create more formulas, sort your spreadsheet data, and change additional format features using other Spreadsheet commands.

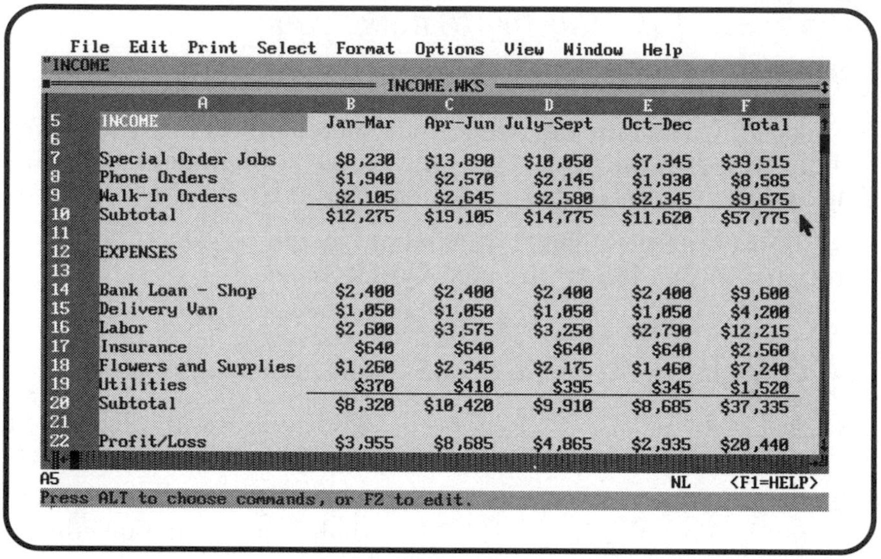

```
        File  Edit  Print  Select  Format  Options  View  Window  Help
    "INCOME
    ═════════════════════════════ INCOME.WKS ═════════════════════════════
              A           B        C        D        E        F
    5    INCOME        Jan-Mar  Apr-Jun July-Sept  Oct-Dec   Total
    6
    7    Special Order Jobs  $8,230  $13,890  $10,050   $7,345  $39,515
    8    Phone Orders        $1,940   $2,570   $2,145   $1,930   $8,585
    9    Walk-In Orders      $2,105   $2,645   $2,580   $2,345   $9,675
    10   Subtotal           $12,275  $19,105  $14,775  $11,620  $57,775
    11
    12   EXPENSES
    13
    14   Bank Loan - Shop    $2,400   $2,400   $2,400   $2,400   $9,600
    15   Delivery Van        $1,050   $1,050   $1,050   $1,050   $4,200
    16   Labor               $2,600   $3,575   $3,250   $2,790  $12,215
    17   Insurance             $640     $640     $640     $640   $2,560
    18   Flowers and Supplies $1,260   $2,345   $2,175   $1,460   $7,240
    19   Utilities             $370     $410     $395     $345   $1,520
    20   Subtotal            $8,320  $10,420   $9,910   $8,685  $37,335
    21
    22   Profit/Loss         $3,955   $8,685   $4,865   $2,935  $20,440

    A5                                               NL     <F1=HELP>
    Press ALT to choose commands, or F2 to edit.
```

Figure 5.13   The completed spreadsheet, rows 1-18 shown.

Saving Your Spreadsheet

It's a good idea to save your spreadsheet every page or so as you are entering data. This is particularly important in areas that are subject to power fluctuations so that you won't lose any of your work.

You may recall from Chapter 2 that all Works files are saved in the same way. Chapter 2 includes a discussion of files and directories, temporary filenames, and saving files. Please refer to Chapter 2 for specific instructions on saving your file.

Save that spreadsheet you have just created now so you can use it again in Chapter 6.

Printing Your Spreadsheet

When you're ready to print your spreadsheet, follow four basic steps:

1. Check the spreadsheet to see that page breaks fall where you want them. If not, you need to move them.
2. Use Print Preview to see how your spreadsheet will look when printed according to the current settings. Pay special attention to page layout, page breaks, headers and footers, and so on.
3. If necessary, change any page layout or margin settings.
4. When all settings are correct, print your file.

Page Breaks

121

As you build your spreadsheet, Works automatically determines where page breaks should fall based on the size of paper and margin settings you're using. When you're using standard 8.5-by-11-inch paper with one-inch top and bottom margins, Works prints 54 spreadsheet rows on a page. Since the rows are numbered, it's easy to check and see where Works will place the page break in a spreadsheet.

Sometimes you may want to force a page break. For instance, if an automatic page break places subtotals for a particular section on the next page, you may want to move the page break back so the entire section—complete with subtotals—moves to the next page. Page breaks must always be moved *backward*, not forward because you can't add printed lines to the page without narrowing the top and bottom margins.

To insert page breaks, use the Insert Page Break command on the Print menu. When you insert a page break, Works inserts the page break marker (>>) on the left side of the spreadsheet next to the row numbers. Page breaks that follow automatically readjust.

Print Preview

The Print Preview feature in Works allows you to see what your printed page will look like based on current print settings. This feature is very helpful for viewing the page layout, page breaks, and so on. Make use of this feature frequently—it can save you a lot of paper. To use Print Preview, select the Preview command on the Print menu. Your window should look like the one shown in Figure 5.14.

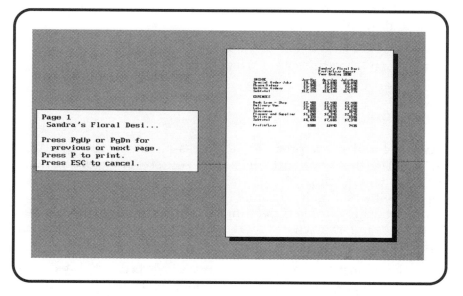

Figure 5.14   The spreadsheet shown using Print Preview.

Notice that the text and numbers in the spreadsheet are difficult to read because the print is reduced, but you don't need to be able to read the text here, just check the page layout, rows, columns, headers, footers, and page breaks.

Page Setup and Margins

Next, you want to make sure your print margins and paper size are set correctly. If you are using standard 8.5-by-11-inch paper and you are printing from top to bottom (portrait style), chances are you won't need to change any settings. The page setup and margins in Works are preset for this size of paper and print direction.

When you want to change the margins or the page size of a document use the Page Setup and Margins command on the Print menu. This command deals with the page areas shown in Figure 5.15.

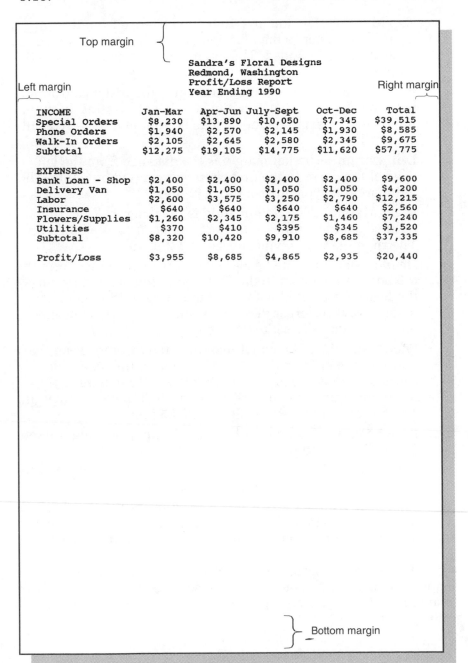

	Sandra's Floral Designs				
	Redmond, Washington				
	Profit/Loss Report				
	Year Ending 1990				
INCOME	Jan-Mar	Apr-Jun	July-Sept	Oct-Dec	Total
Special Orders	$8,230	$13,890	$10,050	$7,345	$39,515
Phone Orders	$1,940	$2,570	$2,145	$1,930	$8,585
Walk-In Orders	$2,105	$2,645	$2,580	$2,345	$9,675
Subtotal	$12,275	$19,105	$14,775	$11,620	$57,775
EXPENSES					
Bank Loan - Shop	$2,400	$2,400	$2,400	$2,400	$9,600
Delivery Van	$1,050	$1,050	$1,050	$1,050	$4,200
Labor	$2,600	$3,575	$3,250	$2,790	$12,215
Insurance	$640	$640	$640	$640	$2,560
Flowers/Supplies	$1,260	$2,345	$2,175	$1,460	$7,240
Utilities	$370	$410	$395	$345	$1,520
Subtotal	$8,320	$10,420	$9,910	$8,685	$37,335
Profit/Loss	$3,955	$8,685	$4,865	$2,935	$20,440

Figure 5.15   The Works page layout and margins.

123

The dialog box for the Page Setup and Margins command is shown in Figure 5.16. If you change paper size or print direction frequently, it's a good idea to check this box from time to time to remind you of the current settings.

Top Margin   The top margin is the distance from the top edge of the paper to the first line of printing, assuming no header text is included. The top margin is typically set to 1 inch.

Bottom Margin   The bottom margin is the distance from the bottom edge of the paper to the last line of printing, assuming no footer text is included. The bottom margin is typically set to 1 inch.

Left Margin   The left margin is the distance from the left edge of the paper to the first character printed on a line. The left margin is typically set to 1.3 inches.

Right Margin   The right margin is the distance from the right edge of the paper to the last character printed on a line. The right margin is typically set to 1.2 inches.

Header Margin   The header margin is the distance from the top edge of the paper to the first line in the header. Because the header is printed within the top margin, the top margin must always be larger than the header margin. The header margin is typically set to 0.5 inch.

Footer Margin   The footer margin is the distance from the bottom edge of the paper to the last line in the footer. Because the header is printed within the bottom margin, the bottom margin must always be larger than the footer margin. The footer margin is typically set to 0.5 inch.

Page Length   The length of the sheet of paper being printed. Typically 11-inch paper is used.

Page Width   The distance from the left edge of the paper to the right edge of the paper, typically 8.5 inches.

First Page Number   This box is used to specify the first number to use to begin page numbering. Typically set to 1, you may want to change it under special circumstances.

If you want to print your spreadsheet on a different size of paper, you need to change some print settings. For example, if you want to print on legal size paper, you need to change the Page Length setting to 14.

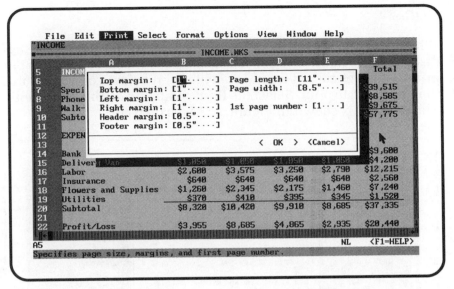

Figure 5.16   The Page Setup and Margins dialog box.

125

If you want to print sideways, or landscape style, on 8.5-by-11-inch paper, you need to change the Page Width to 11 and the Page Length to 8.5. (Note that not all printers are able to print in landscape mode. If you aren't sure about your printer, check your printer manual.)

Even when you are using 8.5-by-11-inch paper in portrait style, you still may need to change some settings. For example, if you use a paragraph header or footer in your document, you probably need to change the Header Margin or Footer Margin to a larger setting. If you want the print area on the page to be wider, you need to set the Right Margin and Left Margin to smaller numbers.

Q Changing Page Setup and Margins

1. Choose the Page Setup and Margins command on the Print menu.

   The dialog box shown in Figure 5.16 is displayed.

2. Type new settings for any of the options in the dialog box, then select OK.

   Works reformats your document to the settings that you change.

Printing

When you've checked your page breaks and all of the settings discussed previously, you're ready to print your spreadsheet. Your printer must be turned on and ready to print before you give Works the command to print. Select the Print command on the Print menu. The dialog box shown in Figure 5.17 is displayed.

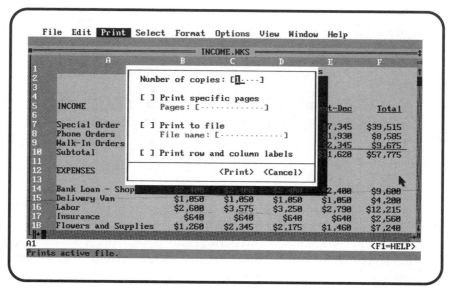

Figure 5.17   The Print dialog box.

Number of Copies   In this field, type the number of copies you want to print.

Print Specific Pages   You don't have to print the entire spreadsheet each time you print. If you want only one page, type that page number. If you want a range of pages, for example, pages 2 through 4, type 2:4. Or if you want a variety of pages, type 1,2,5.

Print to File   When you use this option, Works saves your spreadsheet with all the special printer instructions it needs to print the file. When you save your file this way, you can print it from DOS without having to start up Works. You can also send the file to another computer where it can be printed without having Works.

Print Row and Column Labels   Using this option, you can request that row and column labels be printed on the spreadsheet. You may not want to use this option for your final printing, but for preliminary copies on which you'll be making changes, this feature is especially helpful so you can see exactly which cell or cells need changes.

When all options are set the way you want them, check to see that your printer is turned on and is ready to print, then select `Print`.

What You've Learned

In this chapter you've learned the fundamentals of using the Spreadsheet tool and building a simple spreadsheet. The main points discussed in this chapter are summarized next.

127

► Use the New Spreadsheet command on the Create New File menu to create a new spreadsheet.

► The Spreadsheet work area is a grid made up of rows and columns. The point at which a row and column intersect is called a cell. You work with the *active cell* in the spreadsheet rather than a cursor.

► The keys you use to maneuver through the spreadsheet are similar to those used in the Word Processor tool. When you want to change some aspect of a cell, you must select it first, using either the keyboard or the mouse.

► You can enter text, numbers, or formulas in the cells of a spreadsheet. Formulas are equations that perform calculations on the cells you select.

► It is best to follow a logical process when creating a spreadsheet. The process is outlined in this chapter.

► Works copies duplicate entries to selected cells automatically when you use the Fill command.

► Use the Copy command to copy a cell entry to nonadjacent cells; use the Fill command to copy to adjacent cells.

▶ Use the commands on the Format menu when you want text displayed with commas or as currency, percentage, exponent, and so on. Works offers a total of eight different formats.

▶ Begin each formula by typing an equal symbol.

128

Chapter 6

More About Spreadsheets

In This Chapter

▶ *Changing, deleting, inserting, moving, and copying in the spreadsheet*

▶ *Using cell ranges*

▶ *Formulas: relative versus absolute references*

▶ *Sorting data in the spreadsheet*

In this chapter you'll build on the basic spreadsheet skills you learned in Chapter 5. You'll learn the commands to use to modify spreadsheets, create different formulas and functions, change the format of cells, and sort spreadsheet data. We will be using the sample spreadsheet created in Chapter 5, so if you want to follow along, recall that spreadsheet now.

Editing Your Spreadsheet

You can edit your spreadsheet as you're working or after you have saved it. Editing refers to any kind of text changes you make such as correcting errors, moving, deleting, inserting, or copying. In

Chapter 5 you learned that you need to select cells when you want to make changes to them. In the following sections you'll be selecting cells frequently. Refer to Chapter 5 if you need a refresher on selecting cells.

Changing Text and Numbers in Cells

You can change text, numbers, and formulas in the cells of a spreadsheet whenever you choose. To correct errors as you are entering information in the active cell, press Backspace, which erases characters to the left of the cursor.

If you decide to change an entry once it has been confirmed, select the cell, and Works places a cursor at the far left end of the formula bar. As soon as you begin typing, the previous cell entry is deleted and the new entry you type is placed in the cell when you press Enter.

130

If you prefer, you can use the Edit key, F2, to change cell entries. The F2 key lets you make corrections to the entry shown in the formula bar rather than deleting it entirely. When you press F2, Works places a cursor in the formula bar following the last character. You can press Home to move to the beginning of the line, or use the Right and Left Arrow keys to move the cursor wherever you want it on the line. Make the changes you want, then press Enter. Works overwrites the previous contents of the cell.

If you haven't already, recall the sample spreadsheet that you created in Chapter 5 called *Sandra's Flower Shop, Profit/Loss Report*. Using one of the editing methods just discussed, change the title of the spreadsheet from *Profit/Loss Report* to *Income Statement*.

Clearing Cells

Technically, you can't delete a cell, because a cell is part of a row and column. You can, however, delete the contents of a cell. Works calls this clearing the cell. The quickest way to clear the contents of a cell is to select the cell, press the Spacebar, and then press Enter. The previous cell entry is deleted. To clear a cell, use the following Quick Steps.

Q Clearing Cells

1. Select the cells you want to clear.

   Works highlights the cells you select.

2. Select the Clear command on the Edit menu.

   Works clears the cells you select. ☐

The Clear command removes the cell contents but retains the formatting. When you enter new data into the cells you clear, it will conform to the previous format and style.

Deleting Rows and Columns

When you delete a row or column, it is permanently removed from the spreadsheet. The remaining columns move to the right and the remaining rows move upward to fill the empty space. When the columns and rows shift, Works adjusts the cell references automatically. For instance, if you remove column B, what was previously column C becomes column B and the cells are renamed to B1, B2, B3, and so on. If you delete a row or column referenced by a formula and the formula can no longer be calculated correctly, Works displays ERR in the cell where the formula is located indicating that a formula error exists.

To delete a row or column, use the following Quick Steps.

131

Q Deleting Rows and Columns

1. Select the rows or columns you want to delete.

   Works highlights the rows or columns in your spreadsheet.

2. Select the Delete Row/ Column command from the Edit menu.

   The selected rows or columns are immediately removed from the spreadsheet. ☐

If you don't select the row or column first before selecting the Delete command, Works displays a dialog box asking which one you want to delete. Before you choose one, make certain that the active cell is where you want it. Works will delete either the row or the column of the active cell once you make your choice.

Using the Delete Row/Column command, delete the entire row 14 (Delivery Van) from the sample spreadsheet. Notice that the SUM formulas on row 19 are still able to calculate correctly. So you don't get the ERR entries on this row, Works simply recalculates the subtotals, as shown in Figure 6.1.

File Edit Print Select Format Options View Window Help

INCOME.WKS

	A	B	C	D	E	F
5						
6	INCOME	Jan-Mar	Apr-Jun	July-Sept	Oct-Dec	Total
7						
8	Special Order Jobs	$8,230	$13,890	$10,050	$7,345	$39,515
9	Phone Orders	$1,940	$2,570	$2,145	$1,930	$8,585
10	Walk-In Orders	$2,105	$2,645	$2,580	$2,345	$9,675
11	Subtotal	$12,275	$19,105	$14,775	$11,620	$57,775
12						
13	EXPENSES					
14						
15	Bank Loan - Shop	$2,400	$2,400	$2,400	$2,400	$9,600
16	Labor	$2,600	$3,575	$3,250	$2,790	$12,215
17	Insurance	$640	$640	$640	$640	$2,560
18	Flowers and Supplies	$1,260	$2,345	$2,175	$1,460	$7,240
19	Utilities	$370	$410	$395	$345	$1,520
20	Subtotal	$7,270	$9,370	$8,860	$7,635	$33,135
21						
22	Profit/Loss	$5,005	$9,735	$5,915	$3,985	$24,640

A5

<F1=HELP>

Press ALT to choose commands, or F2 to edit.

Figure 6.1   The spreadsheet recalculates correctly after a row has been removed.

Inserting a Row or Column

Quite often as you are creating a spreadsheet, you'll find that you want to insert a row or a column to make room for something you have forgotten or want to add. You can insert a row or a column anywhere in the spreadsheet by using the Insert Row/Column command on the Edit menu. Works inserts rows above the active cell and columns to the left of the active cell. (You can only insert one row or column at a time.)

To insert a row or column, follow the next Quick Steps.

Q Inserting a Row or Column

1. Select the entire row or the column where you want to insert.

   The entire row or column is highlighted.

2. Select the Insert Row/ Column Command from the Edit menu.

   The new row is inserted above the selected row, or the new column is inserted to the left of the selected column. □

If you don't select the row or column before selecting the Insert command, Works displays a dialog box asking which one you want to insert. Make sure the active cell is where you want it before you make your choice, otherwise Works will insert a row or column where you may not want it.

In the sample spreadsheet, use the Insert Row/Column command to insert a row following row 1. Enter the name of the town for Sandra's Floral Shop, Redmond, Washington, as shown in Figure 6.2.

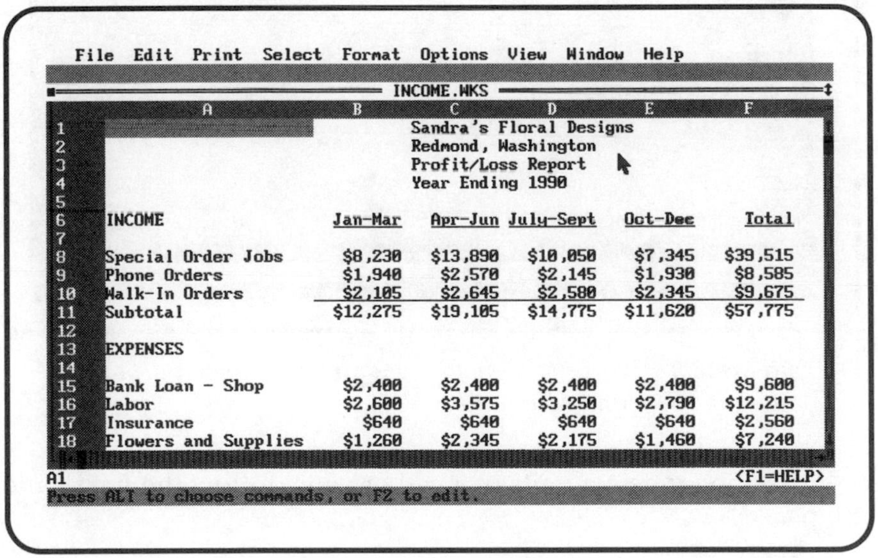

133

File   Edit   Print   Select   Format   Options   View   Window   Help

```
━━━━━━━━━━━━━━━━━━━━━━ INCOME.WKS ━━━━━━━━━━━━━━━━━━━━━━
        A              B        C        D        E        F
1                          Sandra's Floral Designs
2                          Redmond, Washington
3                          Profit/Loss Report
4                          Year Ending 1990
5
6  INCOME              Jan-Mar  Apr-Jun July-Sept Oct-Dec   Total
7
8  Special Order Jobs  $8,230  $13,890  $10,050  $7,345  $39,515
9  Phone Orders        $1,940   $2,570   $2,145  $1,930   $8,585
10 Walk-In Orders      $2,105   $2,645   $2,580  $2,345   $9,675
11 Subtotal           $12,275  $19,105  $14,775 $11,620  $57,775
12
13 EXPENSES
14
15 Bank Loan - Shop    $2,400   $2,400   $2,400  $2,400   $9,600
16 Labor               $2,600   $3,575   $3,250  $2,790  $12,215
17 Insurance            $640     $640     $640    $640    $2,560
18 Flowers and Supplies $1,260  $2,345   $2,175  $1,460   $7,240
```

A1   <F1=HELP>
Press ALT to choose commands, or F2 to edit.

Figure 6.2   Spreadsheet showing row insertion for town name.

Moving Rows, Columns, or Cells

You can move rows, columns, or the contents of cells whether they contain text, numbers, or formulas. If you move cells that contain a formula, Works automatically adjusts cell references in the formula so that it still calculates correctly. If you move a number that is referenced by a formula, the same is also true; Works automatically adjusts cell references in the formula so that it still calculates correctly.

When you move a block of cells, Works uses the upper left cell as the reference point for the new location. When you choose the new location, select the cell where you want the upper left cell to be located (see Figure 6.3).

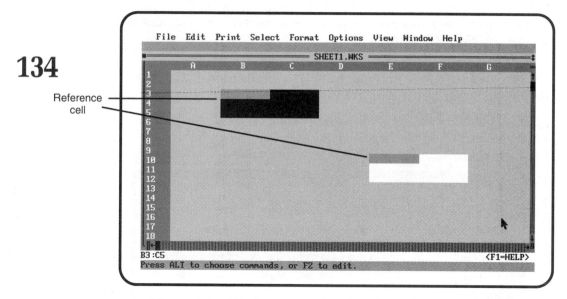

Reference
cell

Figure 6.3   Works screen showing the reference point for moving rows and columns.

To move the contents of a cell or cells, follow the next Quick Steps.

Q Moving Rows, Columns, or Cells

1. Select the cell or cells whose contents you want to move.	The cell or cells are highlighted.
2. Select the Move command on the Edit menu.	The Edit menu disappears and Works returns to your spreadsheet window. The message line tells you to select a new location.
3. Select the new location based on where you want the upper left cell to be located, then press Enter.	The contents of the cell or cells are moved to the new location. □

 Press F3 to move the contents of the selected cell or cells.

135

⊘ **Caution:** When choosing a new location to move cells to, be sure to choose a block of cells that is empty, otherwise the existing entries will be overwritten.

Filling Rows and Columns

In Chapter 5 you learned about the Fill Right and Fill Down commands used for entering repetitive data into rows or columns. When your spreadsheet calls for the same entry in multiple, adjacent cells, you can type it once, then fill the cells to the right or beneath your entry using one of these commands.

Works has another fill command called Fill Series. When you use this command, Works fills adjacent cells with a series of numbers or dates. For example, if you want your spreadsheet columns to be labeled 1/91, 2/91, 3/91, and so on through 12/91, you only have to type the first entry, 1/91, then use the Fill Series command to fill in the rest. When you use the Fill Series command, a dialog box is displayed and asks how you want the entries incremented—by number, by day, weekday, month, or year. The dialog box is shown in Figure 6.4.

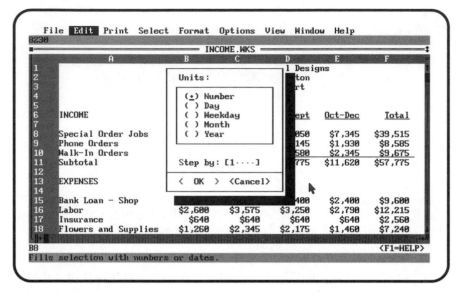

Figure 6.4   The Fill Series Units dialog box.

Number   Enters a series of numbers following the first number you enter. For example, if you enter 25, Works fills in 26, 27, 28, and so on.

Day   Increments your entry by days of the week, including Saturdays and Sundays. For example, 10/1/90, 10/2/90...10/6/90, 10/7/90, and so on.

Weekday   Increments your entry by days of the week, Monday through Friday only. For example, 10/1/90...10/5/90, 10/8/90, 10/9/90, and so on.

Month   Increments your entry by months. For example, 1/91, 2/91, 3/91, and so on.

Year   Increments your entry by years. For example, 1/91, 1/92, 1/93, and so on.

Step by   Specifies the number to increment by. For example, years incremented by 2 would be 1/91, 1/93, 1/95, and so on. (The default setting is 1.)

Q Using the Fill Series Command

1. Enter the number or date (not text) in the initial cell you choose and press Enter.

   Your entry is confirmed in the cell you choose.

2. Select the initial cell and all the cells you want to fill.

The initial cell and the cells you want to fill are highlighted.

3. Select the Fill Series command on the Edit menu.

The Units dialog box is displayed.

4. Make the selections you choose in the dialog box, then select OK.

The cells you selected are automatically filled in according to the settings you chose in the dialog box. □

The spreadsheet you created in Chapter 5 doesn't lend itself well to the Fill Series command because the column headings cover a range of months. However, if you had made the column headings read January, April, July, and October, you could use the Fill Series command. If you want to, move to a blank row in your spreadsheet now and try it. Type January in column A of a blank row, then press Enter. Select that cell and the cells in the same row in columns B, C, and D. Select the Fill Series command. In the dialog box, select Month, and then type 3 in the Step by field. Works fills in the cells in columns B, C, and D with April, July, and October respectively. Be sure to clear these cells before saving your spreadsheet.

137

Copying Cell Contents

In Chapter 5 you learned how to copy the contents of one cell to a new location. You can also copy a block of cells to a new location. Some of the rules you learned for moving cells apply to copying cells as well. For instance, before you choose the location to copy to, make sure the cells in the new location are empty, otherwise the contents will be overwritten. Second, the upper left corner of the cell block is your reference point, so choose the new location based on where you want the upper left cell to be located.

Suppose you want to copy the Expenses section of your spreadsheet to row 30. Select cells A13:F20, then select the Copy command on the Edit menu. The message line tells you to select a new location and press enter. Move the highlight to cell A30, then press Enter. Works copies the Expenses section to cells A30:F37. (Be sure to clear these cells before saving your spreadsheet.)

Sometimes you may want to copy a cell's contents to more than one nonadjacent cell. Copying could become very tedious if you had to reselect the original cell over and over again. Fortunately, you don't have to do that. Once you have copied to the new location, you can select the next location and press Shift+F7 to copy the same selection again. Figure 6.5 illustrates how to use the Copy command to copy to the first location and Shift+F7 to copy to subsequent locations.

138

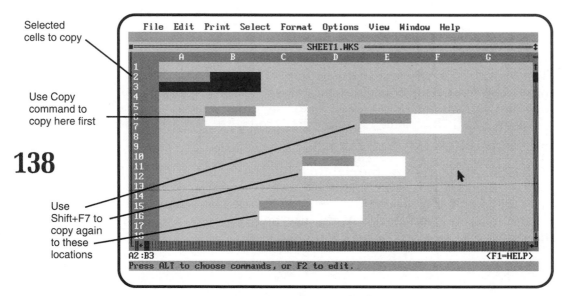

Selected cells to copy

Use Copy command to copy here first

Use Shift+F7 to copy again to these locations

Figure 6.5   Copying blocks of cells to one or multiple locations.

When you use the Copy command, Works copies the cell contents along with the the cell format to the new location. If the cell contains a formula, the formula is copied. What if you want to copy a cell's value instead of the formula? You use the Copy Special command to do this. The Copy Special command can also be used to copy the value in a cell and add or subtract from the value in another cell.

When you select Copy Special, Works displays the dialog box shown in Figure 6.6. To use the Copy Special command, use the following Quick Steps.

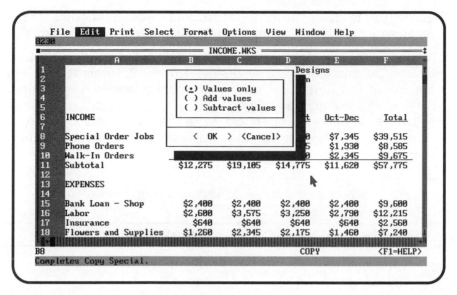

Figure 6.6   The Copy Special dialog box.

139

Copying a Cell Value Rather than Contents

1. Select the cell whose value you want to copy.

   The cell is highlighted.

2. Select the Copy Special command.

   The message line tells you to select the new location, then press Enter.

3. Select the cell you want to copy to, then press Enter.

   A dialog box with three choices is displayed.

4. Choose the Values Only, Add Values, or Subtract Values option, then select OK.

   The value is copied to the cell you select based on the options you choose in the dialog box.   □

Using Formulas

When you created the spreadsheet in Chapter 5, you used some simple formulas to add and subtract values in cells. We told you what to type to create the formulas; now let's look at the rules Works operates by to evaluate formulas so you can create some yourself.

Works follows standard algebraic rules to evaluate the formulas you create. Equations are evaluated from left to right and the contents of the innermost set of parentheses are evaluated first. Works evaluates operators (such as +, −, /, *) in standard order of evaluation. When two operators have the same priority, Works evaluates from left to right. Table 6.1 lists the operators and their order of evaluation.

Table 6.1   Operators and their Order of Evaluation in Works Formulas.

Operator	Order of Evaluation
^ (exponent)	First
− (negative), + (positive)	Second
* (multiplication), / (division)	Third
+ (addition), − (subtraction)	Fourth
=, <>	Fifth
>, <, <=, >=, ~ (NOT)	Sixth
| (OR), & (AND)	Seventh

Relative Versus Absolute Cell References

The formulas you created in Chapter 5 included cell references like =SUM(B4–C9). You were able to copy these formulas to other cells and have them calculate correctly because they use *relative* cell references. Now it's time to find out the difference between relative and absolute cell references.

When you use a relative cell reference in a formula, in effect, you are giving Works maplike directions to follow to find the cells you reference. In Figure 6.7, the formula in cell B6, =C3-B4, tells Works to *take the value from the cell one column to the right and three rows back and subtract from it the value in the cell two rows back.* A formula of this type is said to have relative cell references, because the references change depending on the location of the formula in the spreadsheet. If you copy the same formula to cell D6, the formula references change to =E3–D4. The directions are still the same, but the cells the formula operates on are obviously different ones.

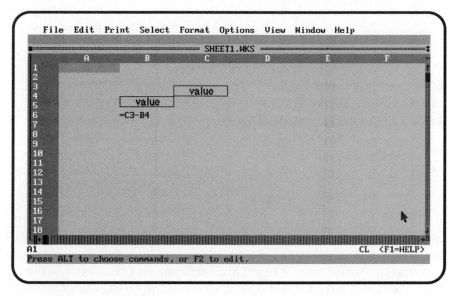

Figure 6.7   Relative cell references give Works maplike instructions to follow.

141

When a formula uses *absolute* references, it means that no matter where the formula is located in the spreadsheet, it always operates on the absolute references it uses. With absolute references, the above formula, =C3-B4, is typed as =C3-B4. The dollar signs ($) before the column letters and row numbers designate the absolute reference. Even if you move this formula to cell H35, it will still subtract the value in cell B4 from the value in cell C3.

In Works you also have the option of making just the column or just the row an absolute reference. These are called *mixed* references. For example, $C3 means that column C is absolute, but row 3 is not. C$3 means that row 3 is absolute but column C is not.

You can enter a relative cell reference in a cell and make it absolute by using the F4 key. As you select the cells for your formula, press F4 to cycle through the following options:

Press F4	For	Example
Once	Relative column, relative row	D6
Twice	Absolute column, absolute row	D6
Three times	Relative column, absolute row	D$6
Four times	Absolute column, relative row	$D6

> **Note:** You must use either the Arrow keys or the mouse to select cells in order for the F4 key to work. If you type the cell references instead, the F4 key is not activated.

Formulas Using Named Cells

In Chapter 5 you learned how to select cells and ranges of cells. In Works you can also name a range of cells. For example, in our spreadsheet, we could name cells B7:B9, *FirstQuarterIncome*, and cells B13:B18, *FirstQuarterExpenses*.

The advantage to naming ranges of cells is that you can use the names as references in formulas. For instance, to calculate the profit/ loss figure in cell B21, we could have created the formula =(FirstQuarterIncome – FirstQuarterExpenses). In cells B10 and B19, we could have used the formulas =SUM(FirstQuarterIncome) and =SUM(FirstQuarterExpenses) rather than =SUM(B7:B9) and =SUM(B18:B18). Creating range names can make it much simpler for you to write formulas.

When you create a name for a range of cells, the dialog box shown in Figure 6.8 is displayed.

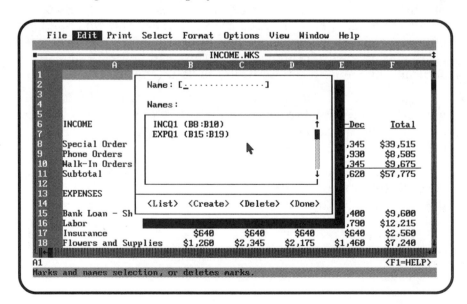

Figure 6.8   The Range Name dialog box.

In the Name field, type the name you want to give the range. The name can be 1-15 characters, but the name itself must not include any single quotation marks. If the name resembles a number, a function name, or a cell reference previously named, you must type a single quotation mark before and after when using the name in a formula. For example, if the name you choose for a range is SUM, then when you want to create the formula, you must type `=SUM('SUM')`. As you can see, using range names that resemble function names, numbers, or cell references can become very confusing, so it's best to choose unique names.

When you have created other names for cell ranges, the names are listed in the Names box. Use this box also to select range names when you want to delete or rename a range.

To name a range of cells, follow the next Quick Steps.

Q Naming Cell Ranges

1. Select the cells you want to name.

   The cells are highlighted on the spreadsheet.

2. Select the Range Name command on the Edit menu.

   The Name dialog box shown in Figure 6.8 is displayed.

3. In the Name field, enter a name using 1-15 characters. Don't use single quotation marks in the name. Select `Create`.

   Works returns to your spreadsheet.

4. If you want to name another range of cells, repeat steps 1-3.

   The other names you have created appear in the Names box. □

When a range of cells has a name, the Go To command recognizes the name. If you want to go to that block of cells, use the Go To command on the Select menu and select the range name you want.

If you decide you no longer want to use a range name that you've created, you can delete the name. Use the following Quick Steps to delete a range name.

Q Deleting a Range Name

1. Select the Range Name command on the Edit menu.

   The dialog box in Figure 6.8 is displayed.

2. Select the name you want to delete from the Name box.

   The name you select is displayed in the Name field.

3. Select `Delete`.

   Works returns to your spreadsheet and deletes the name. If the name was referenced by any formulas in your spreadsheet, Works changes the reference back to the standard format for ranges (such as B6:F9).   □

144

Formulas Using Functions

Aside from creating simple arithmetic and algebraic formulas, you can use any of Works' 57 built-in functions to create formulas. A function is a preset equation designed to solve a specific problem, for instance, finding the average of a range of numbers. Among the 57 functions are mathematical, financial, statistical, and date/time functions. In Chapter 5, you used the SUM function to add numbers in a column. Here is a sampling of some of the functions Works knows:

PV	Automatically calculates present value.
FV	Automatically calculates future value.
$ABS_{(x)}$	Provides the absolute value of x.
AVG	Figures the average of a range of numbers you specify.
COUNT	Counts the number of items in a range of cells.
DDB	Calculates depreciation using the double-declining balance method.
$LOG_{(x)}$	Calculates the base 10 logarithm of x.

For a complete list of functions, refer to the Microsoft Works Reference book, Appendix B, or Help.

Turning Automatic Calculation Off

As you have probably noticed by now, when you enter formulas or change values that formulas operate on, Works recalculates your spreadsheet automatically. In a small spreadsheet, Works calculates almost instantaneously. As your spreadsheet grows and you add more formulas to it, it may take Works longer to recalculate every formula. If you don't want Works to continually recalculate but would prefer to see the recalculation after you've made all your changes, you can turn the automatic calculation off by selecting the Manual Calculation command on the Options menu.

When you select this command, Works only recalculates when you request it. Notice that when you select Manual Calculation, CALC is displayed on the status line. When you're ready to recalculate, select the Calculate Now command on the Options menu. When you want to change back to automatic calculation, select the Manual Calculation command on the Options menu again.

145

Displaying Formulas

As you type formulas into your spreadsheet, you can see the formula in the formula bar. When you select the cell again, the formula reappears in the formula bar and the calculated results appear in the cell itself. If you want to display the formula in the cell, select the Show Formula command on the Options menu. When you select this command, Works displays the formula in the cell rather than the calculated value. To redisplay the calculated value, select the Show Formula command on the Options menu again.

Formatting Your Spreadsheet

Formatting refers to any changes you make to the way the text or numbers look in the cell. In Chapter 5 you learned that you can select a variety of formats for numbers; for instance, currency, percent, or exponential. But format changes also include bold text, italic, underline, a change in font, font size, or alignment of text within the cell. You used the Bold and Underline commands to reformat cells in your spreadsheet in Chapter 5. In this section you'll learn how to change font and font size, and alignment of cell entries.

Changing Text Font and Size

The process for changing font and font size is much the same as changing text to bold, underline, or italic. When you select the Font command on the Format menu, the dialog box shown in Figure 6.9 is displayed. The list of fonts you see on your screen may be different than those shown in the figure. The available fonts are determined by the type of printer you use.

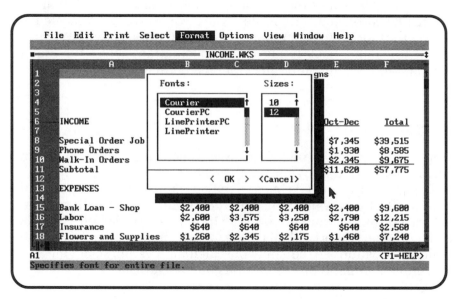

Figure 6.9 The Font dialog box.

Use the following Quick Steps to change the title of your spreadsheet to a different font.

Q Changing the Font in Your Spreadsheet

1. Select the cells whose font you want to change.

   The cells are highlighted in the spreadsheet.

2. Select Font command on the Format menu.

   Works displays the Font dialog box shown in Figure 6.9.

3. Choose the Font and the size you want to use, then select OK.

Works returns to your spreadsheet.

□

You won't see the font change on the screen, but when you print your spreadsheet, the cells you select will be printed in the font you choose.

Changing Character Alignment

The first eight Format commands on the Format menu (General, Fixed, Currency, Comma, and so on) all specify the alignment of an entry in a cell. For example, the General format specifies that text is aligned on the left side of the cell and numbers are aligned on the right. When you want to change the alignment of a cell entry, use the Style command on the Format menu. Works displays the dialog box shown in Figure 6.10.

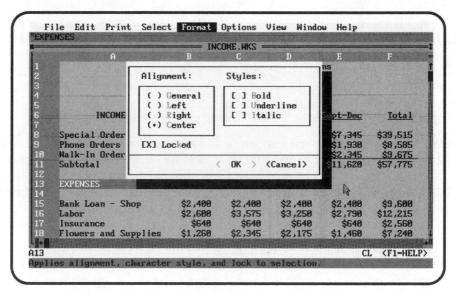

Figure 6.10   Alignment and Styles dialog box.

In Figure 6.10, notice that the alignment of INCOME in cell A6 has been changed to center and EXPENSES in cell A13 is highlighted to be changed. Follow the next Quick Steps to change the alignment of INCOME (A6) and EXPENSES (A13) to center.

Q Changing the Alignment of Cell Entries

1. Select the cell or cells whose alignment you want to change.

The cell or cells you select are highlighted.

2. Select the Style command on the Format menu.

The Alignment and Styles dialog box is displayed, as shown in Figure 6.10.

3. Select the alignment you want: general, left, right, or center; then select OK.

Works returns to your spreadsheet and changes the alignment of the cells you select. ☐

Sorting Your Spreadsheet

Spreadsheets can be easier to work with when information is sorted in different ways. But often, you don't enter the information in the order you would like it sorted. With Works, you can rearrange entries in your spreadsheet either alphabetically or numerically, in ascending or descending order. Works sorts on text as well as numbers, whether they are dates, times, dollars, or other types of numbers.

In Works, you can sort on one, two, or three columns. When items in the first column match, items are sorted on the second column. When items in the first and second column match, items are sorted on the third column. When you select the cells you want to sort and choose the Sort Rows command on the Select menu, Works displays the dialog box shown in Figure 6.11.

Works assumes you want to sort on the first column you select. If you want to sort on a second and third column as well, specify them in the dialog box. Follow the next Quick Steps to sort your spreadsheet.

Q Sorting Your Spreadsheet

1. Select the cells in the column you want to sort by.

Works highlights the cells in the column you choose.

2. Select the Sort Rows command on the Select menu.

The Columns dialog box is displayed. In the first Column field, Works displays the column where you place your cursor.

3. Choose either ascending or descending order for the 1st Column sort.

4. If you want to sort by two or three columns, type the column letters in the appropriate fields, then choose ascending or descending order for each. Select OK.

The dialog box disappears and the columns you select are resorted in the order you choose.

□

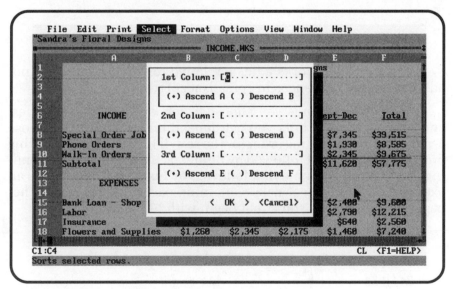

Figure 6.11   The Columns dialog box.

Also use the Quick Steps just previous to sort alphabetically in descending order on the expense items in the sample spreadsheet. Select column A, rows 15-19, then select the Sort command. The spreadsheet now should look like the one shown in Figure 6.12. Notice that the underline from the Utilities row is removed and now appears under the Bank Loan row.

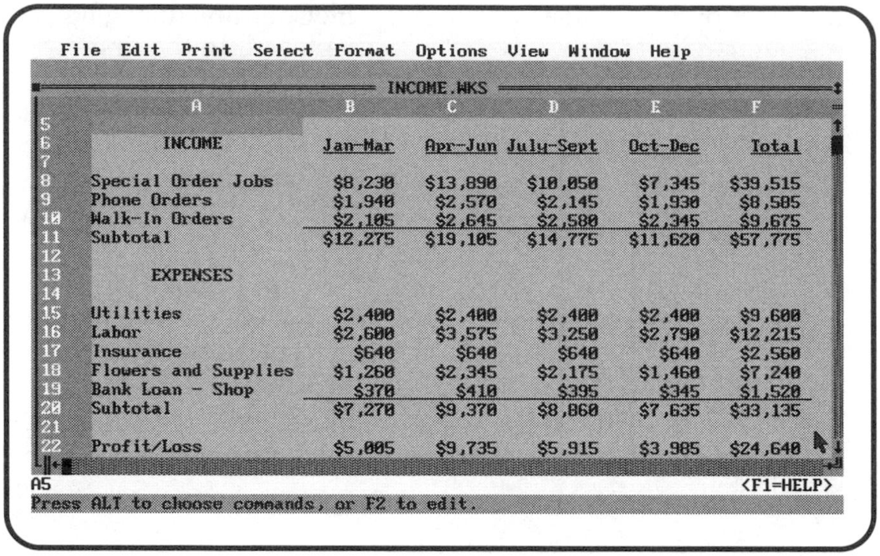

Figure 6.12   The spreadsheet with expense items sorted.

After sorting, Works adjusts relative references but does not adjust absolute references in spreadsheet formulas.

When the columns you choose to sort on contain text, dates, and numbers, the results you get depend on whether you choose ascending or descending order for the sort. If the sort is in ascending order, text comes first followed by numbers. If the sort is in descending order, numbers come first followed by text. The following is an example of spreadsheet data containing part numbers, some that begin with numbers, some that begin with letters:

Part Numbers	Price
99213	$23.99
Z1110X2	$34.90
BN4112S	$10.98
778660	$11.25
NP19899	$33.45
98979	$45.99

When this list is sorted in ascending order, lettered part numbers appear before numbered part numbers, as shown.

Part Numbers	Price
BN4112S	$10.98
NP19899	$33.45
Z1110X2	$34.90
98979	$45.99
99213	$23.99
778660	$11.25

When the list is sorted in descending order, numbered part numbers appear before lettered ones. Notice also that alphabetic items now appear in descending order.

Part Numbers	Price
778660	$11.25
99213	$23.99
98979	$45.99
Z1110X2	$34.90
NP19899	$33.45
BN4112S	$10.98

Isolating Row and Column Headings

When you are working on a spreadsheet that is too large to display on one window, it is often helpful to *freeze* the row and column headings. Freezing the headings allows you to scroll to other parts of the spreadsheet that are not visible in the initial window and still see your row and column headings. When you freeze row and column headings, all rows above the selected cell and all columns to the left of the selected cell are frozen.

In our sample spreadsheet, you would select cell B7 to freeze column A and rows 1-6 (see Figure 6.13). Notice in Figure 6.13 that column C is now displayed alongside column A because column A is frozen.

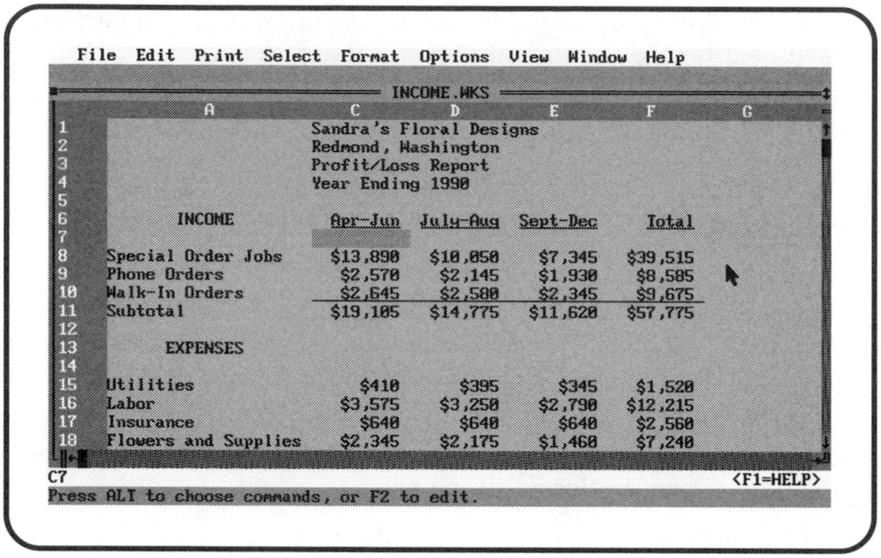

Figure 6.13   A spreadsheet with the column headings and row titles frozen.

What You've Learned

This chapter has built on the basic spreadsheet skills you learned in Chapter 5. In this chapter you have expanded your skills to include editing, reformatting, and sorting your spreadsheet. The following is a list of the main points covered in this chapter.

▶ Change text or numbers in the spreadsheet cells by using the Backspace key, the F2 key, or the Clear command on the Edit menu.

▶ Delete and insert spreadsheet rows or columns by using the Delete and Insert commands on the Edit menu.

▶ Move cell contents or entire rows and columns using the Move command on the Edit menu. The Fill Series dialog box offers you the choice of filling a series in numbers, days, weekdays, months, years, and so on.

► Use the Copy command on the Edit menu to copy blocks of cells to a new location. Use the upper left cell as the reference point for the new location.

► Create formulas in your spreadsheet cells using standard algebraic rules: equations are evaluated from right to left, and values enclosed in parentheses are evaluated first.

► Formulas that contain absolute cell references operate on the values contained in the exact cells specified. Absolute cell references contain dollar symbols before each row and column designator such as: A14.

► Formulas that contain relative cell references operate on relative positions in the spreadsheet. Works might read a relative formula as *take the value in the cell two rows back and one row to the left, and subtract it from the value in the cell one row down and two rows to the right.*

► Name cell ranges by using the Range Name command on the Edit menu. You can use range names as cell references in formulas. Works also recognizes range names when you use the Go To command.

► Change the text font, the font size, and character alignment using the Font and Style commands on the Format menu.

► Use the Sort Rows command on the Select menu to sort your spreadsheet rows. Sort on one, two, or three columns.

► Use the Freeze Titles command on the Options menu to freeze row and column headings. This allows you to scroll to other parts of the worksheet while continuing to display row and column headings.

153

Chapter 7

Charting Your Spreadsheet

In This Chapter

▶ *The eight chart types in Works*
▶ *Choosing the right chart*
▶ *Creating and displaying charts*
▶ *Chart View and Spreadsheet View*

All the data in the world is of little value if it can't be readily understood. Sometimes the best way to understand and interpret data is to see it in a graphical form. The Charting tool in Works lets you present spreadsheet data in the form of charts. Charts can help you understand and interpret numbers quickly, compare data easily, recognize trends, or show you percentages of a whole.

In Works, charts are tied to spreadsheet data. Almost any data that you enter in a spreadsheet can be displayed in a chart of one type or another. You tell Works which data to use to create the chart, and Works creates the chart for you automatically.

Works has eight predefined chart styles for you to choose from. In this chapter you'll learn more about the different types of charts available in Works and how to create them.

Introduction to Works Charts

With the exception of pie charts, all charts have two axes: the x-axis and the y-axis. The x-axis is the horizontal line that forms the bottom edge of the chart, and the y-axis is the vertical line that forms the left edge of the chart (see Figure 7.1). The x-axis often represents time or categories of items. The y-axis often represents dollars or quantity.

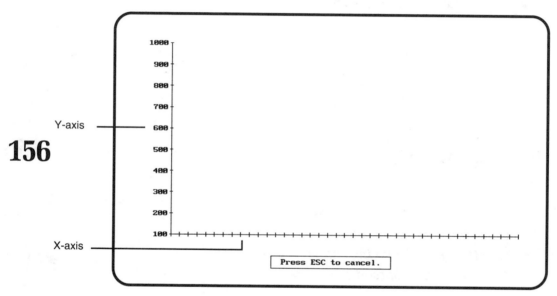

156

Figure 7.1   The x- and y- axes of a chart.

Bar Charts

Bar charts are useful for showing related data at a specific point in time or for comparing categories of data over a period of time. When more than one type of bar is displayed in a bar chart, different categories of data are being compared. Each set of bars usually represents a row or column on the spreadsheet.

In Figure 7.2, income and expenses are being compared over a period of time. The x-axis shows time while the y-axis shows dollars.

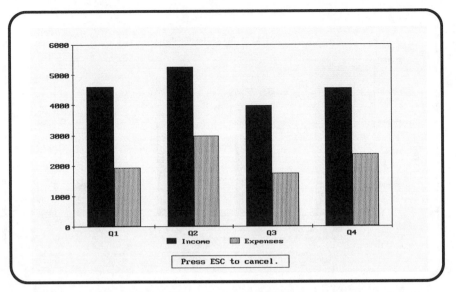

Figure 7.2   A Bar chart showing time on the x-axis and dollars on the y-axis.

157

Stacked Bar Charts

Stacked bar charts illustrate how different categories or types of items contribute to the whole. The total bar in a stacked bar chart represents the whole; the individual bars represent categories or items. The bars that make up the stack usually correspond to a row or column of data in the spreadsheet.

In Figure 7.3, the total bar represents total sales of sporting goods items in a given time period. The individual bars that make up the stacks represent different categories of items sold.

100% Bar Charts

100% bar charts are identical to stacked bar charts except that the y-axis represents percentages rather than dollars or units. The data used to create the bar chart in Figure 7.3 is used again in Figure 7.4 to create a 100% bar chart. Notice that the x-axis is unchanged but the y-axis now measures percentage rather than dollars.

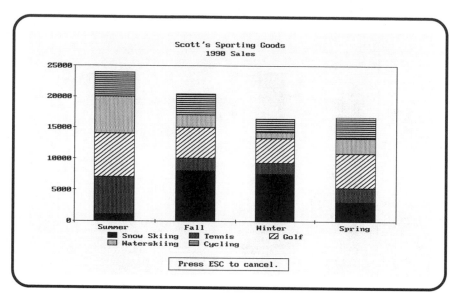

158

Figure 7.3   A Stacked Bar chart.

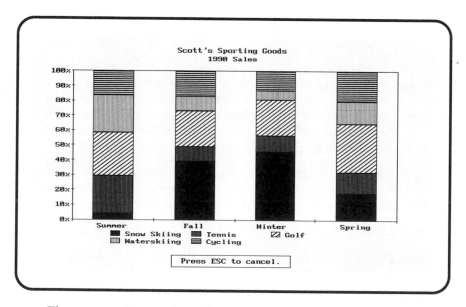

Figure 7.4   A 100% Bar chart.

Line Charts

Line charts work well for showing trends in data, so the x-axis usually represents time. Each line on the chart represents a category which corresponds either to a row or a column of data in the spreadsheet.

The line chart in Figure 7.5 shows how the number of clients in five states has risen or fallen in a four-year period. The x-axis represents years and the y-axis represents numbers of clients.

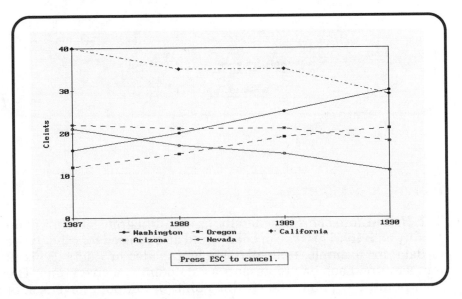

Figure 7.5   A Line chart.

159

Area Line Charts

An *area line chart* is similar to a line chart except that the lines are stacked to show totals in each category. Works adds the values of the first line to the second line, the second line to the third, and so on. The line chart used in Figure 7.5 has been changed to an area line chart in Figure 7.6. Notice that the values of the lines have been added to one another.

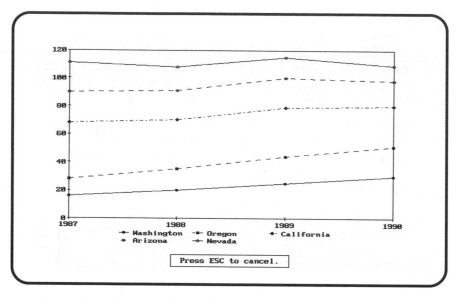

Figure 7.6   An Area Line chart.

Hi-Lo-Close Charts

The *Hi-Lo-Close chart* is generally used to illustrate stock or commodity activity. This type of chart could also be used for other types of data, for example, to display student grades or fluctuations in temperature. Each line represents a data point at a given time. The high point, low point, and closing point (or midpoint, average, or median) are pinpointed on each line. Figure 7.7 illustrates stock activity over a six-month period.

Pie Charts

When you want to show how individual parts contribute to a whole and you only have one category of data, use a *pie chart*. In a pie chart, you can compare the parts to one another or to the whole. The slices correspond to individual values in the spreadsheet; the entire pie corresponds to a total or sum of these values in the spreadsheet. In Figure 7.8, the slices represent individual expenses; the pie represents the total of expenses.

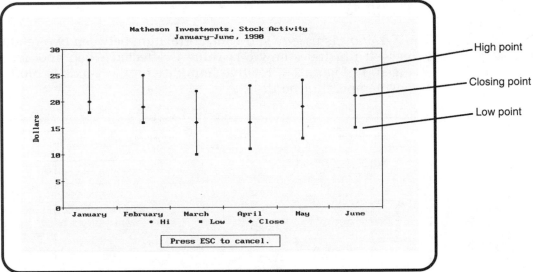

High point

Closing point

Low point

Figure 7.7   A Hi-Lo-Close chart.

161

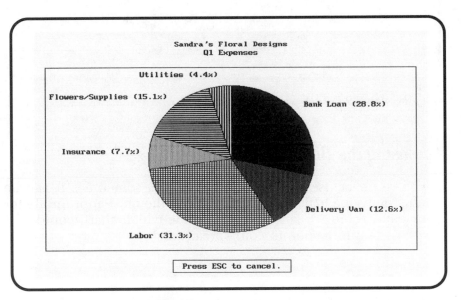

Figure 7.8   A Pie chart.

X-Y Charts

The *X-Y chart* is used to show the correlation between two related values—it illustrates how one value is affected when another is changed. In Figure 7.9, relative humidity on the y-axis is plotted against temperature on the x-axis.

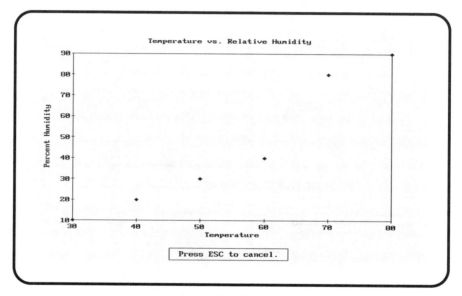

Figure 7.9   An X-Y chart.

Choosing the Right Type of Chart to Use

If you've never used a charting tool before, sometimes it can be confusing trying to decide which chart is the most appropriate for your data. Table 7.1 can help you decide which chart would best display the information in your spreadsheet.

The Parts of a Chart

Most of the eight different types of charts you can create in Works have some common characteristics. These are illustrated in Figure 7.10.

Table 7.1   Chart styles and their uses

Chart Type	Purpose
Bar	To compare related data at a specific point in time, or to show the trend of data over a period of time
Stacked Bar	To show summary data in more than one category over a period of time
100% Bar	To show the percentages that make up the whole at a specific point in time or over a period of time
Line	To show variance in price, quantity, or other entity over a period of time
Area Line	To show the cumulative variance in price, quantity, or other entity over a period of time
Hi-Lo-Close	To show the activity of an entity such as a stock or commodity over a period of time
Pie	To show the percentages that make up the whole for a single category
X-Y	To show one value in relation to another

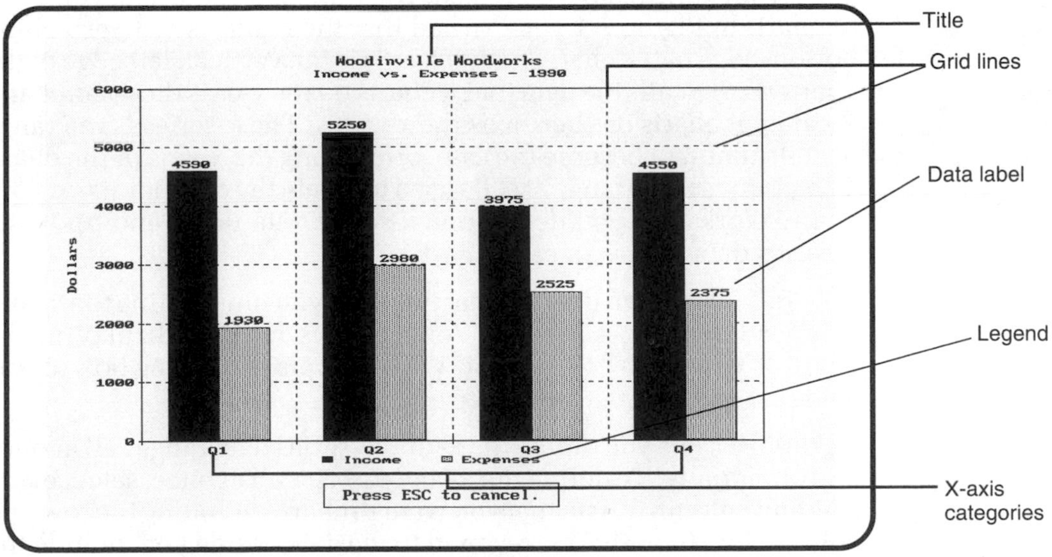

163

Figure 7.10   The different parts of a chart.

Creating Charts

Since charts are linked to spreadsheet data, you must create a spreadsheet before you can create a chart. Works lets you create and save up to eight different charts per spreadsheet. In this section, we'll create a simple chart using the income statement for *Sandra's Floral Designs*. If you'd like to follow along, recall this Spreadsheet file now.

The basic process for creating a chart is as follows:

1. Create the spreadsheet.
2. Select the data in the spreadsheet that you want to chart.
3. Display the chart by entering `Chart View` in the Spreadsheet tool.
4. Add title, legends, data labels, and so on.
5. Return to `Spreadsheet View` and save your file.

Selecting Data to be Charted

Once your spreadsheet is created, you must select the data you want to chart. In Figure 7.1 you learned that the x-axis is the horizontal, bottom edge of the chart and the y-axis is the vertical, left edge of the chart. Works calls the data that it charts on the y-axis the *y-series* and the data it charts on the x-axis the *x-series*. The x-series is the range of cells that will become the categories along the x-axis of the chart. The y-series is the range of cells used to create the data points on your chart. Works lets you define one x-series data range and up to six y-series data ranges in each chart.

Before you can use the Charting tool, you must define the x- and y-series data ranges so that Works knows what to display in the chart. If you don't do this first, Works displays a dialog box saying `Series Not Selected`.

Works lets you define the x- and y-series data ranges all at once or individually. To define the x- and y-series all at once, select every row and column of data that you want to chart, including the row and column headings that correspond to the data. When you include the row and column headings in your selection, Works translates the headings in the first row to the x-series categories. Works translates the headings in the first column to the legend at the bottom of the chart. The legend identifies each of the y-series ranges. This translation process is illustrated in Figure 7.11 using a very simple spreadsheet.

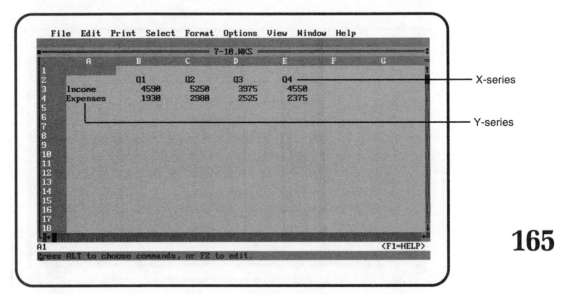

Figure 7.11   Works translates the headings in the first row to the x-series and the headings in the first column to the legend.

To select the x- and y-series data ranges in a spreadsheet, follow the next Quick Steps.

Q Selecting X- and Y-Series Data Ranges

1. Open the Spreadsheet file you want to chart.	Your spreadsheet is displayed on the screen.
2. Select all of the data you want to chart, including column and row headings.	The block of cells you select is highlighted. □

> ▶ **Note:** In order for the data to be plotted correctly on the chart, the block of cells you select must not contain any blank rows or columns. When blank rows or columns exist, blanks will appear in your chart and values in a given row may be plotted against values in the wrong column.

165

Figure 7.12 shows that we have selected cells A6:E9 in our sample spreadsheet to chart the income figures. Notice that the blank row between the column headings and the data has been removed.

Selected cells ──────

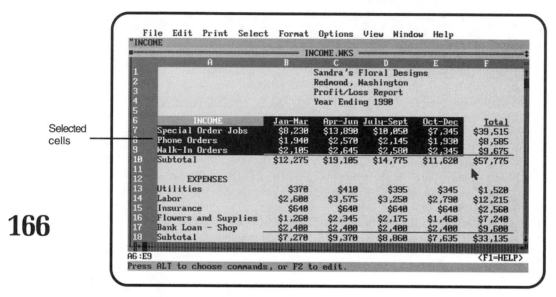

File   Edit   Print   Select   Format   Options   View   Window   Help
"INCOME

INCOME.WKS

	A	B	C	D	E	F
1			Sandra's Floral Designs			
2			Redmond, Washington			
3			Profit/Loss Report			
4			Year Ending 1990			
5						
6	INCOME	Jan-Mar	Apr-Jun	July-Sept	Oct-Dec	Total
7	Special Order Jobs	$8,230	$13,890	$10,050	$7,345	$39,515
8	Phone Orders	$1,940	$2,570	$2,145	$1,930	$8,585
9	Walk-In Orders	$2,105	$2,645	$2,580	$2,345	$9,675
10	Subtotal	$12,275	$19,105	$14,775	$11,620	$57,775
11						
12	EXPENSES					
13	Utilities	$370	$410	$395	$345	$1,520
14	Labor	$2,600	$3,575	$3,250	$2,790	$12,215
15	Insurance	$640	$640	$640	$640	$2,560
16	Flowers and Supplies	$1,260	$2,345	$2,175	$1,460	$7,240
17	Bank Loan - Shop	$2,400	$2,400	$2,400	$2,400	$9,600
18	Subtotal	$7,270	$9,370	$8,860	$7,635	$33,135

A6:E9   <F1=HELP>
Press ALT to choose commands, or F2 to edit.

Figure 7.12   Cells A6:E9 are selected.

Displaying Your Chart

Now that you've selected the x- and y-series data ranges, you're ready to display your chart using the New Chart command on the View menu. When you create a new chart, Works defaults to creating a bar chart. If you want a different type of chart, you can select it later. Use the following Quick Steps.

 Displaying Your Chart

1. Check to make sure you have selected the data in your spreadsheet that you want to chart.

The cells you select are highlighted on your screen. These will be used to define the x- and y-series data ranges in your chart.

166

2. Select the New Chart command on the View menu.

Works creates and displays a bar chart based on the rows and columns you select.

3. Press Esc to return to your spreadsheet.

Works returns to your spreadsheet. □

In our sample spreadsheet, Works translated the headings from row 6, *Jan-Mar*, *Apr-Jun*, *Jul-Sept*, *Oct-Dec*, to the x-series categories, and translated the headings in column A, *Walk-In Orders*, *Phone Orders*, *Special Occasion Jobs*, to the legend. The actual data that appears in cells B7:E9 was used to construct the bars in the chart. B7:E7 is the first y-series, B8:E8 is the second y-series, and B9:E9 is the third y-series. Figure 7.13 illustrates how Works translated the data we selected from our spreadsheet into a chart.

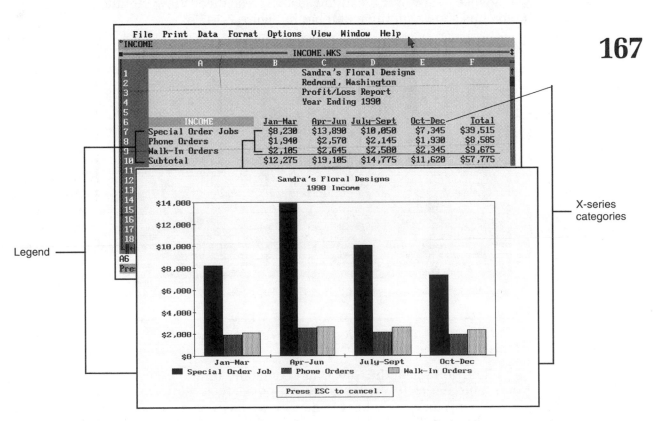

Figure 7.13 *Works translates the data selected from the spreadsheet into the chart.*

Whenever you create a new chart, check it carefully to see that it corresponds to the data you selected and that it looks like you expected. If it doesn't, it may be because the cell range you selected contains blank rows or columns. If you don't want to delete the blank row or column from your spreadsheet, you need to redefine the x- and y-series data ranges (see Changing Data).

Chart View vs. Spreadsheet View

Before you add more information to your chart, you need to learn the difference between Spreadsheet View and Chart View because the menus are different for each.

When you open a Spreadsheet file, Works defaults to the Spreadsheet View of the window. The Spreadsheet View includes the menus shown on the menu bar in Figure 7.14.

168

Menu bar ──

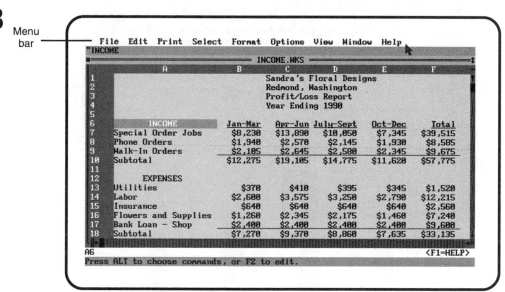

Figure 7.14   The menu bar in Spreadsheet View.

When you select the New Chart command on the View menu, Works automatically switches from Spreadsheet View to Chart View. When Works switches to Chart View, the menus on the menu bar are changed. The change is subtle enough that you may not have noticed it when you created your chart. The menu items in Chart View are shown in Figure 7.15.

Notice also that the status line indicates Chart to let you know you are in Chart View. Take a moment to open each of the menus in Chart View and look at the commands. You will be using many of the commands on these menus in this chapter.

Many of the commands in Chart View are identical to those in Spreadsheet View, but some are different. Look at the Format menu as an example. In Chart View, the Format menu lets you choose the type of chart you want to use whereas in Spreadsheet View, the Format menu lets you format cells. If you want to reform data within the cells, you have to return to Spreadsheet View since the Format command is different in Chart View.

When you are in Chart View and want to return to the Spreadsheet View, select the Spreadsheet command on the View menu.

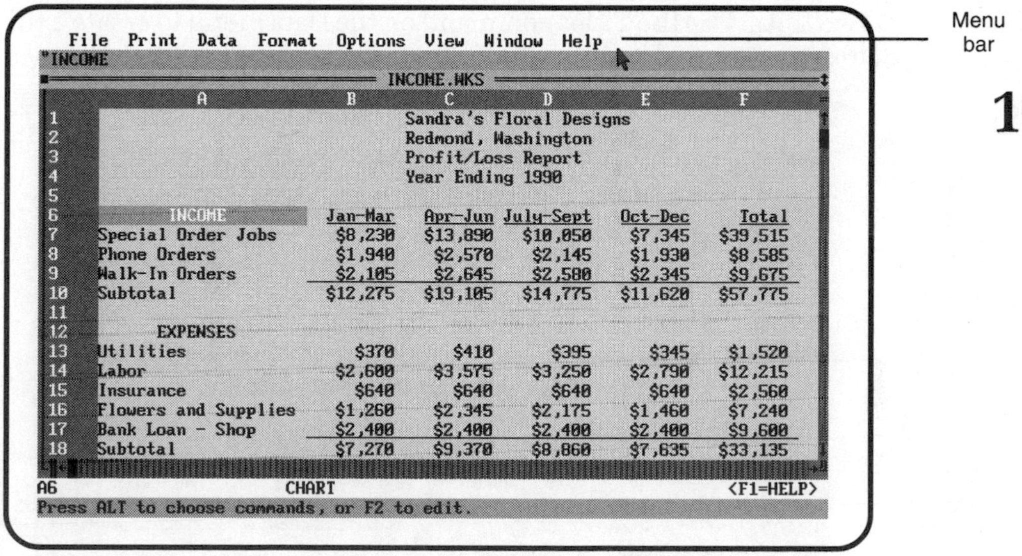

Figure 7.15   The menu bar in Chart View.

▶ **Note:** You cannot enter Chart View unless there is a chart associated with the Spreadsheet file you're working on. If you have not yet created a chart for your spreadsheet, you must select a range of cells to define the x- and y-series, then select the New Chart command on the View menu. If your spreadsheet already has associated charts, select the chart number you want to view from the View menu. You cannot enter Chart View any other way.

Adding Finishing Touches

The important part of your chart—the data—is complete now, but you'll want to add a title and select a font to use. Depending on the data and the type of chart you've used, you may also want to add data labels to describe particular data points.

Adding a Title to Your Chart

Even though your spreadsheet probably has a title, you need to add a title to your chart. Works does not read the spreadsheet title nor automatically insert it into your chart. Your chart title can be one or two lines. Use the Titles command on the Data menu to create a title for your chart. The titles dialog box is shown in Figure 7.16.

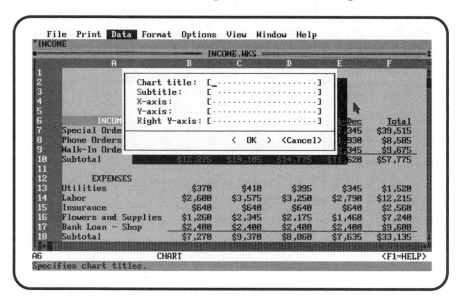

Figure 7.16   The Titles dialog box.

The titles are entered in the first two fields. Follow the next Quick Steps to enter a title.

Q **Adding a Title to Your Chart**

1. In Chart View, select the Titles command on the Data menu.	The Titles dialog box is displayed.
2. Type the first line of your title in the Chart Title field.	The title you type is displayed in the Chart Title field.
3. If you want a two-line title, press Tab to select the Subtitle field, then type the second line of your title.	The second line of your title is displayed in the Subtitle field.
4. If you want to add an x-axis or y-axis title, type the titles in the respective fields. When you have entered all titles, select OK.	Works returns to your spreadsheet. If you want to view your titles, select your chart from the list in the View menu. □

171

If you decide you want to delete a title, select the Titles command from the Data menu to display the dialog box again. Select the title you want to delete, press the spacebar, then select OK.

Selecting Fonts

When you create a chart, Works automatically displays all text and numbers in the 8-point Screen font. This size can be deceiving; it might appear on your screen to be large enough, but when you print your chart, the font may be too small relative to the size of the chart. Works gives you the choice of five different fonts, each in three different point sizes, as shown in Table 7.2.

Table 7.2   *A sample of printable fonts and sizes*

Font	Sizes
Screen	4, 7, 8
Modern C	12, 14, 17
Bold Modern C	12, 14, 17
Italic Modern C	12, 14, 17
Decor A	14, 18, 21

Works lets you change the title font independently of *Other* fonts, which include scale markers on the x- and y-axes, data labels, legends, and x-axis category names. Note that if you use a two-line title, the second line is included under Other fonts.

In Figure 7.17 we have added a title to our sample chart. The first line of the title is displayed in Decor A, 21 points. The Other Font is set to Modern C 12.

172

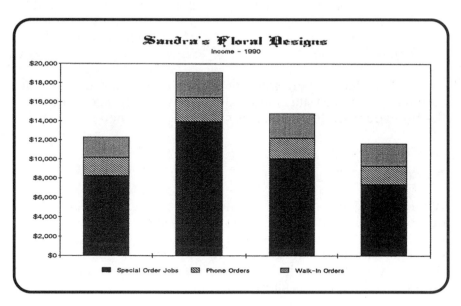

Figure 7.17   *The chart now includes a title.*

Q Selecting Fonts

1. Select the Title Font command on the Format menu.

   Works displays the Font dialog box which lists available fonts and sizes.

2. Select the font you want, then select the size. When you have made your choices, select OK.

   Works returns to your spreadsheet. You do not see the font displayed on the screen, but when you print your chart, the font you select does appear on your chart. □

To change other fonts for your chart, follow the same procedure outlined in the previous Quick Steps, but select the Other Font command on the Format menu.

173

Adding Data Labels

You may find it useful to label the data points in a chart. Data labels provide more precise information by identifying the exact value of lines, bars, or points in your chart. The values for each label are taken directly from the spreadsheet. For example, in Figure 7.18 we have added data labels to each of the highest income bars, identifying the exact values.

The data points in your chart correspond to the y-series ranges you select, so the data labels share the same cell range. For example, if your first y-series is B2:B9, your data label range for that y-series is be B2:B9. You can add data labels to one or multiple y-series data points.

To add data labels to your chart, use the following Quick Steps.

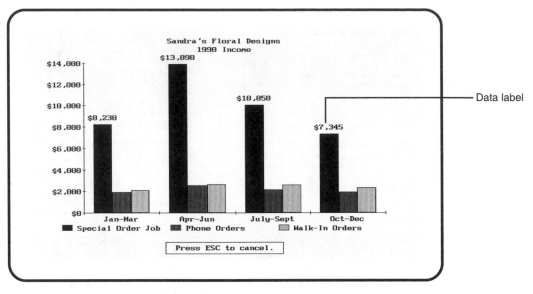

Data label

Figure 7.18   The chart with data labels.

174

![Q] Adding Data Labels to Your Chart

1. In Chart View, select the Series command on the Data menu.

   The Series dialog box is displayed, showing the data ranges you select for each y-series in your chart.

2. Make a note of the current data range for each y-series that you want to label, then select Done to exit the Series dialog box.

   Works returns to your spreadsheet.

3. In the spreadsheet, select the y-series range of cells that you want to label.

   The cells are highlighted on your spreadsheet.

4. Select the Data Labels command on the Data menu.

   The Data Labels dialog box is displayed.

5. Select the y-series you want to label, then select Create.

   Works creates the data label based on the cell range you select and returns to your spreadsheet.

6. Repeat steps 3 through 5 to create additional data labels.

    Works returns to your spreadsheet.

7. To view the data labels, select the chart from the View menu.

    ☐

If you later decide to delete a data label, select the Data Labels command on the Data menu, select the y-series for the label you want to delete, then select `Delete`. When you view your chart again, the data label will be gone.

Adding a Border to Your Chart

175

When you add a border to your chart, Works draws an outline around the chart enclosing all data except titles and legends. A border frames your chart and makes it look more finished. To add a border to your chart, select the Show Border command on the Options menu. If you decide later that you don't want a border, select the Show Border command again to remove the border.

Additional Charts

Sometimes you may want to display the data from one spreadsheet in several different ways by using different types of charts. Or, you may want to display a range of cells in one chart and another range of cells in a second chart. In Works, you can create up to eight charts per spreadsheet. When you create your first chart, Works names it Chart1. As you create additional charts, Works names them Chart2, Chart3, and so on. Works lists the charts you have created in the View menu.

Creating Additional Charts

You can create an additional chart from scratch, or you can create an additional chart by copying an existing one. The method you choose depends on the data you want in the second chart.

If you want to create a new chart using different data from the same spreadsheet, create it from scratch just as you created the first chart. When you are ready to display the new chart, select the New Chart command on the View menu. Works displays the chart and adds it to the list of charts in the View menu.

Copying a Chart

If you want to create an additional chart using the same data ranges but with different titles, fonts, shading, or other characteristics, it is easier to copy the first chart, then modify it. Copying the chart saves you the trouble of having to redefine the data ranges. To copy a chart, follow the next Quick Steps.

176

Q Copying a Chart

1. In Chart View, select the Charts command on the View menu.

   A dialog box is displayed listing all the charts associated with the current Spreadsheet file.

2. Select the chart you want to copy, then choose the Copy command, then choose Done.

   Works adds the new chart name to the chart list in sequential order, then returns to your spreadsheet. To view the chart, select it from the list in the View menu. □

▶ **Note:** You can only copy a chart from the same spreadsheet; you can't copy a chart from one Spreadsheet file to another.

Editing Charts

Editing refers to any kind of changes you want to make to the chart. This includes the values in individual cells in the spreadsheet, the definition of x- or y-series data ranges, legends, titles, data labels, fonts, and so on.

Changing Data

You can update or change data in the cells of your spreadsheet whether you are in Chart View or Spreadsheet View. To change data in the spreadsheet cells, use any of the methods you learned in Chapters 5 and 6, such as removing a row or column, clearing a row or column, editing a cell, and so on.

Whenever you change data in the spreadsheet's cells, Works automatically updates all existing charts that make reference to those cells. The next time you view the chart, it will reflect the changes you make to the spreadsheet. Note that if you change cells that are not referenced in the chart, for instance, the spreadsheet title, the changes will not be reflected in the chart.

177

Changing X- or Y-Series Ranges

When you created your first chart a few pages back, you defined the x- and y-series ranges all at once before viewing the chart. There may be times when you want to delete a series, change a series, or add a series. To redefine data ranges for the x- and y-series, begin by selecting the Series command on the Data menu to display the dialog box shown in Figure 7.19.

This dialog box displays the current data ranges for all of the x- and y-series in your chart. It's a good idea to check this box before changing a series. When you're ready to change a series, use the following Quick Steps.

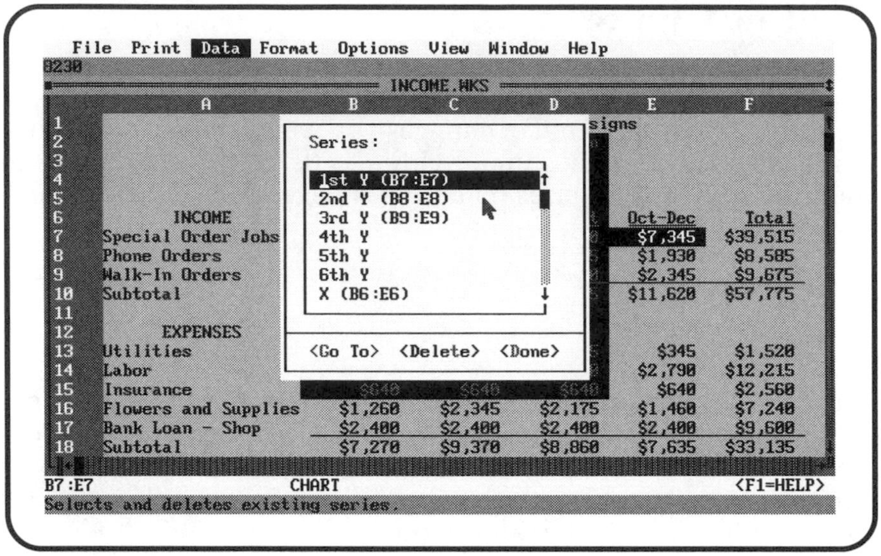

Figure 7.19   The Series dialog box.

178

Q Changing X- or Y-Series Ranges

1. In Chart View, select the cells you want to use to redefine the x- or y-series.

   The cells are highlighted on the spreadsheet.

2. Select the Data menu, then select the x- or y-series you want to redefine.

   Works immediately redefines the series based on the cells you select, then returns to your spreadsheet.

3. Select the Series command on the Data menu to make sure the range you selected is correct, then select Done.

   Works returns to your spreadsheet.

   □

Deleting a Chart

When you no longer need a chart you've created, you can delete it. Since you can only save up to eight charts per spreadsheet, there may be times when you need to delete a chart so you can create a new one. To delete a chart, follow the next Quick Steps.

Deleting a Chart

1. Select the Charts command on the View menu.

   Works displays a dialog box that lists all the existing charts for the current spreadsheet.

2. Select the chart you want to delete, then select `Delete`.

   Works asks if you are sure you want to delete the chart.

3. If you are sure, select `OK`, then select `Done`.

   Works returns to your spreadsheet. The chart you delete is removed from the chart list on the View menu. □

179

Printing Your Chart

Works uses a predefined page setup for printing charts, so you can usually print your chart without changing any print settings. Since most charts are better displayed sideways on an 8.5-by-11-inch page, the predefined page setup calls for landscape mode.

To print your chart, use the following Quick Steps.

Printing a Chart

1. In Chart View, select the Print command on the Print menu.

   The Print dialog box is displayed.

2. Specify the number of copies you want to print, then select `OK`.

   Works returns to your spreadsheet. As Works sends your file to the printer the status line indicates how much of the file has been sent. When the status line reads 100%, the file begins printing. □

As in the Word Processor and Spreadsheet tools, you also may preview your chart by using the Preview command on the Print menu.

If you find that you need to change print settings, select the Print Settings and Margins command on the Print menu.

Naming and Saving Your Chart

If you want to rename your chart before you save it, use the Charts command on the View menu. When you use this command, Works displays a dialog box listing all the charts you have created. In the dialog box, select the chart you want to rename, then select the Rename option and enter the new name. When you are finished renaming charts, select Done.

Because charts are tied to spreadsheet data, your charts are saved whenever you save your spreadsheet. Chapter 2 includes a discussion of files, directories, temporary filenames, and saving files. Please refer to Chapter 2 for specific instuctions on saving files.

What You've Learned

In this chapter you've learned that spreadsheet data can be displayed in the form of charts. You've learned how to create a chart, and add finishing touches such as a title, labels, and a legend. You've learned how to create additional charts, print, and save. The main points discussed in this chapter are summarized next.

▶ Works contains eight predefined types of charts; bar, stacked bar, 100% stacked bar, line, area line, hi-lo-close, pie, and x-y. You can use any of these charts to display spreadsheet data.

▶ Works allows you to save up to eight different charts per spreadsheet.

▶ Charts are tied to spreadsheet data; Works creates the chart based on the range of cells you select in your spreadsheet.

▶ The basic process for creating a chart is as follows:

1. Create the spreadsheet.
2. Select the data you want to chart.
3. Display the chart.
4. Add titles, legends, labels, and so on.
5. Save your file.

▶ The Spreadsheet tool in Works has two different views; Spreadsheet View and Chart View. Each view has its own set of menus.

▶ Charts can be copied or deleted.

▶ Charts can be printed and saved along with the Spreadsheet file.

181

Introducing the Database

In This Chapter

▶ *What is a database?*

▶ *What can it be used for?*

▶ *How to create a database*

▶ *Working with the Database tool in Form View and List View*

▶ *Editing, saving, and printing your Database files*

This chapter introduces you to the Database tool in Works. You'll learn what a database is, what it can be used for, and how to create one.

What Is a Database?

Most of us work with databases all the time without realizing it. Whenever you pick up a phone book, use a card file, or order something from a mail order catalog, you are using a type of database. In its simplest form, a database can be defined as a collection of related information, generally organized in a list format. In a phone book, the related information consists of names, addresses, and phone numbers.

If the Works Database was simply a tool for storing related information, that might not be reason enough to use it, but it can do much more than that. It can help you organize, locate, sort, list, and selectively report on stored information. For example, suppose a database for the mail order catalog included product names, order numbers, prices, and suppliers. You could use the Database tool to locate an order number quickly, sort the database alphabetically by product, list all products with a price of twenty dollars, or generate a report categorized according to supplier.

You can use a database for many different tasks, from sending out a notice to suppliers, to calculating sale prices, to generating sales reports. And when it's time to update the information in the database, you can do it quickly and easily, then select a command to re-sort the data when you're finished.

Records and Fields

184

Databases are made up of *records*. In the example of the mail order product database, a record is equivalent to all the information about one product, that is, its name, order number, price, and supplier. These individual parts that make up the record are called *fields*.

Fields have two components: the field name and the field contents. The field name describes the *type* of information; the field contents is the *specific* information. In the following example, Ski Parka is the field contents for the Product field. The entire collection of information constitutes one record.

Product: Ski Parka
Order Number: S-996
Supplier: Ski Designs
Price: $489.00

It can be quite cumbersome to continually make the distinction between field names and field contents, so they are often simply referred to as fields.

The Database Window

You can access a database from three different views within the Database window. Each one works with the same database information but gives you a different view of it. The two views discussed in this chapter are Form View and List View. (Report View is discussed in Chapter 9.)

Form View

No doubt you have filled out many types of forms, from job applications, to order blanks in catalogs, to tax returns. A form is simply a piece of paper that contains titles or headings and blank spaces to be filled in with information.

The Form View in your database is exactly what it sounds like; it displays your database one record at a time in a formlike manner. The form that you see on the screen looks like it might look on paper—complete with titles or headings and blank spaces where you fill in information. Use Form View when you are creating your database or when you want to view one record at a time.

185

A sample record displayed in Form View is shown in Figure 8.1.

Field name —

Field contents —

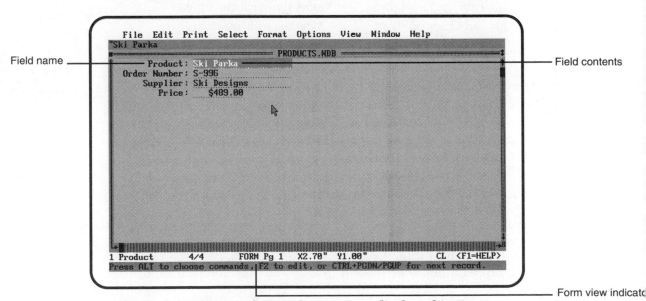

Form view indicato

Figure 8.1   The Works Database screen displayed in Form View.

As you can see in Figure 8.1, when working in Form View, your window resembles the Word Processor window; that is, the work area looks like a page rather than a spreadsheet grid. The window itself has the standard menu bar, scroll bars, status line, message line, and so on, much like the Word Processor window. Notice that the status line displays the word FORM to indicate you are in Form View. In addition, the status line displays the number of the current record and the total number of records in the file.

Before you create your database, you need to know how to move around in Form View. As you are entering field names, your cursor moves one character at a time, just like in the Word Processor tool. Once you have entered field names, you can move from field to field using the Tab key. Table 8.1 shows the complete list of keys and key combinations for maneuvering in Form View.

Table 8.1   Keys and Key Combinations for Maneuvering in Form View

Press	To
Right, Left Arrow keys	Move right, left by field
Up, Down Arrow keys	Move up, down by field
Tab	Move to next field contents
Shift+Tab	Move to previous field contents
Page Up, Page Down	Move up, down one window
Ctrl+Page Up	Move to previous record
Ctrl+Page Down	Move to next record
Home	Move to beginning of field name
End	Move to end of field contents
Ctrl+Home	Move to first record in database
Ctrl+End	Move to last record in database

List View

In List View, you can view multiple records at once rather than viewing one record at a time as in Form View. In List View, the window resembles a spreadsheet with rows, columns, and cells. A sample database displayed in List View is shown in Figure 8.2.

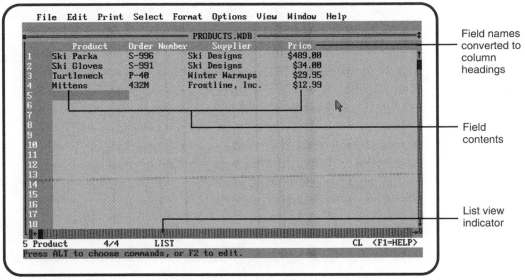

File   Edit   Print   Select   Format   Options   View   Window   Help

━━━━━━━━━━━━━━━━ PRODUCTS.WDB ━━━━━━━━━━━━━━━━

	Product	Order Number	Supplier	Price
1	Ski Parka	S-996	Ski Designs	$489.00
2	Ski Gloves	S-991	Ski Designs	$34.00
3	Turtleneck	P-40	Winter Warmups	$29.95
4	Mittens	432M	Frostline, Inc.	$12.99

Field names converted to column headings

Field contents

List view indicator

5 Product   4/4   LIST   CL   <F1=HELP>
Press ALT to choose commands, or F2 to edit.

Figure 8.2   A sample database displayed in List View.

187

Notice that the title bar, status line, message line, and so on, are the same as those used in the spreadsheet. The word LIST is displayed in the status line to indicate that you are in List View. When you display the database in List View, the field names from Form View are converted to column headings and the field contents now appear in the cells of a single row. Each row represents one record.

List View has other similarities to spreadsheets. In List View, you can change the column width, change alignment of cell contents, copy, move, delete, insert, sort information, and so on. You can perform some of these tasks in Form View as well, but in most cases you can do them faster in List View.

Table 8.2 lists the keys and key combinations for maneuvering through Database records in List View. Many of the keystrokes are similar to those used in the Spreadsheet tool.

Table 8.2   Keys and Key Combinations for Maneuvering in List View

Press	To
Arrow keys	Move up, down one row; right, left one column
Ctrl + Arrow keys	Move by one block of data up, down, right, left
Page Up, Page Down	Move up, down one window
Home	Move to first field of the current row
Ctrl+Home	Move to upper left corner of database
End	Move to end of current row
Ctrl+End	Move to end of last row in the database

Moving Between Form View and List View

While you are working in the Database tool, you'll find it useful to move between Form View and List View quite often. If you are in Form View, select the List command on the View menu to move to List View. If you are in List View, select the Form command on the View menu to move to Form View.

 Press F9 to move instantly from Form View to List View and vice versa.

Planning Your Database

Before you create a database, you need to think about and answer some questions. The planning you do up front can save you hours of time later if you decide to change the data you've already entered. This is not to say that you can't modify the database later, but modifying it can be time-consuming, depending on the changes you make.

Take your time planning your database; don't try to design it in a day. Give yourself a day or two to think about the information you need and how it will all work together. The following are some questions to ask yourself before you begin.

► What kind of information do you want in your database?

► How do you plan to use the information?

► What specific items do you want to keep track of?

► How many characters do you need for each item in the database?

► In what order do you want the items to appear?

► Do you want to include formulas in any of the fields?

► Can you combine two databases into one?

The second question is an important one because you want to include all the fields you think you might want before entering the field contents for each record. While it is possible to add a field to records after they have been entered, it creates a lot of extra work for you to go back to each record and individually add field contents to the new field. This is where careful planning up front can save you time.

The last question is an important one as well because you want to avoid creating multiple databases whenever possible. For example, if you want to send out letters to customers, the only information you need in your database are their names and addresses. But what if you also want to generate reports for each customer showing how much each one purchased in a year? Can you include sales figures as a field in the same database? If so, you can use one database for two different tasks. Combining information into a single database not only saves you the trouble of creating two databases, it saves disk space on your computer as well.

189

Creating Your Database

When you have answered the planning questions, you're ready to begin creating your database. Follow these four steps:

1. Open a new Database file.
2. Create your database form.
3. Enter the field contents for each record.
4. Save your file.

Now, you get to create a database for yourself. Begin by following the next Quick Steps to create a new Database file.

Q Creating a Database File

1. Select the Create New File command from the File menu.

   Works displays a dialog box listing the types of files you can create.

2. Choose the New Database command from the dialog box.

   Works creates a new file called DATA1.WDB and places your cursor at the beginning of the file. □

The Database file that Works creates looks like the one shown in Figure 8.3. The work area is blank and the title is DATA1.WDB, the temporary filename Works assigns to your file. Take the time now to rename the file to CLIENTS.WDB using the Save As command on the File menu.

190

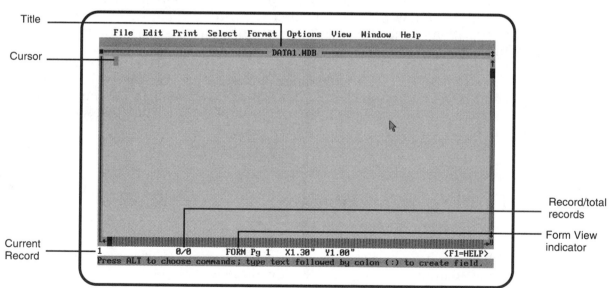

Figure 8.3   A new Database file with the temporary filename DATA1.WDB.

Notice that when you create a new Database file, Works defaults to Form View. This is indicated on the status line.

Creating The Form

In Form View, Works operates much like a word processor; you can enter information anywhere you choose in the work area. You begin by entering field names, as described in the following Quick Steps.

Q Creating the Form

1. Place your cursor where you want to begin entering the first Field Name. Type the name followed by a colon (:).

   As soon as you type the colon, Works displays a dialog box that proposes 20 characters for the field width.

2. If you want the field to be larger or smaller than 20, type the number you need.

   The dialog box also proposes a field height of 1 line.

3. If you want the field to be more than one line, specify the number of lines, then select OK.

   Works returns to the Database window.

4. Repeat steps 1-3 until you have entered all field names, then move your cursor to the first blank field.

191

□

Normally a field height of one line is sufficient for most fields. In some cases, you might want the field height to be more than one line, such as when the field contains a long description.

To create your client database, enter the field names shown in Figure 8.4.

One of the reasons Works provides Form View is so you can make the Database form as easy to work with as possible. This is especially important if you have users who are only entering new records and don't use the database in any other way. They don't necessarily need to understand how the database works, but it should be easy for them to use.

In Figure 8.4, you have all the field names you need, but consider how they are arranged. Perhaps a different form arrangement would make it easier to use, such as that shown in Figure 8.5.

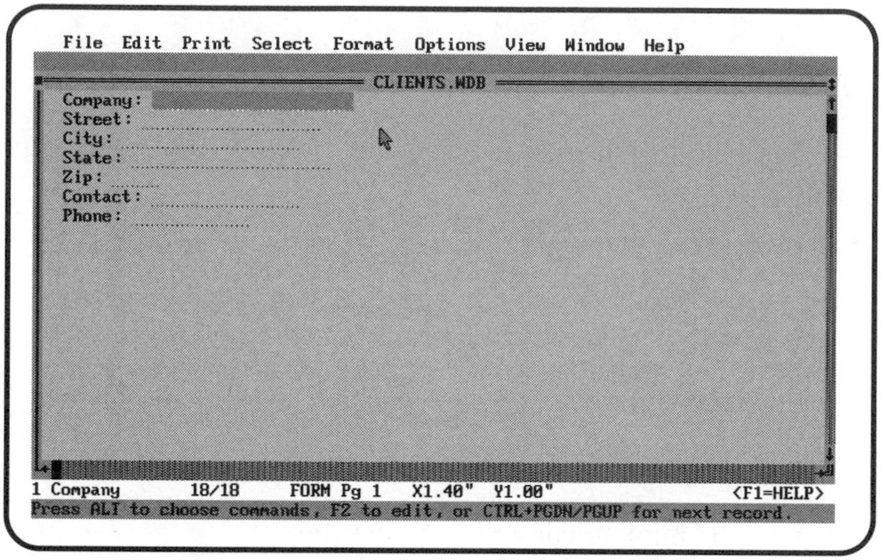

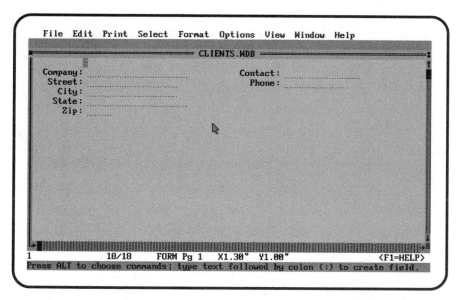

File Edit Print Select Format Options View Window Help

CLIENTS.WDB

Company:
Street:
City:
State:
Zip:
Contact:
Phone:

1 Company   18/18   FORM Pg 1   X1.40" Y1.00"   <F1=HELP>
Press ALT to choose commands, F2 to edit, or CTRL+PGDN/PGUP for next record.

Figure 8.4   Field names for a customer database.

File Edit Print Select Format Options View Window Help

CLIENTS.WDB

Company: Contact:
Street: Phone:
City:
State:
Zip:

1   18/18   FORM Pg 1   X1.30" Y1.00"   <F1=HELP>
Press ALT to choose commands; type text followed by colon (:) to create field.

Figure 8.5   The same form shown in Figure 8.4 with field names rearranged.

To rearrange or move fields in Form View, begin by highlighting the field you want to move. (You can select either the Field Name or the Field Contents line; the two are moved together.) Select the Move Field command on the Edit menu; use the Arrow keys to move the field where you want it; then press Enter. Note that if you want to place a field where another is located you must move it first or insert a blank line using the Insert Line command on the Edit menu.

Arrange the fields in your database like those shown in Figure 8.5.

Entering Text and Numbers

Now you're ready to begin entering information into the field contents. You can enter text, numbers, or a combination of the two in your database fields.

You can use either Form View or List View to make your database entries; each has its advantages and disadvantages. In Form View only one record is displayed at a time while in List View, all records are displayed as you enter information. Experiment with each view to decide which you like best. To enter text or numbers in Form View, follow the next Quick Steps.

193

Q Entering Text and Numbers in Form View

1. Select the first Field Contents line and type your entry.

   If the entry you type is longer than the specified field width, Works displays as much of the entry as it can. In the formula bar, Works adds a double quotation (") to the beginning of text entries.

2. When you have made the first entry, press Tab.

   Works moves the highlight to the Field Contents one line below.

3. Type your entry, then press Tab. Do this for all the fields in your form.

   Works displays each entry, then moves the highlight to the next empty Field Contents when you press Tab.

4. When you have made all of your entries, press Tab at the end of the last entry.

Works brings up a new blank record and highlights the first Field Contents. ☐

Continue entering as many records as you like using these steps. In the status line, you can see that Works increases by one the total number of records each time you complete a new record.

If you choose to enter text and numbers in List View, Works behaves exactly as it does in the Spreadsheet tool. Simply select a cell and type your entry, then press Enter or one of the Arrow keys to confirm the entry in the cell.

Figure 8.6 displays ten records entered in the CLIENT.WDB Database file. If you want to follow along with the example, enter the records shown in the figure into your sample database, making sure to leave the City field in records 9 and 10 blank.

194

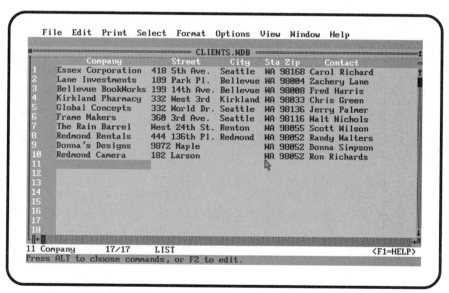

Figure 8.6   The client database.

Correcting Errors

If you make errors as you are typing the field contents, you can change what you've entered using one of three methods. You can retype, you can use the F2 (Edit) key, or you can use the Clear command.

To retype, simply select the field contents (Form View) or cell (List View) you want to change and begin retyping. The new characters you type replace the existing entry entirely.

To use the F2 key, select the field contents or cell you want to edit, then press F2. Works places the cursor at the left end of the current entry. You can use the Right and Left Arrow keys to move your cursor to the character you want to change. Or, you can use the Backspace key to delete characters to the left of the cursor. Works inserts characters wherever you begin typing. When you have finished editing, press Enter and Works changes the entry in the field you select.

To use the Clear command, select the field contents or cell you want to clear, then select the Clear command on the Edit menu. The existing entry is deleted and you can begin typing the new entry.

195

Copying Field Contents

When you are making database entries, often you may have the same field contents for more than one record. In such cases, it's faster and easier to type the entry once, then copy it to the other cells. For instance, if you are creating a product database, you may have several records that list the same supplier. You can copy the supplier name rather than retyping it in each cell.

Copying works best in List View since you can view all your records at once. You can use the Copy command to copy to a non-adjacent cell, and the Fill Down command to copy to adjacent cells. With the Database tool, these commands work exactly like they work with the Spreadsheet. Use the following Quick Steps to copy entries.

Q **Copying from one Cell to Another**

1. In List View, select the cell with the contents you want to copy.	Works highlights the cell.
2. Select the Copy command on the Edit menu.	In the message line, Works instructs you to select a new location, then press Enter.

3. Select the cell where you want to copy, then press Enter.

Works copies the cell contents to the cell you select. □

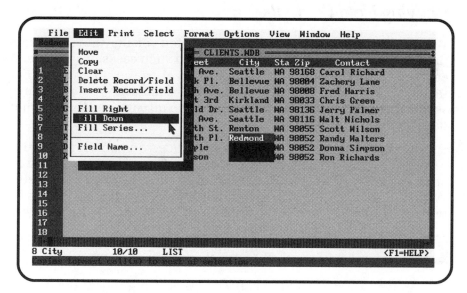 Press Shift+F7 to copy the same entry to another cell.

When you want to fill multiple adjacent cells with the same entry, use the Fill Down command. Begin by selecting the cell you want to copy and all the cells you want to fill immediately below the first cell. Works highlights all these cells. When you select the Fill Down command on the Edit menu, Works copies the entry in the first cell to all the other cells you select.

The Fill Right command works exactly like the Fill Down command, except that you select cells to the right rather than below the cell you want to copy.

Use the Fill Down command to fill in the city for records 9 and 10. Select the City field in rows 8, 9, and 10, then select the Fill Down command as shown in Figure 8.7. Works fills in *Redmond* as the city for records 9 and 10.

196

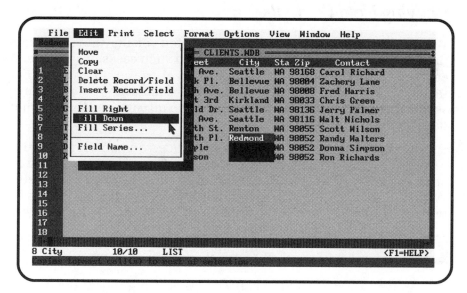

Figure 8.7   Selecting the Fill Down command on the Edit menu.

Editing Your Database

Whenever you want to make any kind of a change to database fields or contents, you are editing. Editing includes reformatting field contents, realigning field names, changing field width, and so on.

You can edit your database in either List View or in Form View. For most editing changes, however, List View is easier and faster. After working with both views, you'll know which view to use for the tasks you perform most often. Quick Steps for each view are provided throughout this section.

Adding and Inserting Records

It is quite common to add new records to your database. When you acquire new products or customers, for example, you need to update your database. If you want to add records, simply go to the end of the database and begin entering new records. When you press Tab in Form View at the end of the last record, Works brings up a blank record. In List View, go to the first empty row and start entering new field contents.

Occasionally you may want to insert records in the middle of your database rather than adding them at the end. To insert records in List View, use the following Quick Steps.

197

Q **Inserting a Record in List View**

1. Select the entire row just below the point where you want to insert the new record.

   Works highlights the row you select.

2. Select the Insert Record/ Field option on the Edit menu.

   Works inserts a blank row above the row you select. Remaining rows are moved downward and renumbered. ☐

If you select only one field instead of the entire row in Step 1, Works displays a dialog box asking if you want to insert a record or a field. Select Record, then select OK. It is perfectly acceptable to add a row this way, it just requires one more step.

Using either List View or Form View, insert record 6 shown in Figure 8.8.

New record ———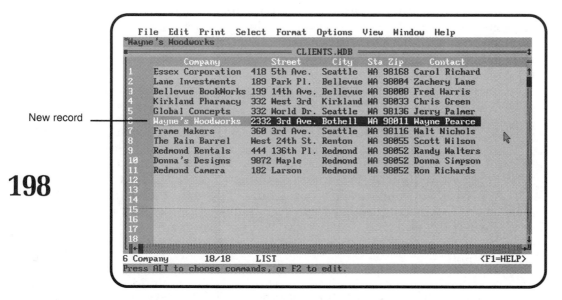

Figure 8.8 A record inserted at row 6 in List View.

To insert a record in Form View, follow the next Quick Steps.

 Inserting a Record in Form View

1. Select the record where you want to insert the new record. (Works inserts the new record just ahead of the record you select.)

   Works displays the record you select.

2. Select the Insert Record command on the Edit menu.

   Works inserts a new, blank record and places the highlight in the first field. □

198

Deleting Records

Just as you may want to add records to your database, you may also want to delete records. For instance, when a client has moved or gone out of business, it's a good idea to delete the record from your database to keep your records current. You can delete records either in List View or Form View. To delete a record in List View, use the following Quick Steps.

Q Deleting a Record in List View

1. Select the entire row that you want to delete.

   Works highlights the entire row.

2. Select the Delete Record/ Field command on the Edit menu.

   Works removes the row you select and moves the remaining rows up to fill the space. The remaining rows are renumbered correctly. □

199

If you don't select the entire row in Step 1, Works displays a dialog box asking if you want to delete a record or a field. Select Record, then select OK.

To delete a record in Form View, follow the next Quick Steps.

Q Deleting a Record in Form View

1. Place the highlight on any field in the record you want to delete.

   Works highlights the field you choose.

2. Select the Delete Record command on the Edit menu.

   Works deletes the record and displays the next record in the database. □

Whether you use Form View or List View, the total number of records displayed in the status line is reduced by one each time you delete a record. But there is no way to retrieve a record once you have deleted it, so be sure you no longer need the record before you delete it.

Inserting Fields

Earlier in this chapter, you learned how important it is to think of all the fields you might need when you plan your database so you can avoid inserting fields later. There may be times when you can't anticipate every field you'll need or when your needs will change, so Works provides a command for inserting fields. You can insert fields in List View or in Form View. To insert a field in List View, follow the next Quick Steps.

Q Inserting a Field in List View

1. Select the column just to the right of the point where you want to insert a new field.

   Works highlights the entire column.

2. Select the Insert Record/ Field command on the Edit menu.

   Works inserts a blank column to the left of the column you select.   □

To insert a new field in Form View, use the following Quick Steps. Note that the command for inserting a new field is *Insert Line* rather than *Insert Field* because in Form View, inserting a field is a two-step process.

Q Inserting a Field in Form View

1. Select the field just beneath the point where you want to insert a new field.

   The field is highlighted.

2. Select the Insert Line command on the Edit menu.

   Works inserts a blank line in every record above the field you select.

3. Place your cursor on the line where you want to enter the new field name and begin typing. When your entry is complete, type a colon (:).

   Works displays the field name you type, then displays a dialog box proposing the field width and height.

4. Enter the field width and height you want, then select OK.

Works enters the new field in the current record as well as all other records in your database. □

When you insert a new field between two fields in Form View, that field appears following the last column when you switch to List View. The reverse is also true; if you insert a new field (column) in List View between two columns, Works places the new field at the *end* of each record in Form View instead of inserting it where you designate. The first time you encounter this it can be somewhat confusing.

The reason Works does this is that in Form View, you are free to arrange your form any way you like. Works does not assume that you want to rearrange fields in Form View just because you inserted a new field in List View. If you want the fields to appear in the proper order in Form View, you must rearrange them yourself. This is a good example of why you want to plan your database carefully so you can avoid inserting fields at a later time.

201

Deleting Fields

After you have used your database for a while, you may find that you don't need a particular field. In such cases, it is a good idea to delete it to save disk space. Before you delete a field, however, be sure you won't need it in the future because you can't bring it back once you delete it; you can only re-create it.

To delete a field in List View, use the following Quick Steps.

Q Deleting a Field in List View

1. Select the Field Name (the entire column) that you want to delete.

Works highlights the entire column.

2. Select the Delete Record/ Field on the Edit menu.

Works deletes the entire column and moves remaining columns to the left to fill the empty space. □

If you don't select the entire column, Works displays a dialog box asking if you want to delete a Record or a Field. Select Field, then select OK.

To delete a field in Form View, follow the next Quick Steps.

Deleting a Field in Form View

1. Select the field you want to delete in any of the records.

   Works highlights the field.

2. Select the Delete Field command on the Edit menu.

   Works displays a dialog box asking if it is OK to delete the data in the field (the field contents).

3. Select OK.

   The field you choose is deleted from the current record, and from all records in the database. □

202

When you delete a field in Form View, Works does not compress the empty line where the field was located. (This is true whether you remove the field in Form View or in List View.) Works does not compress the empty line for the same reason it does not rearrange fields when you insert a field. That is, you are free to arrange the form any way you like, so Works does not assume that you want to remove the empty line just because you remove a field.

Formatting Field Contents

Works allows you to change the format of the field contents in your database. For example, when the field contents represent dollars, you may want to use the Currency format, which displays numbers with dollar signs, commas, and decimal points. If some of your entries represent percentages, you can request that Works display the percent symbol so you don't have to type it.

Works displays all field contents in the General format, described next, unless you specify otherwise. When you choose the Format menu, Works displays the commands shown in Figure 8.9.

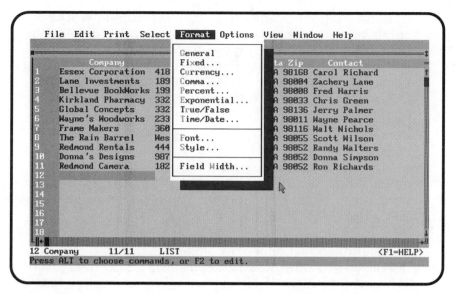

File Edit Print Select **Format** Options View Window Help

Figure 8.9   Format commands on the Format menu.

203

General   Using the General format, Works displays text left-aligned and numbers right-aligned. Numbers are displayed as close to their precise value as possible in the form of integers, decimal fractions, or in scientific notation. Negative numbers are displayed with a minus (–) sign.

Fixed   When you choose Fixed format, you can specify the number of decimal places Works should display. For example, if you specify 0 for the number of decimal places, the number 10992.969 is displayed as 10993. If you specify 2 decimal places, the same number is displayed as 10992.97. Using the Fixed format, Works rounds numbers where appropriate.

Currency   When the numbers in your database represent dollars, you can specify the Currency format so that Works displays dollar signs before each number. In Currency format, Works also inserts commas every 3 places to the left of the decimal point. Works displays the number 8120987 as $8,120,987.00. If you choose to type the $ symbol in the cell, Works recognizes the Currency format and adds commas, but does not add zeros to the right of the decimal point.

Comma   When you choose the comma format, Works adds commas every three places so that the number 8797245 is displayed as 8,797,245. Using this format, you can also specify the number of decimal places. If you choose two, the number is displayed as 8,797,245.00. When you use the Comma format, Works displays negative numbers enclosed in parentheses.

Percent   Numbers are expressed as a percentage when you choose this format. For example, .87 is displayed as 87%. If you choose to type a % symbol following the number you enter, Works recognizes the format and displays the number correctly. Negative numbers are displayed with a minus sign using the Percent format.

Exponential   This format displays numbers in exponential, or scientific, notation. For example, the number 729231 is displayed as 7.29E+05 when you specify 2 decimal places. When you specify 0 decimal places, Works displays the number as 7E+05.

True/False   The True/False format in Works displays numbers in terms of logical values. All non-zero numbers are displayed as TRUE; cells containing zero are displayed as FALSE.

Time/Date   If you want to be able to use times or dates in a formula, use this command. Refer to the Microsoft Works Reference book for more details.

You can change the format of field contents in your database in either Form View or List View. Follow the next Quick Steps, using either view.

Q Formatting Field Contents

1. Select the field contents you want to change.	Works highlights the field you select.
2. Select the Format menu.	Works displays the list of format commands on the menu.
3. Select the format option you want to use.	The dialog box specific to the option you choose is displayed.

4. Specify the changes you want to make in the dialog box, then select OK if necessary.

Works returns to your database and reformats the selected field contents to the format you choose. □

Saving Your Database

Use the same procedure to save a Database file that you use to save other Works files. Begin by renaming your file using the Save As command on the File menu. (You have already done this for the sample database you created.) Remember, you don't need to add a file extension; Works adds the .WDB file extension to all Database files. Once you have renamed your file using Save As, you can use the Save command to save the file in the future.

Chapter 2 includes a discussion of files, temporary filenames, and saving files. Refer to Chapter 2 for detailed instructions on saving your file.

205

Printing Your Database

In Works, you can print your Database file from either Form View or List View. Works uses predefined print settings for printing on standard 8.5-by-11-inch paper in portrait (top to bottom) style. Top and bottom margins are set to one inch. As with other Works tools, you should be able to print most Database files without having to change these settings. If you need to change print settings, use the Page Setup and Margins command on the Print menu. Figure 8.10 shows the default print settings from the Page Setup and Margins dialog box.

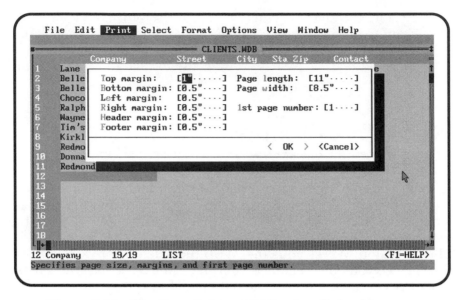

Figure 8.10   The Page Setup and Margins dialog box.

Print Preview

The Preview command on the Print menu allows you to see how your printed page will look based on the current print settings. This feature is very helpful for viewing the page layout, page breaks, margins, and so on. Use this command before you print to double-check how your printed page will look.

Printing in Form View

In Form View, you can print one record at a time, all records, or you can print a blank database form. When you select the Print command on the Print menu, Works displays the dialog box shown in Figure 8.11.

The first three items in the dialog box should be familiar to you from the Works Word Processor and Spreadsheet tools. The rest of the items (Page breaks between records, Print which records, Print which items) are unique to Form View in the Database tool. These items are defined following Figure 8.11.

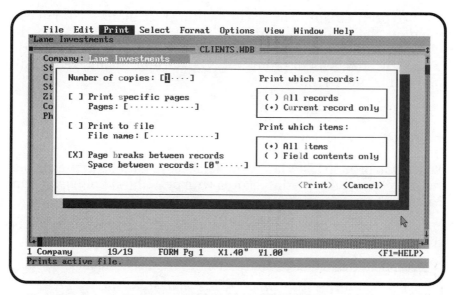

Figure 8.11   The Print dialog box for Form View.

Page Breaks Between Records   This option allows you to print each record on its own page. When you don't want an individual page for each record, you can specify how much space you want between records.

Print Which Records   This option gives you the choice of printing all records or the current record only.

Print Which Items   This option gives you the choice of printing all items or field contents only.

To print in Form View, use the next Quick Steps. Be sure to check the settings under the Page Setup and Margins command and change them if necessary before you print.

Q **Printing in Form View**

1. From List View, select the Print command on the Print menu.

   Works displays the dialog box shown previously in Figure 8.11.

2. Select the print options you want to use to print your Database file, then select Print.

   Works returns to your database and prints your file based on the settings you choose.   □

To print a blank database form, bring up a blank record in your window, then follow the previous Quick Steps. When Works displays the Print dialog box, select the Current option under Print which records. Works prints only the current (blank) record displayed in your window.

Printing in List View

When you print in List View, your database resembles a spreadsheet. In List View, you can print records with or without field names and row numbers.

When you select the Print command on the Print menu, Works displays the dialog box shown in Figure 8.12.

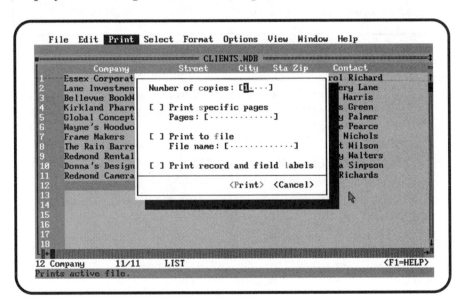

Figure 8.12   The Print dialog box for List View.

This dialog box resembles the Print dialog boxes used in the Spreadsheet and Word Processor tools. The last option is specific to printing a database in List View. Use this option when you want your printed page to include field names and row numbers.

To print in List View, use the next Quick Steps. Be sure to check the settings in the Page Setup and Margins dialog box before you print.

Q **Printing in List View**

1. From List View, select the Print command on the Print menu.

   Works displays the dialog box shown previously in Figure 8.12.

2. Select any of the options in the dialog box, then select Print.

   Works returns to your database and prints the file according to the options you choose. □

What You've Learned

This chapter gives you an introduction to databases and how to create them. The main points covered in this chapter are summarized next.

209

▶ A database is a collection of related information organized in a list-type format.

▶ A database is made up of records; records are made up of fields.

▶ You can use the Works Database tool in either Form View or List View. Form View displays one record at a time in a word processor-type format, while List View displays all records at once in a format similar to a spreadsheet.

▶ There are four steps to creating a database. Be sure to take the time to plan your database before you begin creating it.

   1. Open a new Database file.
   2. Create your database form.
   3. Enter the field contents for each record.
   4. Save your file.

▶ As you are entering field contents, you can retype, use the F2 (Edit) key, or the Clear command to make corrections to what you've entered.

▶ When you have multiple records with the same field contents, you can use the Copy or Fill Down commands to enter information quickly.

► Database files are saved much like any other type of Works file. Be sure to rename your file the first time you save it. Works saves Database files with a .WDB extension.

► You can print your database in List View or Form View. When you print in List View, the database resembles a spreadsheet. In Form View, you can print records consecutively on a page, one record per page, and you can print a blank database form.

210

Chapter 9

More About Databases

In This Chapter

▶ *Using formulas in a database*
▶ *Selecting records and sorting your database*
▶ *Using the reporting feature in the Database tool*

This chapter introduces you to some of the more sophisticated features of the Database tool. You'll learn how to include formulas in Database fields, select particular records, and sort a database in various ways. You'll also learn how to work with Database reports, a feature that brings you one step closer to generating the precise information you want from your database. Later you'll be using the Database file you created in Chapter 8, CLIENTS.WDB. Recall that file now if you want to follow along.

Using Formulas in Database Fields

In Chapter 8 you learned that you can enter text and numbers as field contents in your database, but you can also enter formulas. Suppose you had an employee database that included fields for Hourly Rate and Hours Worked. And perhaps you'd like to have the Database tool calculate the Wages for you. You can do that by entering a formula in the Wages field to multiply the Hours Worked by the Hourly Rate.

The formula would look like the one shown in Figure 9.1.

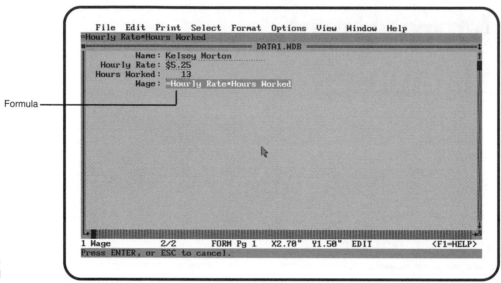

Formula

Figure 9.1   A database field that contains a formula.

To create a formula that calculates the wage, move the highlight to the Field Contents for Wage and type =Hourly Rate*Hours Worked. You must type the equal symbol first to indicate that this is a formula entry. You must also type the exact field names; the asterisk is the symbol for multiplication. As soon as you press Enter after typing the formula, the Wage is calculated for the first record. When you enter the Hours Worked and Hourly Rate for the following records, the Wage is calculated and filled in automatically.

This is an example of just one type of formula you can use in the Database tool. You can enter many other types of formulas, including many of the 57 built-in functions in Works. Refer to the Works Reference for a list of supported functions.

Selecting Records

Sometimes you may want to work with a smaller set of records, a *subset*, rather than the entire database. For example, in your client database suppose you want to display only those customers that are located in the city of Seattle, or in the ZIP code of 98052. In Works, you can select such a subset of records in one of two ways: using the Query command or the Hide Records command. Use Query when you want to tell Works to display a set of records that have common field contents, such as Seattle in the City field. Use Hide Records when you want to choose one or more records for Works *not* to display; a subset of records that may or may not have common field contents.

Using the Query Command

To display a specific group of records, or subset, and hide the rest, use the Query command on the View menu. When you select the Query command, Works displays a blank Database form on your screen. Choose the type of field from which you'll create the subset of records you want displayed. For example, to select only your Seattle clients from your client database, type Seattle in the City field of the blank form, then select the List command on the View menu to display the amended database. Your database should look like the one shown in Figure 9.2.

213

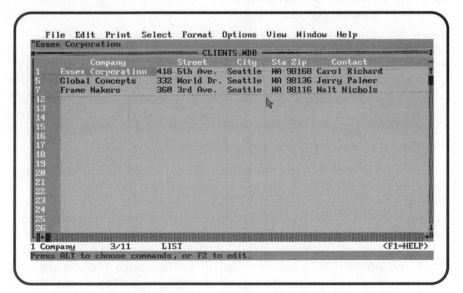

Figure 9.2   The database displaying a subset of records with the common City field contents of Seattle.

The rest of the records in the database have not been deleted, they're just not displayed. To redisplay *all* records, select the Query command on the View menu, and clear the City field. Then, when you select List command, all records in the database are displayed again.

Hiding Records

When you have a subset of records you want to hide that don't have any common field contents, you can use the Hide Record command on the Select menu rather than the Query command. Just select the records you want hidden, then select the Hide Record command on the Select menu. The records you select are temporarily removed from the display. (Note that their row numbers are missing from the sequence.) Again, as with the Query command, these records are not deleted, they are simply hidden. To redisplay these records, simply select Show All Records on the Select menu.

214

Sorting Your Database

In Works, you can rearrange, or *sort*, records in your database by whatever field you choose, in alphabetical, numeric, ascending, or descending order. For example, you might want to sort your customer list in alphabetical order by company name or city. Or, you might want to sort it numerically by ZIP code. Works sorts by text as well as numbers, whether they are dates, times, dollars, or other types of number entries.

When you select the Sort Records command, Works displays the dialog box shown in Figure 9.3. Works lets you sort by up to three fields in ascending or descending order. When you choose to sort by multiple fields, Works sorts all records by the first field. When entries in the first field match, Works sorts on the second field; and when entries in the second field match, Works sorts on the third field. When you sort alphabetically, Works does not distinguish between upper- and lowercase; all entries are sorted as if they are entered in the same case.

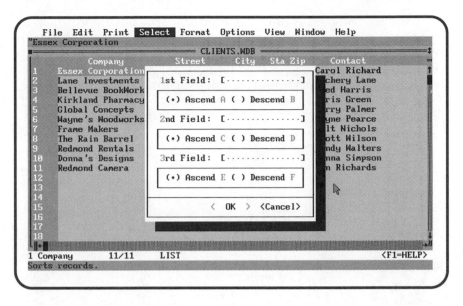

Figure 9.3   The Sort dialog box.

The steps for sorting a database are the same whether you are using Form View or List View. Use the following Quick Steps.

Q Sorting Your Database

1. Select the Sort Records command on the Select menu.

   Works displays the dialog box shown in Figure 9.3.

2. Works proposes to sort by the first field in your database in ascending order. If correct, select OK. If not, type a different field name and choose ascending or descending order.

   Works displays the entry you type in the dialog box.

3. If you want to sort on a second or third field, enter the field names and the sort order you want, then select OK.

   The dialog box disappears and Works automatically resorts the records in your database according to the fields you choose.   □

Suppose, for example, you want to sort your client database alphabetically by city; then alphabetically by company. Select the Sort dialog box on the Select menu, choosing City as the first field and Company as the second field. Choose to sort both in ascending order. Your dialog box should look like the one shown in Figure 9.4.

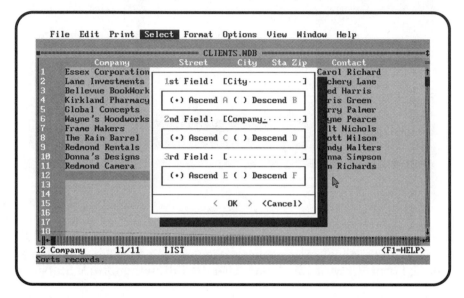

Figure 9.4   The Sort dialog box set up to sort alphabetically on City, then Company.

Works sorts the database alphabetically first, which groups together all companies with the same city name. Then Works sorts alphabetically by company name so that within each city, company names appear in alphabetical order. The sorted database is shown in Figure 9.5.

How the Database Report Works

In Chapter 8 you learned that you can print your database in Form View or in List View. A printed copy from List View is adequate for some purposes, but the Report command in Works offers some additional features that may be important to you. For instance, using the Report command, you can add a title to your report and blank lines for spacing. You can display records in categories and enter subtotals for selected columns. If you want your report to include only selected fields or records, you must use the Report command to print your report.

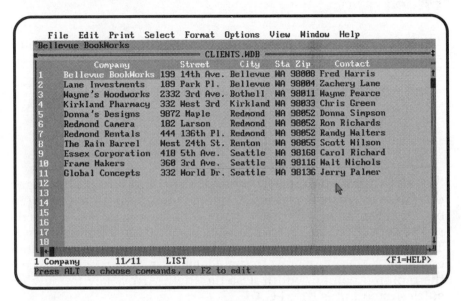

File Edit Print Select Format Options View Window Help
"Bellevue BookWorks
════════════════════════ CLIENTS.WDB ════════════════════════

	Company	Street	City	Sta	Zip	Contact
1	Bellevue BookWorks	199 14th Ave.	Bellevue	WA	98008	Fred Harris
2	Lane Investments	189 Park Pl.	Bellevue	WA	98004	Zachery Lane
3	Wayne's Woodworks	2332 3rd Ave.	Bothell	WA	98011	Wayne Pearce
4	Kirkland Pharmacy	332 West 3rd	Kirkland	WA	98033	Chris Green
5	Donna's Designs	9872 Maple	Redmond	WA	98052	Donna Simpson
6	Redmond Camera	182 Larson	Redmond	WA	98052	Ron Richards
7	Redmond Rentals	444 136th Pl.	Redmond	WA	98052	Randy Walters
8	The Rain Barrel	West 24th St.	Renton	WA	98055	Scott Wilson
9	Essex Corporation	418 5th Ave.	Seattle	WA	98168	Carol Richard
10	Frame Makers	360 3rd Ave.	Seattle	WA	98116	Walt Nichols
11	Global Concepts	332 World Dr.	Seattle	WA	98136	Jerry Palmer
12						
13						
14						
15						
16						
17						
18						

1 Company   11/11   LIST   <F1=HELP>
Press ALT to choose commands, or F2 to edit.

Figure 9.5   The database sorted by City, then Company.

217

The report feature in the Database tool works much like the chart feature in the Spreadsheet tool. Works creates standard reports for you automatically and lists them in the View menu. You can create and store up to eight different reports for each Database file. This gives you the flexibility to create and print several different reports from a single database. Whenever you change data in the database, Works automatically updates the reports. When you don't need a report any longer, you can delete it and create a new one.

Works creates reports using a *report definition*. The report definition is a kind of blueprint or a roadmap for the report layout. It gives Works instructions for creating your report by defining different types of rows to use in the report. The report definition contains a list of the types of rows that are included in your report.

Works uses a *preset* report definition to create *standard* reports. The preset report definition is somewhat like the preset printer settings in Works. It makes creating reports convenient and easier for you, but if you want to change the settings, you are free to do so.

When you change the settings to add special features to your report, you are *customizing* the report definition.

The Preset Report Definition

The preset report definition sets up a report with the following items, and in the order shown.

- ▶ Two introductory report rows
- ▶ Two introductory page rows
- ▶ One record row
- ▶ Two summary rows

218

Each time you create a new report, Works uses this report definition to create the report. A sample preset report definition for our client database is shown in Figure 9.6. The rows described in the report definition list just previously appear to the left of column A. The descriptions for the contents of these rows appear in subsequent columns. (Columns F and G are not visible on the screen because of the required column width. Use the Right Arrow key to view the entries in columns F and G.)

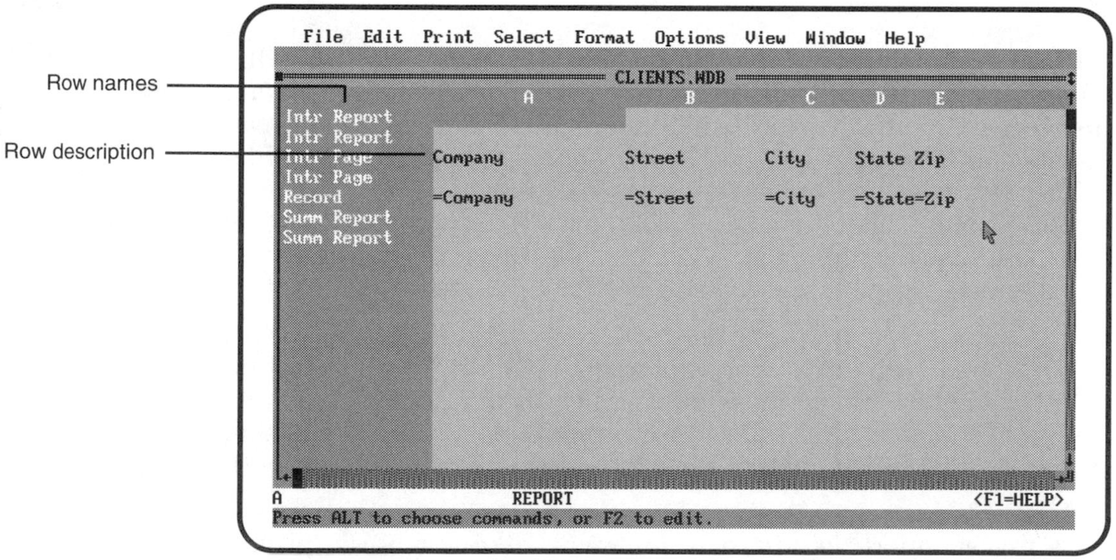

Row names ——

Row description ——

File   Edit   Print   Select   Format   Options   View   Window   Help

═══════════════════ CLIENTS.WDB ═══════════════════

	A	B	C	D	E
Intr Report					
Intr Report					
Intr Page	Company	Street	City	State Zip	
Intr Page					
Record	=Company	=Street	=City	=State=Zip	
Summ Report					
Summ Report					

A   REPORT   <F1=HELP>
Press ALT to choose commands, or F2 to edit.

Figure 9.6   The preset report definition for our client database.

Take a closer look at the parts of the report definition shown in Figure 9.6. For now, ignore the row descriptions in columns B-G. To the left of Column A, Works displays the following row names. Each one represents a type of row that is included in a Database report.

Intr Report   This abbreviation stands for *introductory report row*. The preset report definition includes two of these rows at the top of your report. These rows are used for either a one- or two-line title. The information you type in these rows is shown only on the first page of the report.

Intr Page   This abbreviation stands for *introductory page row*. The preset report definition includes two of these rows immediately following the Intr Report rows. Works automatically places the column headings (field names) in the first Intr Page row. The second Intr Page row is generally left blank to provide spacing between the headings and the data that follows, or you can add column headings here, too.

Record   This row indicates which fields from each record are to be displayed. In this row, field names are always preceded by an equal sign (=).

Summ Report   This abbreviation stands for *summary report row*. The preset report definition includes two of these rows and leaves them blank.

219

Some of these rows require no definition, while others include definitions in columns A-G. In our example shown in Figure 9.6, only the first Intr Page and the Record rows include definitions. Works takes the field names from the database and places them in the Intr Page row for column headings. The entries in the Record row are identical to these field names except for the equal symbol preceding them, which instructs Works to insert the actual data.

Creating a Database Report

Since Works provides the preset report definition for you, creating a report is really quite easy; in fact, it's automatic. Follow the next Quick Steps to create a report.

Creating a Database Report

1. Open the Database file for which you want to create a report, and choose either Form or List View to display the database.

   Works displays the Database file you choose.

2. Select the New Report command on the View menu.

   Works creates the report based on the preset report definition and displays the first page of the report.

3. Press Enter to see additional pages; Esc to see the report definition; or F10 to return to List or Form View.

   □

220

That's all it takes; it's that easy to create a report. Works names the new report Report1 and adds it to the Report list on the View menu. Follow the Quick Steps just previous to create a report from your client database. Your report should look like the one shown in Figure 9.7.

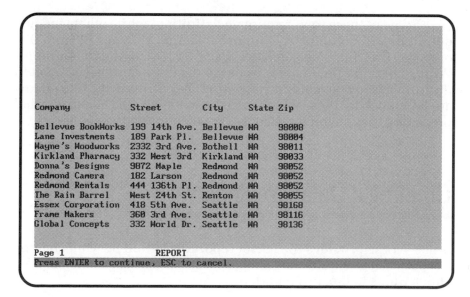

Figure 9.7   A standard report created with the preset report definition.

▶ **Note:** When you use the preset report definition, Works includes every field in the report, but the last visible field on Page 1 is the ZIP code. Press Enter twice to display Page 2 where the Contact and Phone fields appear. Press Enter twice again to return to the preset report definition.

Customizing a Database Report

If you want to change anything about the report—the title, the records or columns that are displayed, the spacing between sections—you need to customize the report definition. In general, you customize a report by adding or deleting rows in the report definition. You can have as many of one type of row in a report definition as you want.

221

Adding a Title to a Report

As figure 9.6 illustrates, the preset report definition provides two Intr Report rows. The second one provides the blank line before the report data; the first one can be used to enter a title for your report. Move your cursor to column B in the first Intr Report row and type the title Client List.

If you want a two-line title and still want to retain the blank line between the title and the data, you need to add another Intr Report row to your report definition. When you select the Insert Row/Column command, Works displays the dialog box shown in Figure 9.8.

Add an Intr Report row to your client database now. Use the following Quick Steps to do it.

Q Adding a Report Row to a Report Definition

1. Select the entire row below the point where you want to insert the new row.

   Works highlights the row you select.

2. Select the Insert Row/ Column command on the Edit menu.

Works displays the dialog box shown in Figure 9.8.

3. Select the type of row you want to insert, then select OK.

Works returns to your report definition and inserts the row type you select. ☐

If you don't select the entire row in Step 1, Works displays a dialog box asking if you want to insert a row or column. Select Row.

Now you're ready to enter the second line for your report title. Move your cursor to the second Intr Report row in Column B and type 1990 as the second line of your title. Select both title entries and use the Style command on the Format menu to center the titles. Your report definition should now look like the one shown in Figure 9.9.

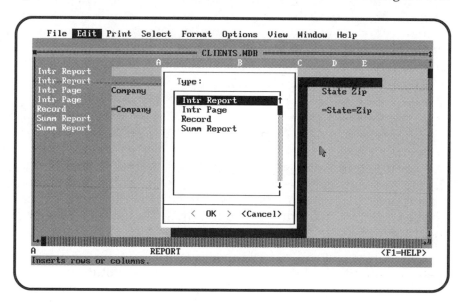

Figure 9.8   The dialog box used for selecting the type of row to insert.

To display your title, select Report1 on the View menu, then press Esc to return to the report definition.

Selecting Fields

The preset report definition automatically displays all fields from the database in your report, but by customizing the report, you can display only selected fields. In your client database, create a report that displays only the company name, contact, and the phone number. In Report View, edit the Record row of the preset report definition to match the one shown in Figure 9.10.

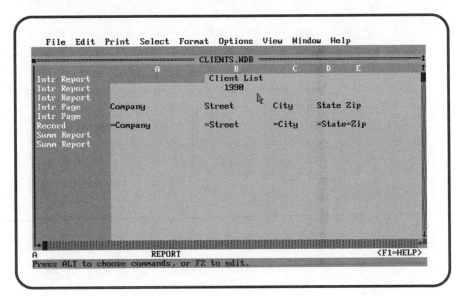

Figure 9.9   The report definition with a two-line title.

You can use any editing method you like—clearing fields, deleting columns, or just retyping entries. You may also want to change the column widths for your final report display. When you are finished editing, redisplay your report by selecting it from the View menu. It should look like the one shown in Figure 9.11.

Selecting Records

Using the Query command you learned in Chapter 8, you can include only selected records in a report. Suppose you want your report to display the company name and address, but you only want records whose city is Seattle. Begin by applying a Query requesting Seattle in the City field, then display the report by selecting it on the View menu. Now your report should look like the one shown in Figure 9.12.

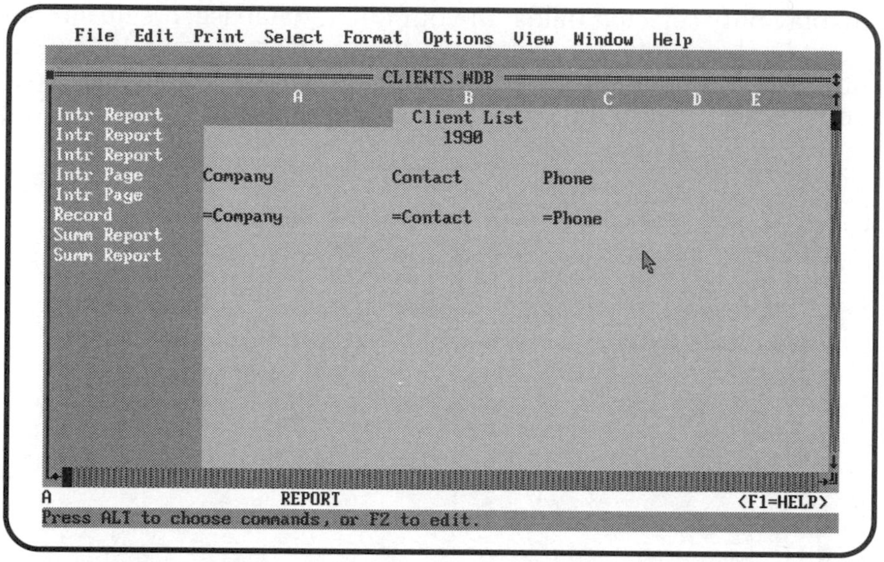

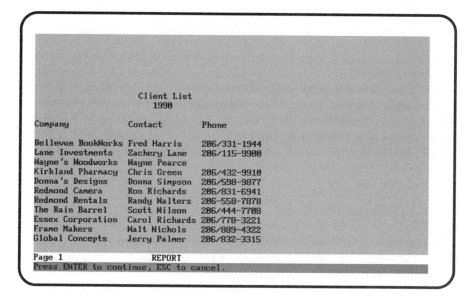

Figure 9.10   The report definition used to display the Company, Contact and Phone fields only.

Figure 9.11   The report showing only the Company, Contact, and Phone fields.

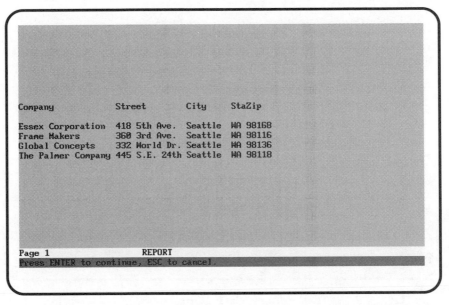

```
Company            Street       City     StaZip

Essex Corporation  418 5th Ave. Seattle  WA 98168
Frame Makers       360 3rd Ave. Seattle  WA 98116
Global Concepts    332 World Dr. Seattle  WA 98136
The Palmer Company 445 S.E. 24th Seattle  WA 98118
```

```
Page 1                    REPORT
Press ENTER to continue, ESC to cancel.
```

225

Figure 9.12   The report showing only Seattle records, with just company name and address for each.

Creating Additional Reports

You have learned how to customize the preset report definition by modifying the standard report settings. But you may find that you want to create more than one report per database so you can present different data in different ways. The report you just created (and modified) is listed on the View menu as Report1. You can create additional reports by selecting the New Report command on the View menu. When you select this command, Works creates a new report using the preset report definition. Works lists this as Report2 on the View menu. Additional reports are numbered sequentially. You can customize the second report just as you did the first. When you want to recall any of the reports you create, just select it from the View menu.

Deleting a Report

When you no longer need a report, you can delete it from your Database file by selecting the Reports command on the View menu. When you select this command, Works displays the dialog box shown in Figure 9.13.

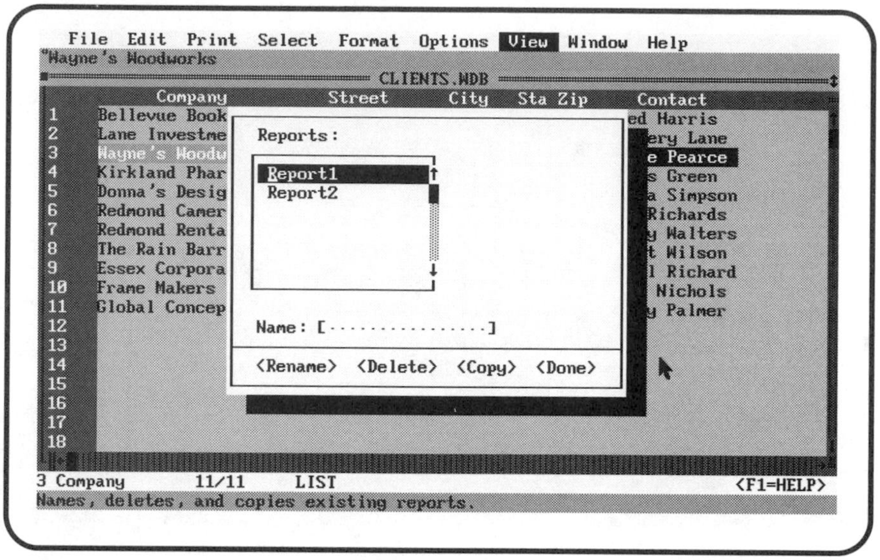

Figure 9.13   The Reports dialog box.

All the reports that belong to the current Database file are displayed in the dialog box. Select the report you want to delete, select Delete, then select Done. Works deletes the report and removes it from the report list on the View menu.

Printing a Database Report

In Chapter 8 you learned that you can print your database in Form View or List View. You can also print your database in Report View. As with Form View and List View, Works uses predefined print settings for printing on 8.5-by-11-inch paper in portrait style. Top and bottom margins are set to one inch. You should be able to print most reports from Report View without having to change these settings. If you need to change these settings, use the Page Setup and Margins command on the Print menu.

To print your report using the standard settings, begin by selecting the report you want to print from the reports listed on the View menu. When you are finished viewing the report and the report definition is displayed on your screen, select the Print command from the Print menu. Works displays the dialog box shown in Figure 9.14.

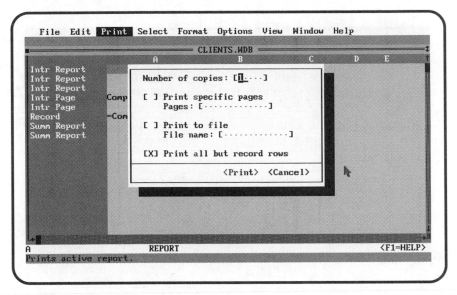

Figure 9.14   The Print dialog box.

227

By now, this dialog box should be very familiar to you. It is almost identical to the dialog box used in the Word Processor and Spreadsheet tools. The only difference in this dialog box is that the last line allows you to print your report without any data—only title, column headings, and other information you have added will be printed. Use the following Quick Steps to print a Database report.

Printing Database Reports

1. From Report View, select the Print command on the Print menu.

   Works displays the dialog box shown in Figure 9.14.

2. Select the print option you want for printing your report, then select Print.

   Works removes the dialog box and prints the report you request.

Saving a Database Report

In Chapter 8 you learned that you save Database files the same way you save other Works files: rename the file and use the Save As command the first time you save the file. After that, use the Save command to save the file. Since Database reports are tied to the Database file, any reports you create are saved when you save the Database file.

For a complete discussion of files, directories, and how to save files, refer to Chapter 2.

What You've Learned

228

In this chapter you learn some of the more advanced features of using the Database tool. The main points discussed in this chapter are summarized next.

▶ You can enter a simple formula in a Database field to calculate a figure in another field. For example, you could enter a formula such as =*Hourly Rate*Hours Worked* to calculate a Wage.

▶ You can display selected records in your database while hiding others. Use the Query command to display subsets of records that have common field contents. Use the Hide Records command to hide records that have no common field contents, or to hide one or more records selectively.

▶ Use the Sort command to rearrange records in your database according to field contents. You can sort on one, two, or three fields at a time, in ascending or descending order.

▶ To create printed copies of your Database records in a professional, report-style format, use the Report View. Works uses a preset report definition to create your first Database report. You can modify, or customize, the report by adding spacing between lines, adding a title, or choosing just specific records and fields you want included in your report.

Chapter 10

Using Communications

In This Chapter

▶ *What is required to use the Communications tool*

▶ *What you can do with the Communications tool*

▶ *The process used in every communication session*

▶ *Setting up your PC for communications*

▶ *Using your PC as a terminal, capturing text, and transferring files*

Communications is a somewhat advanced topic for an introductory level book, so you won't find an exhaustive discussion of the procedures for using the Communications tool in this chapter. But since Communications is one of the four Works tools, this chapter gives you an overview of the tool and teaches you some of the simpler communication tasks that you're most likely to use.

Using the Communications tool requires special hardware for your computer. You must have a modem, either built-in or attached to your PC. A modem connects to your telephone on one end and to your PC on the other. It converts the computer's digital signals to the telephone's analog signals and back again so that two computers can *talk* to each other over telephone lines.

What You Can Do With Communications

The Communications tool in Works allows you to connect your computer to another computer so you can share or exchange information. Some of the things you can do using Communications are the following:

- ▶ Use your PC as a terminal to a mainframe or mini-computer.
- ▶ Capture text on your PC as you're viewing it from the mainframe.
- ▶ Send information from your PC to another computer.
- ▶ Receive information from another computer.

230

Let's look at each of these in more detail.

Use your PC as a terminal   You can use the Communications tool to connect your PC to a mainframe or minicomputer. When you connect to one of these computers, you are using your PC as if it were a terminal directly connected to that computer system. For example, if you have a PC at home and use a mainframe computer at work, you can connect your PC to that mainframe as if you were logged on to that system directly. You can do your work from home just as you would from your terminal in the office.

Another way to use your PC as a terminal is to access local bulletin board systems (BBS) or, for a fee, commercial data services such as Dow Jones, CompuServe, or Prodigy. These types of services offer information on a variety of topics—from the latest news and weather, to travel information. You can even use services like these to shop electronically. You must be a member to access most commercial services.

Capture text   When you use your PC as a terminal to a mainframe or minicomputer, you may want to capture some of the information you are reading on that system. When you capture text you save it in a file on your PC so you can recall the file whenever you want to use the information again. For example, if you are reading from the Dow Jones service about a company's stock performance, you may want to capture that information in a file on your PC so you can include it in a report.

Send files   When you want to send information to another computer, you use one of two Works commands. One command lets the computer you're connected to receive a text file, or *ASCII* file, from you without saving it; the other command lets the computer receive a non-ASCII, or *binary,* file from you and save it. ASCII files contain text only while binary files usually contain special codes for formatting, such as bold or centered text. Because of the special codes contained in binary files, the two computer systems must use compatible file transfer software so that they each understand the codes contained in binary files. The file transfer software defines the rules for communicating and helps to ensure that all the data being transferred is received correctly.

This chapter deals with these three most commonly used Communications tasks—using your PC as a terminal, capturing text, and sending files. Before you can perform any of these tasks, you need to know the process for communicating with another computer.

231

Steps in the Communication Process

Follow the same basic steps no matter which type of Communications task you perform. These steps are outlined next.

1. **Create a Works Communications file or open an existing one**   You must use a Communications file to connect to another computer, regardless of the task you perform. The Communications file stores the communication settings as well as the phone number Works uses to dial the other computer.

   If you will be communicating with more than one computer, create and save a Communications file for each computer. Once you have created a file for a particular computer, you can simply open that file again rather than create a new one.

2. **Choose the communication settings**   This is something you most likely have to do only once—the first time you create a Communications file. But even when you are using an existing file, from time to time you may want to change some of the communication settings.

3. **Start a communication session** A communication session refers to the entire time you are connected to another computer. You must start a session so that Works can dial the other computer and make the connection.

4. **Perform communication tasks** Once you are connected to the other computer, you are free to do whatever type of communication tasks you choose, from capturing text to transferring files.

5. **Close the communication session** When you are finished working and are ready to disconnect, you must close the communication session. This disconnects the phone and *hangs up* your modem. This is an important step to remember, especially if you are calling long-distance.

Creating a Communications File

As you have just learned, you must create a Works Communications file to communicate with another computer for the first time. To create a Communications file, select the New Communications option from the File menu. Works creates a file called COMM1.WCM (see Figure 10.1). You use this file exclusively for the system to which you are connecting. When you create the file, the first thing to do is to set the communication settings to match those of the system to which you are connecting. Once you have chosen communication settings, rename the file and save it so you can recall it whenever you need to communicate with that same system.

If you will be communicating with more than one system, create a new Communications file for each system.

Setting Up Your PC for Communications

When you open a Communications file, you must set up your PC to match the communication settings used by the other computer. These settings ensure that you can make a connection, that the two computers can *talk* to each other, and that the data you send or receive is as error-free as possible. You must check with the person operating the other computer to find out what communication settings their computer uses. If you are connecting to a commercial data service, the communication settings should be described in the membership information they send you when you subscribe to the service.

To change communication settings in Works, use the three commands on the Options menu: Phone, Terminal, and Communication.

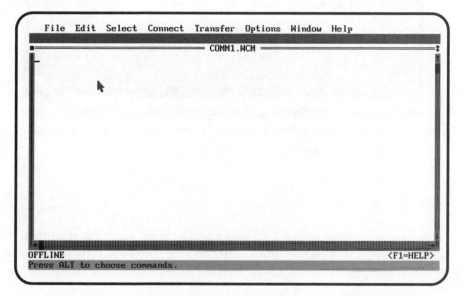

Figure 10.1 *A Works Communications file with the temporary filename of COMM1.WCM.*

Phone

The Phone command is used to enter phone numbers for dialing and special modem instructions. The dialog box for this command is shown in Figure 10.2.

In the Phone number field of the dialog box, type the phone number of the computer you're dialing. If you must dial 9 first, type 9 followed by a comma, then the area code, if required, and phone number. You can include dashes or parentheses in the number if you like but they are not required. Leave the Modem setup field blank. Select either Tone or Pulse for the type of phone you have. Automatic Answer is used for answering incoming calls. You can ignore this setting for now.

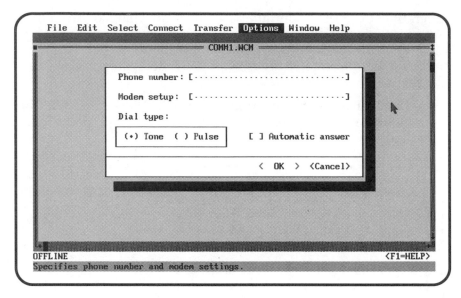

Figure 10.2   The Phone dialog box.

Terminal

The Terminal command lets you specify how your computer displays the data it receives. The dialog box for this command is shown in Figure 10.3.

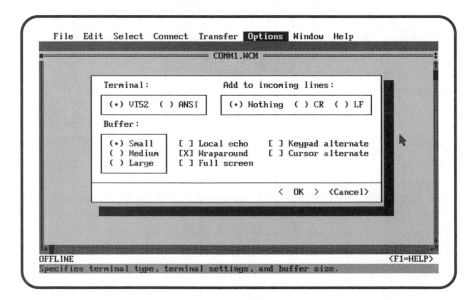

Figure 10.3   The Terminal dialog box.

In the Terminal field of the dialog box, select either VT52 or ANSI for the terminal type used by the system to which you are connecting. VT52 is most similar to a Zenith Z19 terminal; ANSI is most similar to the DEC VT100 or VT220/240 terminals.

In the Add to Incoming Lines field, select either CR (carriage return), LF (line feed), or Nothing. In most cases you should be able to use Nothing.

The Buffer is a temporary storage area on your PC for the information you receive from the other computer. If the information you expect to receive is less than 100 lines, select Small; if it is up to 300 lines, select Medium; if it is up to 750 lines, select Large.

When you select the Local Echo option, the characters you type are displayed on the screen. Since most PCs already display the characters you type, you don't need to select this option.

If you seem to lose characters at the right margin because the lines are too long, select Wraparound. This wraps the extra characters at the right margin down to the next line so you can read them.

235

When you select Full Screen, Works removes the menu bar, status line, and message line from your screen.

When you select Keypad Alternate with either VT52 or ANSI terminal types and you press NUMLOCK, your keypad works as it would in the application you're using on the system to which you're connected.

When you select Cursor alternate with the ANSI terminal type and you press NUMLOCK, your cursor works as it would in the application you're using on the system to which you're connected.

Communication

The Communication command is used to set up how the two computers connect and pass data back and forth. You can think of these settings as the *rules* for communicating. The Communication dialog box is shown in Figure 10.4.

Before you can connect to another computer, you must know the settings (shown in Figure 10.4) the other computer is using. Don't be too concerned about what these settings mean; just make sure your settings match those of the computer to which you're connecting.

Baud Rate   The speed at which data is transmitted. The baud rate is usually set to 300, 1200, or 2400.

Stop Bits   The number of bits used to mark the end of a character and the beginning of another. This is usually set to 1.

Data Bits   The number of bits used to represent one character. The most common setting is 8.

Handshake   A setting that controls the flow of information during a communication session.

Parity   A communication setting used to control errors during transmission.

Port   The communication port on the back of your system box where your modem cable is connected.

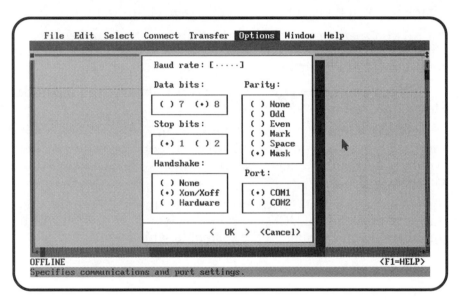

Figure 10.4   The Communication dialog box.

Saving Your Communications File

If you are creating a Communications file for a system that you will communicate with again, take the time now to save the file using the Save As command. Choose a filename that will remind you of the system you are connecting to. You don't need to type the file extension .WCM; Works adds it for you.

Starting a Communication Session

You've created your Communications file and chosen all the necessary settings (Phone, Terminal, and Communication) and saved the file under a new filename. Now you're ready to start your communication session—the time during which you are connected to the other system. You begin each session by placing the phone call to the other system and you end each session by disconnecting.

To begin the session, select the Connect command on the Connect menu. A clock on the status line begins counting time as soon as Works dials the phone number. At this point you can hear your modem dialing the phone number you stored in your Communications file. As soon as the other computer answers, you usually see some type of a welcome message on your screen. If not, you see a prompt for your user identification number or a password. The status line clock continues to count time as long as you are connected.

237

We have just described what happens when you connect to a computer system for the first time: you create the Communications file; you choose the appropriate settings and save the file; then you select the Connect command.

To communicate with the same computer again, select the Communications file you created earlier for that computer using the Open Existing File command on the File menu. When you select the file and Works opens it on your screen, you see a dialog box asking `Connect to other computer?` Select `OK` if you are ready to begin. Should you need to change any of the communication settings in your file, select `Cancel`, then choose the Connect command on the Connect menu when you're ready to begin your session.

Using Your PC as a Terminal

Most Works users employ the Communications tool to connect, or log on, to local or commercial information services such as CompuServe. You must be a member of the service to log on to the system. The service sends you dialing instructions and communication settings when you subscribe. They also send you an identification number (ID) and a password. You need to have these handy when you're ready to connect.

To log in to the mainframe or minicomputer, follow the previous instructions listed under *Starting a Communication Session*. As soon as Works says you are connected, you can log in to the system using the ID number and password given you. When you are finished using the system, be sure to log out according to the instructions given you by the service.

> ▶ **Note:** Logging out is not the same thing as ending a communication session; you must do both to end the phone connection.

238 Capturing Text

Often you may be connected to another computer and want to save the information you are reading. You can use the Capture Text command on the Transfer menu to do this. When you capture text, Works saves the incoming text in a Works file so that you can recall it when you want to use it.

Captured text is saved as an ASCII file. An ASCII file doesn't contain any special formatting characters. If the file requires editing, you can use the Word Processor tool in Works later to edit the file. To capture text, follow the next Quick Steps.

Capturing Text

1. When connected to the other system, select the Capture Text command on the Transfer menu.

Works displays a dialog box.

2. In the directories box, select the directory where you want the file to be saved, then type the filename and extension in the Save File As field and select OK.

If the file you select already exists, Works displays a dialog box asking if you want to append or replace the file.

3. If you want the captured text to be added to the existing file, select Append. If you want the captured text to replace the existing file, select Replace.

The incoming text is saved to the file you name.

4. When you have received all the text you want to capture, select the End Capture Text command on the Transfer menu.

Works stops capturing text displayed on your screen. Your communication session is still open. □

239

Sending Information

Works has two commands on the Transfer menu for sending information, Send File and Send Text. The first one, Send File, is used for sending files that contain special formatting; for instance, tabs, bold or underlined text, or the dollar signs and commas used to display numbers in a spreadsheet. Most Works files with file extensions .WPS, .WKS, .WDB, and .WCM contain special formatting. These files are often referred to as binary files.

Use the Send File command when you want to send a Works file to another Works user. When you use the Send File command, any file you send is automatically captured (saved) by the receiving computer.

The other command, Send Text, is used for sending information that is purely text, meaning information that contains no special formatting codes. This includes text that you type or text files. Text files usually have a .TXT file extension, which is explained later in this section.

Use the Send Text command when you want to send information to a non-Works user. Unlike the Send File command, the Send Text command does not ensure that the text is saved by the receiving computer. The person at the receiving end must select the proper command on their computer to capture the text.

> ▶ **Tip:** The Send File and Send Text command names can be somewhat confusing because you can send files using either command. It's helpful to remember that when you want to send binary files, you must use the Send File command; otherwise use the Send Text command.

Until now, you have saved all your files in Works with .WPS, .WKS, .WDB, or .WCM file extensions. Now you'll learn about .TXT files. You create them by choosing the Text format option on the Save or Save As menu. When you choose this option, Works adds a .TXT file extension to the filename you choose and saves only the text. Any special characters or formatting such as tabs or bold text are not saved. Use the text format option when you want to send a file to a non-Works user.

You may be wondering why Works has two different commands for sending files. The reason is that you can send text files easily to almost any type of computer because all computers understand text. All computers don't, however, understand special formatting. When you send a file that contains special formatting, the two computers must use the same communication procedures, or *protocol*, so that the receiving computer can interpret the special formatting codes you're sending. The protocol Works uses is called XMODEM. The other computer must also use this protocol for you to use the Send File command.

In the following sections you'll learn how to send a simple text file to another computer using the Send Text command, and how to send a Works file to a Works user using the Send File command.

Sending Text

When you want to send text to another computer, you need to make sure the person at the receiving end is prepared to receive your message at a specific time. Always contact the person at the receiving end to make sure your computers are set up to communicate with

240

each other, and to agree on a time to send the message. If you are sending a message to a communication service, they may have a menu option you can use to alert them that you are going to send a message.

Once you have alerted the other system, use the Send Text command on the Transfer menu, which displays the dialog box shown in Figure 10.5.

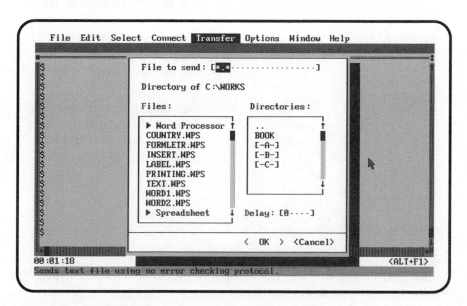

241

Figure 10.5   The dialog box used for sending a text file.

You use this dialog box to select the name of the file you want to send. This dialog box should be familiar to you except for the Delay option. Sometimes the computer you are sending to can't receive data as fast as your PC sends it. The Delay causes Works to pause at the end of each line while it is sending information. Using the Delay option gives the receiving computer a chance to catch up. Delays are specified in tenths of a second. For example, if you specify 3, Works pauses .3 of a second at the end of each line during transmission.

Use the following Quick Steps to send a text file.

Q Sending Text

1. Notify the operator at the receiving end that you are ready to send a text file.

2. Select the Send Text command on the Transfer menu.

   Works displays the dialog box shown in Figure 10.5.

3. From the dialog box, select the text file you want to send.

   Works places the name of the file you select in the File to Send field of the dialog box.

4. If you want to specify a delay, type the number you choose in the Delay field, then select OK.

   The dialog box is removed and Works returns to your Communications file to begin sending the text. □

242

Sending a Works File

When you want to send a Works file to another Works user, use the Send File command on the Transfer menu, which displays the dialog box shown in Figure 10.6.

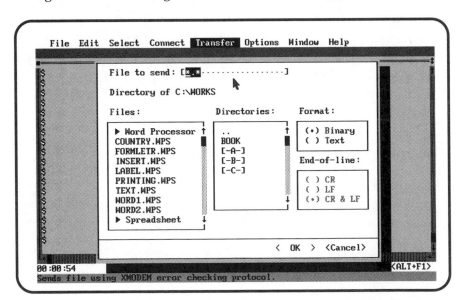

Figure 10.6   The dialog box used for sending a Works file.

This dialog box is similar to the one shown in Figure 10.5 except that you can specify the type of file, including binary, in the Format box.

Before you begin, remember to contact the receiving computer to alert it that you are about to send a message. To use the Send File command, follow the next Quick Steps.

 Sending a Works File to Another Works User

1. Once connected to the other computer, select from Works the Send File command on the Transfer menu.

   Works displays the dialog box shown in Figure 10.6.

2. In the dialog box, select the directory and the file you want to send.

   Works displays the filename you choose in the File to Send field.

3. Select either Binary or Text in the Format box. If the file you want to send is a Text file, select either CR or LF in the End-of-Line box. If you aren't sure which you need, select both, then select OK.

4. Works begins to transfer the file and displays a status box (see the following Figure10.7) telling you how much of the file has been transferred.

   The status alternates between SEND and WAITING as the file is being transferred.

5. When the file has been completely transferred, select OK to continue the communication session.

   The status line clock continues to count time as long as you are still connected to the other computer. □

243

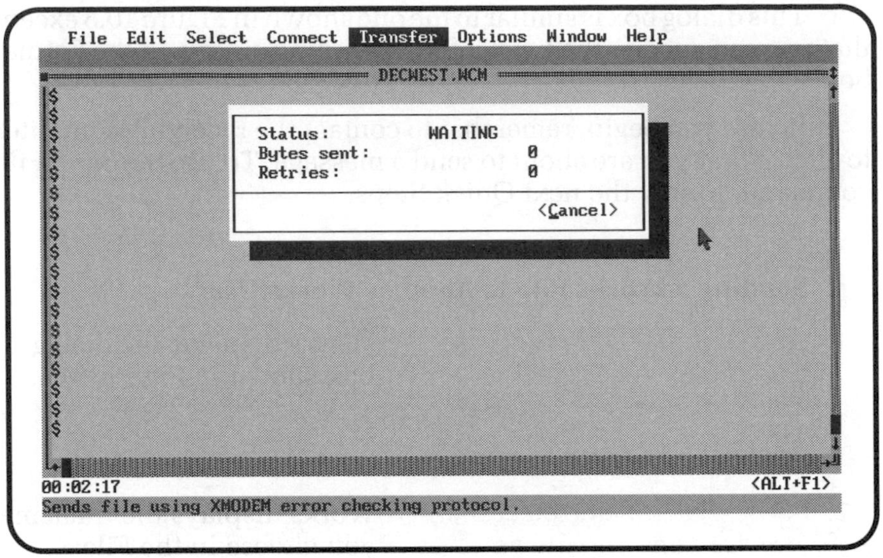

Figure 10.7   *The status box Works displays while sending a file.*

Closing a Communication Session

When you are finished communicating with the other computer, close the communication session. Closing the session disconnects your phone and hangs up your modem. If you are connected to a mini or mainframe computer or a communication service, be sure to log off of that system before you disconnect.

When you are ready to end the communication session, select the Connect command on the Connect menu. The Connect command toggles on and off; when you are connected, a marker appears to the left of the command name on the menu. When you select Connect again, Works removes the marker and disconnects your telephone. You know you are disconnected when the clock on the status line stops counting.

What You've Learned

In this chapter you learn that you can use Works to connect your computer to other computers to transfer and share information. The main points covered in this chapter are:

▶ Using the Communications tool in Works, you can use your PC for a variety of tasks. You can use it as a terminal to a mini or mainframe computer. You can capture text in a file as you're viewing it from the mainframe so you can use it later. And, you can transfer files between your PC and the system to which you're connected.

▶ When you capture text on your PC, Works saves the information you receive in a file under a filename you choose.

▶ No matter what type of communication task you are performing, you follow the same basic steps for a communication session.

245

1. Create a new Communications file or use an existing one.
2. Choose the communication settings.
3. Start the communication session.
4. Carry out the communication tasks you want to perform, such as transferring a file, and so on.
5. Close the communication session.

▶ Use the Send Text command to transfer text (.TXT) files; use the Send File command to transfer binary files.

▶ Close the communication session by logging off the main-frame if you are logged on to one, then select the Connect command on the Connect menu to disconnect your modem.

Chapter 11

Making the Works Tools Work For You

In This Chapter

▶ *Using the Works window feature to your advantage*
▶ *Creating documents using multiple Works tools*
▶ *Creating form letters using Database and Word Processor files*

In Chapter 1 you learned that Works is referred to as integrated software because it combines four software tools into one package. If you've read through most or all of the chapters in this book, you've learned something about each of the four Works tools. In Chapter 2 you learned that Works has a built-in window system that allows you to work on more than one file at a time. You can move, resize, and rearrange windows on the screen however you choose, but until now, you haven't worked with more than one window at a time. In this chapter you'll work with multiple windows and discover that the real power of Works lies in the ability to copy from one window to another.

Using the Tools Together

There is quite an advantage in being able to copy from one window to another. You can create documents that contain information from multiple tools without having to retype the information. For instance, if you want to include part of a Spreadsheet file in a letter you have in a Word Processor file, you begin by opening both files on your screen (Works creates a separate window for each file). Then select the portion of the spreadsheet you want to copy and insert it into your letter. If you want to insert a chart to back up the Spreadsheet data you've inserted, select the chart, then insert it into your letter.

Sound easy enough? Now you'll get the chance to try it yourself using some of the files you've created in previous chapters. In the following sections, you'll create a new letter using the Word Processor tool and include Spreadsheet data and a chart from files you created in previous chapters.

Inserting a Spreadsheet into a Word Processor File

Suppose you have applied for a business loan at your local bank. The bank has reviewed your application and is now requesting a breakdown of your income for the year 1990. You want to write a letter to the bank that includes a portion of your income statement and a chart illustrating those figures.

Begin by creating a new Word Processor file and renaming it BANKLTR.WPS using the Save As command. Then type the letter as shown in Figure 11.1.

Now that you have typed your opening paragraph, you're ready to include the figures from your spreadsheet. Using the Open Existing File command on the File menu, recall the Spreadsheet file you created in Chapters 5-7, INCOME.WKS. When you open this file, Works creates a separate window for the spreadsheet. The Spreadsheet window appears on top of the Word Processor window, leaving its title bar visible. Both windows are shown in Figure 11.2.

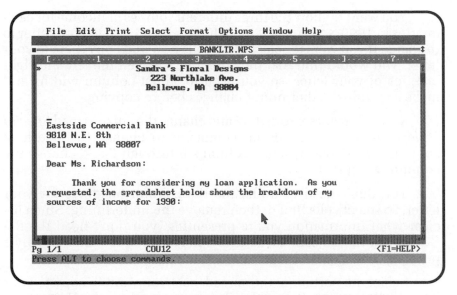

Figure 11.1   The beginning of your letter to the bank.

249

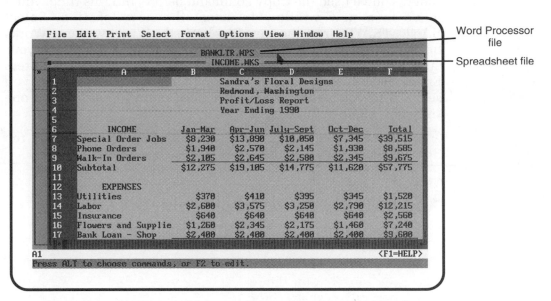

Figure 11.2   The Spreadsheet window overlying the Word Processor window.

You want to show the three different sources of income for each quarter in 1990, so you want to include cells A6:F10 in your letter to the bank. If you were to select these cells now and copy them to your letter, you would find that they don't fit between the left and right margins of your letter, so you need to adjust column widths and make a couple of other minor changes before copying.

Move your cursor to cell A7 and change the entry to read *Special Orders*, then use the Format command to change the width of column A to 15. Next, select columns B through F and change the column width to 9.

You don't need to underline the column headings for your letter, so select cells B6:F6, then remove the underlining. Since it's clear what information you're presenting, you don't need the INCOME heading in cell A6, so delete it. Now you're ready to copy a range of cells to your letter.

Select the portion of the spreadsheet you want to copy to your letter, cells A6:F10. Select the Copy command on the Edit menu. Notice the status line tells you to select the new location, then press Enter. You've used the Copy command before, but this time, you'll move to a new window to select the new location. Select BANKLTR.WPS from the open files list in the Window menu. Works brings the Word Processor window to the foreground. Move your cursor to the line below the last sentence in your letter, then press Enter. Works copies the portion of your spreadsheet that you selected to your letter. Your letter now should look like the one shown in Figure 11.3.

The following Quick Steps describe how to copy from the Spreadsheet window to the Word Processor window.

Q Copying From the Spreadsheet to the Word Processor

1. Open an existing Word Processor file or create a new one.	Works opens the Word Processor file in its own window.
2. Enter new text for the letter; or if you are using an existing file, place the cursor where you want to insert spreadsheet information.	

3. Select the Open Existing File command on the File menu to open your Spreadsheet file.

Works opens the Spreadsheet file in its own window, overlying the Word Processor window.

4. Select the portion of the spreadsheet you want to copy to the Word Processor document, then select the Copy command on the Edit menu.

The status line tells you to select the new location, then press Enter. Move to a new window to select the new location.

5. To reopen your Word Processor file, select the filename from the Window menu.

Works redisplays your Word Processor file.

6. Move your cursor to the location where you want to insert the spreadsheet data, then press Enter.

Works inserts the spreadsheet data into your Word Processor file. ☐

251

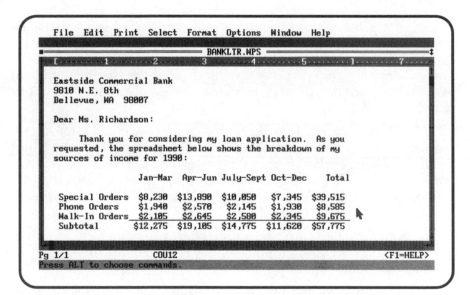

Figure 11.3   A Word Processor letter that includes a selected portion of a spreadsheet.

In our example, we altered the column width to make sure the spreadsheet data would fit into our letter. If you find the information you copy doesn't fit quite right, use the Undo command on the Edit menu to undo the copy, then return to your Spreadsheet window to make the necessary changes.

Inserting a Chart into a Word Processor File

In your sample letter, you're ready to enter another paragraph that introduces the chart that you'll be inserting. Directly below the spreadsheet data you just inserted in your letter, enter the following paragraph:

```
The chart below presents this information in a graphical
form.
```

As you recall from Chapter 7, charts are tied to spreadsheet data. Whenever you copy a chart, it reflects the most recent spreadsheet data, so when the chart is not correct, you need to update the spreadsheet before you copy the chart. Both the Spreadsheet and Word Processor files must be open in order to copy a chart to a Word Processor file.

To insert a chart in a Word Processor file, place your cursor where you want to insert the chart, then select the Insert Chart command from the Edit menu. Works displays the dialog box shown in Figure 11.4. The dialog box lists the Spreadsheet files that are currently open as well as the charts associated with that spreadsheet.

From the Charts box, select the chart you want to insert, then select OK. Works inserts a placeholder for the chart in your Word Processor document.

Now you're ready to try it yourself. To copy the chart of your spreadsheet data into your letter, place your cursor one line below the last paragraph, then select the Insert Chart command. The only Spreadsheet file you currently have open is INCOME.WKS, so this is the only file listed in the dialog box. Select Chart1 from the Charts box, then select OK.

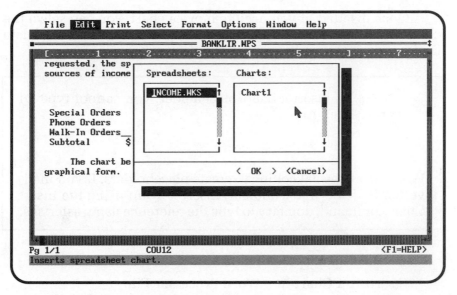

Figure 11.4   The Insert Chart dialog box.

253

Works inserts a placeholder in your letter where the chart is to be inserted when you print the letter. If you want to view the chart, use the Preview command on the Print menu.

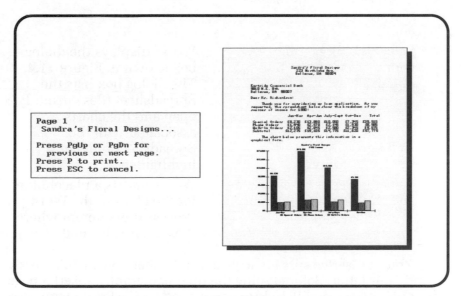

Figure 11.5   The letter displayed using the Print Preview command.

Once inserted, if you need to move a chart, you can select the chart placeholder and move it to a new location. If you want to delete it, simply select the placeholder and delete it.

▶ **Note:** To insert a chart placeholder, you cannot type an entry like:

```
*chart filename.WKS:Chart1*
```

Works uses special coding to create placeholders. If you inadvertently delete a placeholder, insert it again using the Insert Chart command; don't try to type the reference using asterisks.

Q Inserting a Chart in a Word Processor File

1. Open the Spreadsheet file for the chart you want to insert, then open the Word Processor file.

   Works opens a separate window for each file, overlying the last file you open on the first.

2. Place the cursor in the Word Processor file where you want to insert the chart.

3. Select the Insert Chart command from the Edit menu.

   Works displays the dialog box shown in Figure 11.4. The dialog box lists the Spreadsheet files currently open and the charts associated with the Spreadsheet file that's highlighted.

4. Select the spreadsheet data and the chart you want to insert, then press OK.

   Works inserts a placeholder for the chart in the Word Processor document where the cursor is located. □

You've inserted spreadsheet data and a chart; now you're ready to end your letter. Before typing the final paragraphs, insert a page break using the Insert Page Break command on the Print menu. The page break appears as a dotted line across the document. Now add the final paragraphs shown in Figure 11.6 and save the file.

```
 File  Edit  Print  Select  Format  Options  Window  Help
═══════════════════════ BANKLTR.WPS ═══════════════════════
[········1·········2·········3·········4·········5·········]········7····
    Special Orders   $8,230  $13,890  $10,050   $7,345  $39,515
    Phone Orders     $1,940   $2,570   $2,145   $1,930   $8,585
    Walk-In Orders   $2,105   $2,645   $2,580   $2,345   $9,675
    Subtotal        $12,275  $19,105  $14,775  $11,620  $57,775

       The chart below presents this information in a
    graphical form.

                    *chart INCOME.WKS:Chart1*

 »···································································
       Please let me know if you require further information.
    I look forward to hearing from you soon.

    Sincerely,                                    ▸

    Sandra Simpson

 Pg 2/2                    COU12                       <F1=HELP>
 Press ALT to choose commands.
```

Figure 11.6   The final paragraphs are added to the letter.

255

Your letter is now complete, and you have learned how to insert spreadsheet data as well as a chart using the window feature of Works.

Using the Database to Create Form Letters

In the examples above, you learned how to bring spreadsheet data and a chart into a letter that is to be mailed to one bank. Suppose you want to send the same letter to four prospective investors. Using the Database and Word Processor tools in Works, you can create form letters. Form letters are identical to one another except for the personalized information such as the name and address. Whenever you want to send the same letter to several people, use a form letter.

To create a form letter, you use two documents: the letter itself (a .WPS file) and a Database file containing names and addresses (a .WDB file). In the Database file, you select all the companies you want to send a letter to. In the Word Processor file, you type the common parts of the letter and insert placeholders for the name and address. The placeholders are sometimes called fields because they are the identical fields taken from the Database file. When Works sees the field placeholders in the Word Processor file, it inserts the actual name and address for each company selected from the Database file.

In this section, you'll see how the bank letter you just created can be altered slightly and sent to several prospective investors. You can follow along with your own files. Use the letter you just wrote as well as the database you created in Chapters 8-9, CLIENTS.WDB.

Your Database file, CLIENTS.WDB, contains two records for investment companies. Recall the CLIENTS.WDB file now and add two more records to the database. Enter the following records in the database as shown next.

Record 12	Record 13
Anderson Investors	The Palmer Company
1499 N. Third	445 S.E. 24th
Bellevue, WA 98007	Seattle, WA 98118
Rick Anderson	Alex Palmer
206/873-2281	206/521-2994

You want to send the letter to these two new companies as well as to *Lane Investments*, record 2, and *Essex Corporation*, record 9. To select only these records, you must hide the rest. Select record 1, then select the Hide Records command on the Select menu. Works hides but does not delete record 1. Do the same for records 3-8 and records 10 and 11. The database now looks like the one shown in Figure 11.7.

Now it is time to create the form letter to send to these four companies. Use the same letter you made for the bank, except for some minor changes. Recall the letter BANKLTR.WPS. To make a copy of the letter, use the Save As command to save the file under the name INVSTRS.WPS.

In the file INVSTRS.WPS, delete the inside name and address of the bank. Change *Dear Ms. Richardson:* to *Gentlemen:*. The letter now should look like the one shown in Figure 11.8.

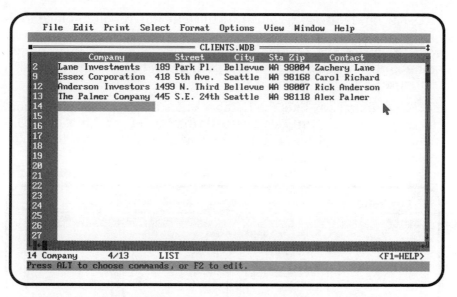

Figure 11.7   A select group of investors from the CLIENTS.WDB Database file.

257

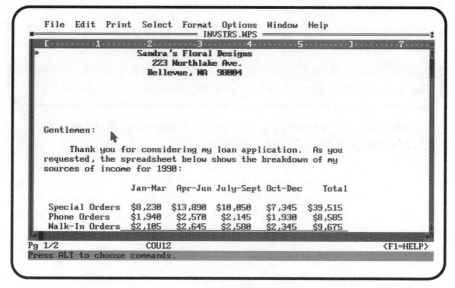

Figure 11.8   The bank letter altered to be sent to investors.

The only things missing from the letter are the field placeholders for name and address. Place the cursor in the letter where you want to insert the company name, then select the Insert Field command on the Edit menu. Works displays the dialog box shown in Figure 11.9.

The dialog box lists the Database files that are currently open. In our example, the only Database file that's open is CLIENTS.WDB. When you select CLIENTS.WDB, Works displays only the fields associated with that Database file.

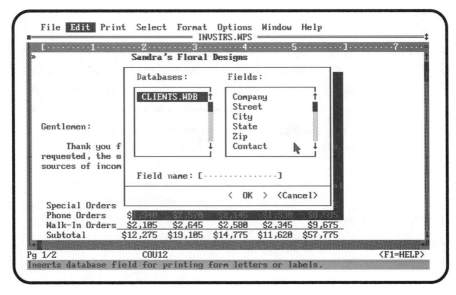

Figure 11.9 *The dialog box used for inserting field placeholders in a Word Processor file.*

To insert a placeholder for the company name, select Company from the Fields list in the dialog box, then select OK or press Enter. Works returns to your Word Processor file and inserts a placeholder like the one shown next.

<<Company>>

▶ **Note:** Just like the chart placeholder you inserted earlier, this field placeholder is specially coded by Works. You cannot insert a field by typing the field name enclosed in the left and right double arrows, you must use the Insert Field command.

The rest of the fields are inserted in exactly the same way. Remember to move your cursor to the exact location where you want to insert the field, then select the Insert Field command. To insert the Street field, move your cursor to the next line. Move to the next line and insert the City field, but instead of going to the next line, type a comma and a space to separate the City field from the State field. After you have inserted the State field, type two spaces, then insert the ZIP field.

Q Inserting Field Placeholders in Form Letters

1. Open the Database file used for the form letters, then open the form letter file.

   Works opens two windows on your screen.

2. If the form letter file is not the active file, select it from the Window menu. Then place your cursor where you want the first field placeholder inserted in the letter.

259

3. Select the Insert Field command on the Select menu.

   Works displays a dialog box listing the Database files that are currently open. The Database fields are listed in the Fields box for the Database file that is highlighted.

4. Select the field you want to insert, then select OK or press Enter.

   Works returns to your letter and inserts a placeholder for the field you select.

5. If you want to insert more field placeholders, move your cursor to the location where you want to insert the field, then repeat steps 3 and 4. When you are finished inserting fields, Works returns to your letter.

   ☐

After inserting the Company, Street, City, State, and ZIP fields from the CLIENTS.WDB database, your sample letter should now look like the one shown in Figure 11.10.

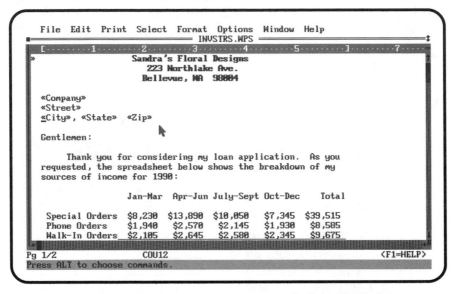

260

Figure 11.10   *The letter to investors including field place-holders.*

That's all there is to it. If you need to move the fields, you can select and move them just like any other text. If you want to delete a field, delete it just like any other text.

Printing Form Letters

You've taken all the necessary steps to create the form letters, now it's up to Works to merge the database information with the field placeholders to create the final letters. Works does this during the printing process. If you want to view the letters before printing them, you choose the Print to File option on the Print menu shown in Figure 11.11.

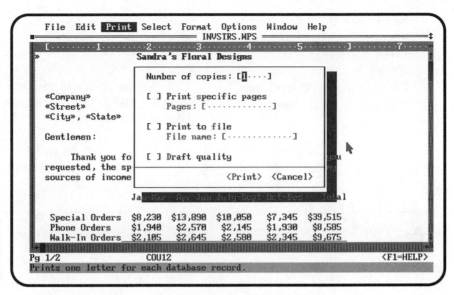

Figure 11.11   The Print dialog box.

Works displays this dialog box when you select the Print Form Letters command on the Print menu. The options in the dialog box should be familiar to you from previous chapters.

To print form letters, use the following Quick Steps.

Q Printing Form Letters

1. Open the Database file used for the form letters, then open the form letter file.

   Works opens two windows on your screen.

2. If the active file is not the form letter file, choose it from the Window menu.

3. Use the Print menu to change any print or margin settings.

4. Select the Print Form Letters command on the Print menu.

   Works displays a dialog box listing the Database files that are currently open.

5. Select the Database file you want to use from the Database box, then select OK.

Works displays the Print dialog box shown in Figure 11.11.

6. Choose the print options you want, then select OK.

Unless you select the Print to File option, Works begins printing the letters. □

When Works begins printing, the status line displays the total number of letters to be printed and the number that are already printed.

> ▶ **Tip:** If you want to print a trial copy of one letter before printing all the form letters, select the Print command instead of the Print Form Letters command on the Print menu. When you select this command, Works prints a letter that contains the field placeholders rather than actual names and addresses.

What You've Learned

In this chapter you learn that the real power of Works is in its capability to copy between windows. Because you can copy from one window to another, you can create documents that contain text, spreadsheet data, database records, or charts. The main points covered in this chapter are summarized next.

- ▶ When you are copying from one tool to another, each of the files you are using must be open at the same time.
- ▶ Once both files are open, you can copy information from one tool to another by using the Copy command on the Edit menu.
- ▶ Insert charts in a Word Processor document by using the Insert Chart command on the Edit menu.
- ▶ Use your Works Database and Word Processor files to create form letters.

Appendix A

Installation and Startup Instructions

Before you can use Works on your computer, you must install it on a hard or floppy disk. On a hard disk system, Works is installed directly on drive C. On a floppy disk system, the installation process prepares a *working copy* of Works on a floppy disk so you can start-up Works quickly and easily whenever you want to use it.

If you have a hard disk on your system, follow the hard disk installation instructions. If you don't have a hard disk on your system, follow the procedures for installing Works on the floppy disk.

As soon as you insert the first disk and begin the installation, Works guides you on the screen through the installation process. You are asked some questions and told when to remove and insert Works disks. The installation takes ten to fifteen minutes, depending on the disk system you are using.

What You Need to Begin

Before you begin the installation procedure for either hard or floppy disk, you need to know some important information about your computer. During the installation procedure, you are asked what printer port you are using as well as what kind of printer, video card, and mouse you have. If you aren't sure of the brand name, you should know the type (such as an EGA or VGA video card).

To install Works on a hard disk system, you need the eight original Works disks listed next.

Setup	Spell & Help	Learning Works 2
Program	Thesaurus	Learning Works 3
Accessories	Learning Works 1	

To install Works on a floppy disk system, you need the four original Works disks listed next.

Setup	Spell & Help
Program	Accessories

In addition, you'll need a blank, formatted floppy disk.

> ▶ **Note:** If you are installing on a floppy disk system, you'll be able to use the Thesaurus and the tutorial when you run Works, but you don't need the disks during the installation process.

Before you install Works for the first time, be sure to make backup copies of all the Works disks.

Installing Works on a Hard Disk

To install Works on your hard disk, follow the next instructions.

1. Turn on your computer and insert the Works Setup disk in drive A.
2. At the DOS prompt, C:\, type a:setup and press Enter.
3. Follow the instructions on the screen.

At this point, you are also asked what type of video card, printer, and mouse you have as well as the printer port you use. Answer the questions as best you can. If you aren't sure, select the default option that Works chooses.

Works also tells you when to remove and insert Works disks so that files can be copied to the hard disk. You are given the option of installing the Learning Works disks. All Works files are copied to a directory called C:\WORKS unless you specify otherwise.

Works displays the message `Setup is finished` when the installation is complete.

Starting Works on a Hard Disk System

265

1. Turn on your computer.
2. At the DOS prompt, `C:\`, change to the directory where Works is installed. (Unless you specify otherwise during the installation process, Works is installed in C:\WORKS.) To change to this directory, type `cd works`, then press Enter.
3. The DOS prompt is now `C:\WORKS`. At the prompt, type `works` and press Enter. Within a few seconds you'll see the opening Works screen. From this screen you can create a new file, open an existing file, or use the Works tutorial if you installed it.

Installing Works on a Floppy Disk

Works does not require a hard disk; you can install Works on a floppy drive system. To do so, you must have your original DOS disk and a blank, formatted disk. Formatting a disk prepares it to receive and store information. If you have not formatted a blank disk yet, follow the instructions given next. Formatting a disk takes only a few minutes.

Formatting a Blank Disk

1. Insert your DOS disk in drive A and turn on your computer.
2. At the DOS prompt, `A>`, type `format a:` and press Enter.
3. Remove the DOS disk and insert a blank disk in drive A.
4. Follow the instruction given on the screen.
5. When the disk is formatted, remove it from drive A and set it aside until you are asked to insert it again.

During the installation process, Works refers to the disk you just formatted as the *working disk*.

If the disk you are formatting is a 3 ½ inch disk or a high-density (1.2 megabyte) 5 ¼ inch disk, you can install DOS and Works on the same disk so you can start both DOS and Works from the same disk.

To copy DOS to the disk you are formatting, type `format a: /s` at step 2 above, then follow steps 3 and 4. Later, when you begin the installation and are asked to insert the working copy disk, insert this disk and continue to follow the rest of the installation procedure as usual.

266

Installing Works on a Floppy Drive System

To install Works on a floppy drive system, use the following steps.

1. Insert your DOS disk in drive A and turn on your computer.
2. When the DOS prompt, `A>`, appears on your screen, remove the DOS disk from drive A.
3. Insert the Works Setup disk in drive A.
4. At the DOS prompt, `A>`, type `a:setup` and press Enter.
5. Follow the instructions on the screen.

At this point, you are also asked what type of video card, printer, and mouse you have as well as the printer port you use. Answer the questions as best you can. If you aren't sure, select the default option that Works chooses.

Works also tells you when to remove and insert Works disks. When asked to insert the working disk, insert the blank, formatted disk. This floppy disk becomes your working copy of Works.

Works displays the message Setup is finished when the installation is complete.

Starting Works on a Floppy Drive System

267

To start Works on a floppy drive system, follow the steps given next.

1. Turn on your computer and insert the DOS disk in drive A.
2. At the DOS prompt, A:, remove the DOS disk and insert your working copy of Works in drive A. If you have a second drive, insert a blank, formatted disk in drive B. Works will store your files there.
3. At the DOS prompt, type works and press Enter.

Within a few seconds you'll see the opening Works screen. From this screen you can begin using Works.

Common Works Functions

A *function* is a preset equation that Works provides to save you time entering a formula in a spreadsheet. Works includes 57 different functions of various types from mathematical, to statistical, to financial. This appendix lists 22 of the most common functions. For a complete list, see Help by pressing F1 from anywhere in Works.

ABS(x)

ABS gives you the absolute value (positive value) of the number *x*.

Example: When you enter the formula =ABS(−8), Works gives you 8 as a result.

AVG(RangeReference0,RangeReference1,...)

Works adds the values specified by the RangeReferences and divides by the number of values. Range references can include numbers, formulas, and cell or range references.

Example: If the values in A1, A2, and A3 are 25, 14, and 15 and you enter the formula =AVG(A1:A3), the result is 18.

COLS(RangeReference)

COLS gives you the numbers of columns in a RangeReference.

Example: The formula =COLS(B5:E9) gives you 4 as a result. If the range B5:E9 is named ExpQ1, the formula =COLS(ExpQ1) also gives you 4 as a result.

COUNT(RangeReference0,RangeReference1,...)

Works counts the number of cells in a range reference that contain values. Those that are blank are not counted.

Example: If cells A1:A7 all contain values except for cell A7, the formula =COUNT(A1:A7) gives you a result of 6.

When you use a specific cell rather than a range reference, Works counts the blank cells.

Example: If cells A1:A7 all contain values except for cell A7, the formula =COUNT(A1:A6,A7) gives you a result of 7.

CTERM(Rate,FutureValue,PresentValue)

Works calculates the number of compounding periods required for an investment at a fixed interest rate to grow from its present value to a future value. The Rate represents the interest rate for a single compounding period. (If interest is compounded monthly, and the interest rate is 12%, the monthly Rate is 1% per month.)

Example: If you invest $1,000 at an annual interest rate of 8.25%, you would double your investment in 101.16 months, about 8.5 years. The formula is expressed as =CTERM(8.25%/12,2000,1000).

DDB(Cost,Salvage,Life,Period)

Works uses the double-declining balance method to find the amount of depreciation in a specific Period. Cost is the amount you paid for the asset; Salvage is the amount you expect the asset to be worth when you sell it; Life is the amount of time (usually years) you expect to use the asset; and Period is the amount of time over which you want to find the depreciation amount.

Example: The formula =DDB(15000,9000,10,3) is used to calculate the amount of depreciation for a car that costs $15,000, and that you expect to be worth $9,000 at the end of the Period of 3 years. The Life of the car is 10 years. This formula results in a depreciation expense for the third year of $600.

FV(Payment,Rate,Term)

Works calculates the future value of an annuity of equal payments that earns a fixed interest rate, compounded over several terms. Future value is based on the first payment occurring at the end of the first period.

Example: If you deposit $1,000 each year for the next five years in a savings account that pays 7.75% interest, compounded annually, how much money would you have in your account at the end of five years? The formula to calculate this is =FV(1000,7.75%,5) and the result is $5,837.43.

INT(x)

INT gives you the integer portion of x. INT deletes the digits to the right of the decimal point without rounding to the nearest integer.

Example: The formula =INT(8.75) gives the result of 8.

LOG(x)

LOG gives you the base 10 logarithm of x where x is a positive number.

Example: The formula =LOG(10) gives the result of 1.

MAX(RangeReference0,RangeReference1,...)

Works finds the largest number contained in the RangeReference. RangeReferences may be numbers, formulas, cell references, or range references. When you use a cell reference, blank cells are treated as zero. When you use a range reference, blank cells are ignored. In all references, text is treated as zero.

Example: If cells C3:C7 contain the values 9, 7, 13, blank, and 5, the formula =MAX(C3:C7) gives the result of 13; while the formula =MAX(C3:C7,25) gives the result of 25.

MIN(RangeReference0,RangeReference1,...)

Works finds the smallest number contained in the RangeReference. RangeReferences may be numbers, formulas, cell references, or range references. When you use a cell reference, blank cells are treated as zero. When you use a range reference, blank cells are ignored. In all references, text is treated as zero.

Example: If cells C3:C7 contain the values 9, 7, 13, blank, and 5, the formula =MIN(C3:C7) gives the result of 5; while the formula =MIN(C3:C7,2) gives the result of 2.

272

PI()

When you use PI() in a formula, Works inserts the number 3.14159... for the mathematical constant π.

PMT(Principal,Rate,Term)

PMT calculates the periodic payment for an investment or loan. The Principal is the amount of the loan; the Rate is the fixed interest rate that compounds over a given Term. The function assumes that payments are made at the end of periods of equal length.

Example: If you wanted to buy a $15,000 boat over a 36-month period at 9.5% interest per year, the formula to calculate this is =PMT(15000,9.5%/12,36). The monthly payment is $480.49.

PV(Payment,Rate,Term)

Works calculates the present value of an annuity of equal payments that earns a fixed interest rate, compounding over several years. The function assumes that the first payment is made at the end of the first period.

Example: Suppose you were to receive $1,000 each year for the next five years and you expect the annual inflation rate over the next 5 years will be 9%. The formula to calculate the present value of the $5,000 is =PV(1000,9%,5), which equals $3,889.65.

RATE(FutureValue,PresentValue,Term)

Works finds the fixed interest rate per compounding period needed for an investment at present value to grow to its future value over the term.

Example: If you purchase rental property today at $200,000 and expect to sell it five years from now for $375,000, the annual rate of return on your investment is 13.4% based on the formula =RATE(375000,200000,5).

273

ROUND(x,NumberOfPlaces)

Works rounds x to the number of places you choose. When the NumberOfPlaces is positive, Works rounds x to the chosen number of decimal places to the right of the decimal point.

Example: The formula =ROUND(4.43,1) is rounded to 4.4.

When the NumberOfPlaces is negative, Works rounds x to the number of places to the left of the decimal point.

Example: The formula =ROUND(789,–2) is rounded to 800.

When NumberOfPlaces is zero, Works rounds x to the nearest integer.

Example: The formula =ROUND(3.62,0), is rounded to 4.

ROWS(RangeReference)

Works finds the number of rows in the RangeReference.

Example: The formula =ROWS(B5:E9) gives the result of 5. If the range B5:E9 is named ExpQ1, the formula =ROWS(ExpQ1) also gives you 5 as a result.

SLN(Cost,Salvage,Life)

Works calculates the amount of depreciation for one period using the straight-line depreciation method. Cost is the amount paid for the asset; Salvage is the amount you expect the asset to be worth when you sell it; Life is the amount of time (usually years) you expect to use the asset.

Example: The formula =SLN(15000,2000,10) is used to calculate the amount of depreciation for a car that costs $15,000, and that you expect to be worth $2,000 at the end of its Life, or 10 years. This formula results in a straight-line depreciation expense of $1300.

SQRT(x)

SQRT calculates the square root of x. If x is a negative number, Works gives the error value ERR.

Example: The formula =SQRT(144) gives the value of 12.

SUM(RangeReference0,RangeReference1,...)

Works calculates the total of all values in RangeReferences. Range references may be numbers, formulas, and cell or range references. When you use range references, Works ignores blank cells. When you use cell references, Works treats blank cells as zero.

Example: If cells A2:A6 contain the values 14, 13, 20, 10, and blank, the formula =SUM(A2:A6) gives the result of 57. If 13 is the value in cell A9, the formula =SUM(A2:A6, A9) gives the result of 70.

TERM(Payment,Rate,FutureValue)

Works calculates the number of compounding periods necessary for a series of Payments earning a fixed interest Rate to reach the FutureValue amount.

Example: If you put away $400 each month in a savings account that pays 8.5% interest, it will take 23.10 months, or almost 2 years, for your savings account to reach $10,000, based on the formula =TERM(400,8.5%/12,10000).

VAR(RangeReference0,RangeReference1,...)

Works calculates the variance of the numbers in the RangeReference. RangeReferences may be numbers, formulas, or cell or range references. When you use a cell reference, Works treats blank cells as zeros. When you use any other type of reference, text is treated as a zero.

Example: If cells B2:B7 contain the values 97, 83, 78, blank, 97, and 98, formula =VAR(B2:B7) gives the result of 70.64.

Index

278

281

282

284

285

Reader Feedback Card

Thank you for purchasing this book from SAMS FIRST BOOK series. Our intent with this series is to bring you timely, authoritative information that you can reference quickly and easily. You can help us by taking a minute to complete and return this card. We appreciate your comments and will use the information to better serve your needs.

1. Where did you purchase this book?

☐ Chain bookstore (Walden, B. Dalton)　　☐ Direct mail
☐ Independent bookstore　　　　　　　　☐ Book club
☐ Computer/Software store　　　　　　　☐ School bookstore
☐ Other _____

2. Why did you choose this book? (Check as many as apply.)

☐ ·Price　　　　　　　　　　　　　　☐ Appearance of book
☐ Author's reputation　　　　　　　　☐ SAMS' reputation
☐ Quick and easy treatment of subject　☐ Only book available on subject

3. How do you use this book? (Check as many as apply.)

☐ As a supplement to the product manual　☐ As a reference
☐ In place of the product manual　　　　☐ At home
☐ For self-instruction　　　　　　　　☐ At work

4. Please rate this book in the categories below. G = Good; N = Needs improvement; U = Category is unimportant.

☐ Price　　　　　　　　　　☐ Appearance
☐ Amount of information　　☐ Accuracy
☐ Examples　　　　　　　　☐ Quick Steps
☐ Inside cover reference　　☐ Second color
☐ Table of contents　　　　☐ Index
☐ Tips and cautions　　　　☐ Illustrations
☐ Length of book
☐ How can we improve this book?_____
☐ _____

5. How many computer books do you normally buy in a year?

☐ 1–5　　　　　☐ 5–10　　　　　☐ More than 10
☐ I rarely purchase more than one book on a subject.
☐ I may purchase a beginning and an advanced book on the same subject.
☐ I may purchase several books on particular subjects.
☐ (such as _____)

6. Have your purchased other SAMS or Hayden books in the past year? _____
If yes, how many _____

7. Would you purchase another book in the FIRST BOOK series? _____

8. What are your primary areas of interest in business software? _____

☐ Word processing (particularly _____)
☐ Spreadsheet (particularly _____)
☐ Database (particularly _____)
☐ Graphics (particularly _____)
☐ Personal finance/accounting (particularly _____)
☐ Other (please specify _____)

Other comments on this book or the SAMS' book line: _____
_____

Name _____
Company_____
Address _____
City _____ State _____ Zip_____
Daytime telephone number _____
Title of this book _____

Fold here
- -